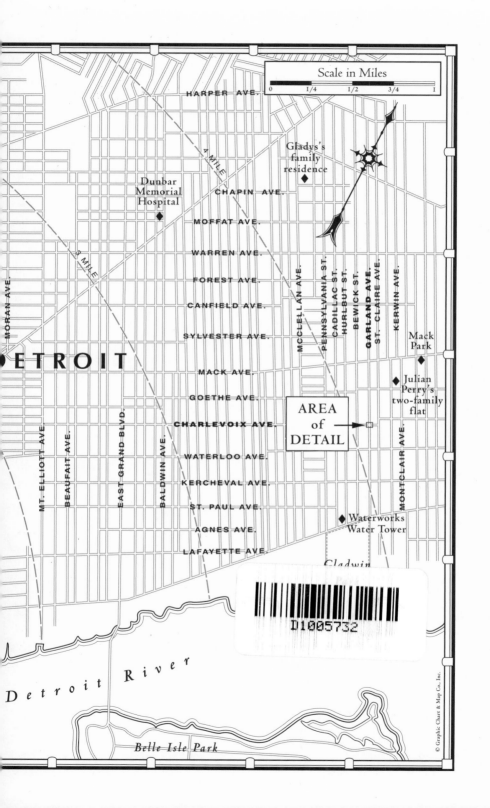

Scale in Miles

0   1/4   1/2   3/4   1

HARPER AVE.

Gladys's
family
residence ◆

Dunbar
Memorial
Hospital ◆

4 MILE

CHAPIN AVE.

MOFFAT AVE.

WARREN AVE.

3 MILE

FOREST AVE.

CANFIELD AVE.

DETROIT

SYLVESTER AVE.

MCCLELLAN AVE.

PENNSYLVANIA ST.
CADILLAC ST.
HURLBUT ST.
BEWICK ST.
GARLAND AVE.
ST. CLAIRE AVE.
KERWIN AVE.

Mack
Park ◆

MACK AVE.

GOETHE AVE.

Julian
Perry's
two-family
flat ◆

MT. ELLIOTT AVE.
BEAUFAIT AVE.
EAST GRAND BLVD.
BALDWIN AVE.

CHARLEVOIX AVE.

AREA
of
DETAIL → □

WATERLOO AVE.

KERCHEVAL AVE.

MONTCLAIR AVE.

ST. PAUL AVE.

AGNES AVE.

◆ Waterworks
Water Tower

LAFAYETTE AVE.

Gladwin

D e t r o i t   R i v e r

Belle Isle Park

© Graphic Chart & Map Co., Inc.

One Man's Castle

ALSO BY
PHYLLIS VINE

Families in Pain:
Children, Siblings, Spouses, and Parents
of the Mentally Ill Speak Out

•

Household and Kin:
Families in Flux
(COAUTHOR)

Amistad

An Imprint of HarperCollins*Publishers*

One Man's Castle

CLARENCE DARROW
IN DEFENSE
OF THE
AMERICAN DREAM

Phyllis Vine

HarperCollins books may be purchased for educational, business, or sales promotional use. For information, please write: Special Markets Department, HarperCollins Publishers Inc., 10 East 53rd Street, New York, NY 10022.

Grateful acknowledgment is made to Random House, Inc., for permission to reprint "I, Too, Sing America." From *The Collected Poems of Langston Hughes*, copyright © by the Estate of Langston Hughes. Used by permission of Alfred A. Knopf, a division of Random House, Inc.

FIRST EDITION

Designed by Deborah Kerner

Map by © Graphic Chart Co., Inc.

Printed on acid-free paper

Library of Congress Cataloging-in-Publication Data

Vine, Phyllis.
One man's castle : Clarence Darrow in defense of the American dream / Phyllis Vine.—1st ed.
p. cm.
Includes bibliographical references and index.
ISBN 0-06-621415-7 (acid-free paper)
1. Sweet, Ossian, 1895–1960—Trials, litigation, etc. 2. Darrow, Clarence, 1857–1938. 3. Trials (Murder)—Michigan—Detroit. 4. African Americans—United States—Civil rights—History—20th century. I. Title.
KF224.S8V56 2004
305.8′00973—dc22   2003045116

04 05 06 07 08 BVG/RRD 10 9 8 7 6 5 4 3 2 1

FOR GARY

I, TOO, SING AMERICA

I, too, sing America.

I am the darker brother.
They send me to eat in the kitchen
When company comes,
But I laugh,
And eat well,
And grow strong.

Tomorrow,
I'll sit at the table
When company comes.
Nobody'll dare
Say to me,
"Eat in the kitchen,"
Then.

Besides,
They'll see how beautiful I am
And be ashamed, —

I, too, am America.

—LANGSTON HUGHES, 1926

CONTENTS

One Man's
Castle

PROLOGUE

ONE FALL MORNING IN OCTOBER 1925 FOUR MEN FROM THE
National Association for the Advancement of Colored People knocked
on the door of a brownstone in New York City. They were looking for
Clarence Darrow, who had just come in from Chicago and was resting
upstairs at the home of Arthur Garfield Hays. Darrow was expecting
them, but when he came downstairs to greet them, he looked as rum-
pled as the clothes in which he had been sleeping.

James Weldon Johnson led the delegation for the NAACP that had
come to urge Darrow, to beg him if necessary, to take a case for someone in need. A black doctor, along with ten friends and family members, had been arrested the month before in Detroit. They had been
defending themselves against an attack led by Ku Klux Klan sympathizers. Someone in the mob, a man named Leon Breiner, died, and
Dr. Ossian Sweet now faced murder charges. The trial would start in
five days, and they needed an attorney.

For most of September the NAACP had been gathering facts to
build a defense for Dr. Sweet. Now in New York, James Weldon Johnson led Darrow through the high points of their research. He told
Darrow that on the day the Sweets moved into a home in a so-called
white neighborhood, the local police had been assigned to protect
them. By noon, on this hot and humid day, a group of white neighbors
had gathered outside the house while others surrounded the block. Dr.
Sweet and his wife, Gladys, were not so naive that they were expecting
the neighbors to welcome them with iced tea and peach pie. But neither did they expect anybody to throw bricks.

After Breiner's death, the mood in Detroit was tense. SLAYING LEADS TO NIGHT RIOT, blurted the *Detroit News*. The local press claimed that the Sweets bought the house to provoke a fight, that their motives were impure, intending to mix races on streets where blacks were not wanted. The press portrayed the shooting as premeditated and unprovoked.

Johnson and the NAACP believed these stories were false. But it was not enough for them to know that Dr. Sweet had bought the house four months earlier. Or that from the windows on the second floor, Ossian Sweet and his brother Henry could look through a crack in the curtains and see the police standing idle at an intersection while clusters of pedestrians mingled, some throwing rocks.

The NAACP needed a lawyer who could use these facts to prove Dr. Sweet's innocence to a jury of twelve, someone who could also weave them into an indictment of state-sponsored residential segregation through attacks on black homeowners nationwide. Cleveland, Los Angeles, Washington, D.C., and Staten Island were among the most recent places to experience similar provocation. Several racial clashes, in which whites forced blacks out of homes, had taken place in Detroit during the summer after Dr. Sweet bought his house, after he put down a nonrefundable $3,500 for a three-bedroom home on an ordinary street.

The NAACP was searching for someone with a reputation that could engender the support of the larger constituency of liberal whites and middle-class blacks. They did not want a lawyer who employed fancy legal tricks to defend bootleggers or gangsters. The man the association hired to represent Dr. Sweet had to know how to reach beyond personal tragedy to expose the spread of residential segregation, to denounce mobs that were arrogating the power of the police while threatening, intimidating, and terrorizing people in their own homes. Properly defended, the case could potentially be as important to America's twelve million blacks as it was to the eleven people awaiting trial in Detroit's jail.

Johnson knew Darrow was a seasoned tactician and strategist, a friend of the oppressed. He had a reputation for eloquence, humor, and satire. They were looking for someone like him who believed strongly that courts and the law could tame injustice. But time was running out. The defendants faced a trial before Judge Frank Murphy the following week. Would Darrow defend them?

Darrow had just finished defending a high school science teacher, Thomas Scopes, for teaching evolution in Tennessee. The trial took the better part of July, and the withering heat and humidity had left him exhausted. Just before the Scopes Monkey Trial, he had represented admitted killers Nathan Leopold and Richard Loeb in a harrowing Chicago case. For more than one year the pace had been intense. Now, at the age of sixty-nine, he was looking forward to slowing down. What he really wanted to do was to go back to bed after his trip to New York from Chicago.

Darrow might not have considered even seeing them that morning had mutual friends not helped the NAACP make the appointment. But now he was intrigued. Though not without his flaws, he was the era's most effective advocate for justice and the rights of the downtrodden. His childhood hero was John Brown, the abolitionist who led the attack at Harper's Ferry. Now a case involving racial discrimination appealed to his sense of mission, as well as to his vanity. Yet he was too fatigued to give them an answer right away. He would need time to think. He would give them a decision in a few days.

Before the NAACP's representatives left, Darrow turned to Arthur Spingarn, a Jewish lawyer who headed their legal committee. With warmth and sincerity, Darrow told Spingarn he "knew full well the difficulties faced by his race." Spingarn, with a dark complexion and curly hair, had to explain that he was not black. Trying to make light of this blunder, Darrow turned to Charles Studin, another dark-skinned, curly-haired lawyer, and said something like "Well you know what I mean." But Darrow erred once again, and embarassment set in. Like Spingarn, Studin was dark-skinned and Jewish. Walter White, the assistant secretary to the NAACP, sensed the desperate moment when Darrow turned to him and said, "Well with your blue eyes and blond hair, I could never make the mistake of thinking you colored." White was amused, actually, as he wrote about this in his autobiography, because he had to tell Darrow he had guessed wrong for a third time. "I am colored," White told him.

Darrow ended that meeting with an improved understanding of the subtleties of race. He was a leathery-skinned midwesterner who was born in Iowa but spent most of his life in Chicago. He had seen the prairie settle and the frontier close, and from his trial work as a defense attorney, he had learned about caste, class, and privilege, about labor, anarchists, and a state that could be repressive. But until that morning he had never tackled racism and the law, nor had he personally experienced its complexity, the way it scripted expectations, defied appearance, challenged intuition. Darrow now realized that he had many of the misconceptions that were as illusory as Spingarn's or White's appearance.

At no time in American history had the nation come as close to an outright race war as it did in the teens and twenties. By 1925 conflict occurred with such remarkable frequency that newspapers buried stories about racial atrocities. People who wanted to know could find Jim Crow's imprint in accounts of lynchings, riots, massacres, and kangaroo courts, along with state-sponsored legislation to eliminate voting rights, civil rights, and property rights. Nothing did more to corrupt the American dream, deny hope, and destroy an individual's potential than myths of merit based on race.

Of the countless stories that lay bare the nation's shameful toleration of racial violence, Ossian Sweet's is among the tragic. That may be why Darrow, exhausted as he was, took the case. Sweet's story reveals an exceptional man, an astonishing individual whose pursuit of the

American dream ended in catastrophe. Had he been white, his accomplishments, his hard work, his pursuit of education and an ambitious career would place him among the heroes of the past. Because he was black, his struggle and the dashing of his dreams have been largely ignored.

Sweet's struggle was not an isolated relic of a bygone era. Many gifted people who sought to sidestep the pervasive opprobrium of racial apartheid wrestled with the devil in America's Garden of Eden. Chattel slavery is America's Original Sin, and its sorrowful legacy survives in continuing policies such as racial profiling, red-lined neighborhoods, police brutality, the color of death row, and so-called achievement tests that unlock but also lock doors. The story of Ossian Sweet offers a unique insight into this history. It permits us to understand the personal as political, the historical in the contemporary. It is a reminder that the past challenges us in the present. His experience was that of a promising, intelligent, and gifted person who found himself in society's whirlpool, one he could neither avoid nor control, for which reason the trials of Ossian Sweet are as relevant for our time as they were in his.

Florida: "Incomparable and Indescribable"

When he was seven years old, Ossian Sweet witnessed a lynching. It was spring in the Peace River Valley, a time for recitals, fishing, and garden parties. Sweet was meandering home along the banks of the Peace River in Bartow, Florida, when he saw a mob escorting a black hostage named Fred Rochelle. The very sight of Rochelle sent him under cover near the river's shore, where he hid, quiet as a rock, under the freckled canopy of a cypress tree while the white men went about the business of claiming their vengeance.

Rochelle's crime was murder. Late in the month of May he had brutally killed a white woman, Rene Taggart, a hometown favorite and bride of the local baker. One morning she had been fishing in the Peace River, and by noon she had had as much of the Florida sun as she could take. As her boat came closer, Rochelle, a drifter, stood alert, watching her from the bridge spanning the river. Perhaps he accidentally passed by, but locals believed he followed her to settle a vendetta against her husband.

When Taggart stepped onto land, Rochelle lunged at her. He came from behind but she fought back. He pulled her down but she struggled to get up, to run away toward the swamp. She lost her footing. Stronger and faster, he overpowered her and slit her throat. Then he fled, running into the woods, leaving her on shore to bleed to death. It happened so fast that the only thing the single eyewitness could do was run for help.

It took little time to form a posse, while white and black men gathered a team of bloodhounds to follow his trail. For the next day and a half, rumor and anticipation sputtered through town. The *Courier-Informant* announced LYNCHING ALMOST CERTAIN long before the bloodhounds picked up his scent. The local paper proved prescient. Lynchings were ubiquitous in the land of Dixie, especially when a white woman was the victim and a black man was said to be at fault. Florida had its share. Because racial hostility was not as apparent in Bartow as in other Florida towns, locals fostered the conceit that somehow their town remained above the violence.

Townsmen focused on finding Rochelle. Two black men in the posse took him captive. They brought him back to town and turned him over to the sheriff. Ten minutes later, vigilantes whisked him away.

Everybody knew Rochelle would be lynched. As was the custom, white children were escorted to a local waterfall, Kissingen Springs. It was a bucolic setting, three miles out of town, popular with locals and tourists. The adults expected youngsters to fish, picnic, and leap from the diving platform, while at home they took care of business.

Sweet stood by as the sun was setting, watching the mob bring in Rochelle, who was tied and bound on horseback. Sweet saw them methodically and purposefully prepare a pyre. First they placed a barrel on the bridge over the Peace River, at the same spot where Rochelle stood before he attacked Rene Taggart. Then they arranged a combustible heap, piling scraps of wood and kindling around the barrel, which they doused with coal oil so it would ignite and burst into flames quickly when brushed by fire.

When the entire posse had assembled, Rochelle was dragged to the spot and tied securely. The mob poured drinks for spectators while he cried for mercy. They ignored him and instead behaved as if they were guests at one of the popular outdoor parties. Eventually Mr. Taggart was ready, and they took their places so he could strike a match. For the next eight minutes, Rochelle shrieked. Flames climbed up his legs, formed a curtain around his torso, draped his face. After the flames died back, souvenir hunters pocketed pieces of his charred remains—a digit, a part of his femur, a piece of his foot.

The orderliness of this ritual would have terrified anybody. It is hard to imagine what went through the mind of a young Ossian Sweet. He could not have understood how the event was based on the bizarre etiquette of frontier justice, governed by a set of informally sanctioned rules of racial retribution as binding as any codified by legal doctrine. But it was routine. Accounts of lynchings usually portrayed mobs with a mannered courtesy that belied their brutal violence, and convention implied that justice was at work, that the mob was the equivalent of a jury in deliberation. The ritual brought them pride.

Rochelle's lynching and the children's trip out of town were part of a scripted protocol, as was the convention that dictated the charade of justice when the posse handed Rochelle over to the sheriff who, in turn, handed him to the mob. As always, the *Courier-Informant* described the mob as "quiet but determined."

Not much was ever learned about Rochelle except that a sister lived in nearby Tiger Bay. Rumors spewed forth from the white community about why he did it, but the best they could figure was Rochelle was settling some kind of grudge against Mr. Taggart. Prominent members of the black community tried to portray Rochelle's crime as the inexplicable act of a deranged man, lest the stigma brush them with shame.

Newspapers from Sacramento, California, to New York City carried the story on their front pages. Indictments may have been reflected in the national spotlight, but on Bartow's front porches blacks and whites hoped to put the event behind them. Elected officials tried to pacify the black community with an invitation for the African Methodist Episcopal Church, suggesting it hold its annual convention in Bartow. Local black church officials were not so sure this idea was good, referring to Bartow as "a hot-bed of South Florida 'crackerdom' accentuated by a human barbecue."

Whatever leaders of the black and white communities did to blunt the aftermath, it did little to diminish the impact of the horrifying scene for Ossian Sweet. Twenty-five years later, he would recall the details of the sickly smell of cooked flesh for a jury in a packed courtroom.

O ssian Sweet grew up in a middle-class enclave of a segregated town in Bartow, south-central Florida. His family lived on the east side, which had been ceded to black newcomers like his parents who arrived in the 1890s when cattlemen roamed freely. A vast forest—hardwood trees such as oak, ash, and hickory, and the softer pine—still brushed the sky, giving shape to the earth's cathedral. By the time the Sweets settled in Bartow, the railroads had laid track and built depots on land as flat as the sea. It looked like a painter's palette with shades of green. There was the emerald-green of the chubby saw grass and the hunter-green of the five varieties of waxy palm fronds. But it was the muted silver-green of Spanish moss, delicate as a bridal veil shrouding the mighty oak, that conveyed the paradox of Florida's robust frontier. To some admirers, to those who loved the land of Polk County, no description was good enough. It had "no counterpart on the globe," wrote the *Florida Times Union* in 1890. "It must be seen to be understood and appreciated as it is incomparable and indescribable."

The Sweets moved to Bartow after a record freeze began one night in December 1894. The air started blowing cold quite suddenly, and powder dusted the yellow and green oranges. Beginning in Canada's Northwest, the front swept southward and plunged Christmas Day temperatures from the normal eighty degrees to twelve in Tallahassee, fourteen in Jacksonville, eighteen in Orlando. By New Year's Eve the front blanketed plump, fragrant fruit. As farmers examined their groves, they saw row after row of oranges dangling from broken branches, split or lying on the ground. By the time the temperature climbed back into the normal range, three days later, it was too late. The crop was gone. Farmers used the six weeks it would take to collect the fallen fruit to gather resolve. These were frontier families, and affliction would not stop them. They would prune the branches, then settle the earth and begin anew.

Then came another cold spell. This time it was a root-killing, sap-stopping freeze. And it covered Florida. Far worse than the first, it was like a wizard's bolt cracking the tree trunks, splitting them to the ground. It froze the folded buds where the fruit had started to grow again. Groves were destroyed. So, too, the spirits of growers. The press called it A STORY OF RUIN. After 1895, it seemed, everybody moved one town to the south. From Jacksonville they slammed their doors shut, loaded the wagons, hitched the mules, and moved to cities the railroad made. From Fort Meade, Plant City, Lakeland, and Homeland they moved to Tampa, later to Miami.

The Sweets moved south from Orlando. They could have chosen any one of several destinations, each with its own personality. Mulberry had been a sawmill town, then a turpentine town, but now it seemed depleted. Homeland was best known for its wealthy black cattlemen and the biracial families who formed a community on its perimeter. Tampa, on the coast, was a commercial seaport, but it still carried the stigma of a yellow-fever epidemic. And Bartow was genteel.

If any frontier town deserved to be recognized for its gentility, it would be Bartow. With bicycle races on clay-paved streets and a lending library in the middle of the village, it was the largest town in Polk County, adjacent to the nonnavigable Peace River, forty miles from Tampa Bay. Bartow boasted fine things, respect for progress. It was the first town to receive electricity. It was made up of families, not of hurly-burly, boardinghouse bachelors like Mulberry. The antisaloon league actually outlawed drink and enforced prohibition with a vigilance that led to the recall of a mayor who liked to sneak into illegal bars for a jigger or more of moonshine. Of the dozen churches, four were predominantly black, including the nearly new St. James African Methodist Episcopal Church.

Careful with his family, stubborn with his future, Henry Sweet was deliberate with his choices. It is unlikely that serendipity guided him and his wife, Dora, when they packed their belongings and moved their three young children, Ossian, Otis, and Delocca, to Bartow.

Bartow was in the middle of a transformation brought first by the railroad, then by the discovery of phosphate, a mineral used for fertilizer. Workers who built the tracks put down roots in the late eighties, remaining with the railroad to become its conductors, firemen, or ticket takers. Others mined phosphate, and they turned a dusty crossroad en route to places such as Tampa Bay, Jacksonville, or Orlando into an economically viable town.

Florida's phosphate fields were graveyards for the ancient mastodons, crocodiles, turtles, shark, and rays. For fifteen million years remnants rested undisturbed, deep in the limestone beds of the Peace River Valley. Within a decade of discovery it all changed. Adventurers pulsed the valley, tapping outcroppings or digging along the swamp's muddy edge. When phosphate was discovered, speculative fever brought delusions of cascading wealth. Miners speared the earth's crust to measure the find, paid the exorbitant price of $5 a day for a hired horse, and deliriously calculated the profits they could unearth. They pounded together shanties near company sites and packed pistols for self-defense. Exuberant and often drunk, they chased dancehall girls and dubbed a drink the "phosphate cocktail." Saloons and brothels, the staple of booming frontier towns, abounded.

With these workers came hotels and hotel operators. Banks needed tellers, and all land booms create realtors. There were two restaurants, one near the railroad depot, the other in town; a manicurist; and two milliners. T. L. Hughes, a merchant, owned the Bartow Opera House on Main Street. E. M. Law, commander of the Confederate Veterans of the State, published the weekly newspaper, the *Courier-Informant*.

The local press predicted phosphate mines "will equal if not surpass the famous beds that have been so profitably worked in the vicinity of Charleston." They would enhance the area's appeal based on "the vast herds of cattle and the numberless orange groves and truck farms." And so it was. Of the twenty companies in Florida, three had located in Bartow to explore the riverbed.

Phosphate created the same delirium in Polk County that gold had created the generation before in California's foothills. Any male who wanted a mud-splattering job could have one prospecting. So strenuous was the work that professional ditch diggers from Ireland, it was said, lasted no more than three days. The Peace River itself was partly to blame. Sometimes cresting seventeen feet higher in summer than in winter, it could swing moods like an angry foe, first in one direction, then in the opposite, then back abruptly. Vessels were grounded where inlets and sandbars formed. But the lure was irresistible. Just as much as had the railroad, the discovery of phosphate left an indelible mark that would thereafter influence the region's size and shape. The full benefit of one of these industries would have been impossible without the other.

Phosphate mining in the Peace River Valley after the Civil War depended on unskilled, dependent labor, like a large antebellum plantation. From morning to sunset work crews made up of local black men aimed water guns against the earth. They pumped thousands of gallons into the ground, carving, drilling, making pits ever bigger, wider, deeper, shaping them into small canyons measuring fifty feet deep, hundreds of feet broad. The rest of the digging was done by hand, with crowbars, shovels, and oyster tongs. Whites held jobs as foremen and managers, permitting the maintenance of an antebellum racial hierarchy to ease the Peace River Valley's transition into the new century without disrupting the status quo.

But Henry Sweet was fiercely independent and resolutely self-reliant, and he would remain distant from any hierarchy topped by white industrialists from afar or their overseers on the job. If Sweet's neighbors chose to work for absentee captains of industry financing the phosphate industry or the railroads, that would be their decision. He would remain outside the reach of any hierarchy presuming to tell him what to do.

Henry Sweet told people he was born in Eufala, Alabama, in 1867. But nobody then, and nobody now, knows anything more about his background than that. His name does not appear in a federal census or one from Alabama or Florida between 1860 and 1890. He had walnut-colored skin and wavy brown hair and a seventh-grade education, an indication, perhaps, of advantages reserved for the racially mixed children of the planter class. He never said. But stern silence could not quiet suspicions that, like so many in Florida, he was part Spanish.

A picture that has been passed down to his children and grandchildren shows a handsome, cultured-looking man. Dark eyes glance skyward; his hair is combed to one side with a single, soft wave above his forehead. A V-shaped mustache neatly edges his thin upper lip. He wears a horseshoe-shaped diamond stickpin in his tie and a Masonic pin on his lapel. He has a serious, pensive bearing.

A picture of Dora from about the same time, perhaps it was her wedding, shows a spare-looking woman, pencil-thin, wearing a dress with a high neck, long sleeves, and gentle folds falling to her ankles. A large piece of jewelry, perhaps a watch or a bracelet, hangs from her right hand just below the wrist. Her gaze is intense, her lips drawn tight, and her hair parted in the middle, secured at the back, covering her ears. Even though she is petite, she looks formidable in a handsomely fitted dress with a tight bodice, which, as an accomplished seamstress, she probably made herself. With prominent cheekbones, dark eyes, and thick, dark hair highlighted by shades of red, she looks part Indian, perhaps Creek, many of whom lived in northern Florida. The photos were probably taken to commemorate the marriage of Ossian Sweet's parents in 1891. She was fifteen, he twenty-four.

Ossian's father's background may have been obscure, but his mother's most certainly was not. Dora descended from slaves who were brought to Florida's northern counties from North Carolina by their owners in the 1850s. Her parents, Lizzie Argrett and Remus Devaughn, married in the 1870s, and relatives on both sides threw themselves into building a strong community protective of their freedom. One uncle became a minister in the militant African Methodist Episcopal Church. Two others were elected to Florida's legislature during Reconstruction. One still represented Wakulla County in the lower house when, in 1885, a conservative majority rescinded liberal Reconstruction law during Florida's constitutional convention. Governor Ossian B. Hart remembered that he owed his election to black voters, the Argretts and Devaughns among them, and appointed yet another uncle as justice of the peace in Leon County. Dora paid homage to the closeness between her family and the governor's by naming her first two sons after Hart and his brother. Oscar, the firstborn, died in infancy, and Ossian (pronounced Osh-an) was born in 1894.

The legacy of Dora Sweet's family was that of leadership and access to power, while Henry's gift was staunch, almost defiant independence.

He would neither seek the company of whites nor buckle before them. The self-reliance some considered the trademark of Florida's frontier guided his life and the lives of his children. He supported his family by working as a woodcutter, a human bulldozer in the timber industry. It was the third largest industry in Florida's economy. Working alone or with one of his children, he would carve tunnels through the evergreen darkness, or bring down the cypress and the cedar, open a window for the sun to shine on a dark swamp. He made room for roads and towns and pastures and railroad tracks. When he was done clearing, done fighting the chiggers, the mosquitoes, and the heat, he sold the wood. It would be up to others to make boxes, crates of all sizes, furniture like chests and bed frames, shingles and railroad ties. Oak made good posts. Scrap, mostly yellow pine, went for firewood that Sweet sold from his own yard. Sometimes he cleared just a few acres, sometimes hundreds. One time Ossian helped him clear five hundred. Choosing to work independently, he painstakingly insulated himself.

Boldly, he demanded the same independence for his family. He ignored Southern vagrancy laws that former Confederate states drafted between 1890 and 1910 under the pretense of promoting industry and preventing idleness. They were really designed to regulate the activities of black Americans by placing their work under white authority. Someone like Dora, who did not work for others, remained outside the purview of that white surveillance, and could be considered suspect, idle, and profligate instead of middle-class like her white counterparts. Sweet's distrust of whites led him to resolve never to let his daughters launder, cook, or clean across town. They, too, might have been at risk because they made themselves unaccountable. Elsewhere men like Henry Sweet might be called provocative. His neighbors thought him proud and independent; and Bartow's whites, descended from the first generation of cattlemen, seemed more at ease than whites in other towns with their black citizens, perhaps because so many were kin.

Within one year of his arrival Sweet settled his family on the edge of town, bounded by the South Florida Railroad tracks on the west and the meandering Peace River on the east. He paid $240 for a wood-framed house, with a front porch and bedrooms with fireplaces. When Henry and Dora Sweet moved in with their three children, it probably seemed enormous.

No family need starve in Polk County. Anybody with a shotgun could hunt deer, rabbit, or possum; anybody who could walk could collect wild berries. Or go over to the lake—there were two hundred nearby—and throw a fish line. Or trap a gator. The Sweets were more resourceful. They had two and one half acres, enough for a small citrus grove that averaged eighty trees to an acre. There was land enough for Dora's flower beds, a vegetable garden, a chicken coop, and an underground cellar where they would cure and store beef slaughtered from their own herd.

The Sweets lived surrounded by a close community, near other woodcutters and phosphate miners, teachers, ministers, and one book dealer. Some neighbors drove ice wagons, others made and laid bricks, one managed a stable, and many farmed groves of citrus, pineapple, or snap beans. A few artisans, cabinetmakers and the tailor found jobs with whites across town. Altogether, they infused the community with stability while they supported four churches, a nurse, a midwife, a barber, a butcher, a couple of grocers, and one music teacher. Vitality permeated East Bartow's Palmetto Street, which ran east to west, with a restaurant, hotel, movie hall, and an Odd Fellows Lodge. Years later big bands and other entertainers would perform on Palmetto Street and stay overnight before continuing their trip to Tampa.

Good wages and a demand for labor fanned employment, allowing stability. But segregation also produced uncontested inequality that distinctions of class could not buffer. "For Colored Only" hung over doors at the municipal building. Consensus sent black children fishing and swimming at their own marked section of Polk Lake. Elected officials did not send the convict labor to pour concrete sidewalks or to set clay highways on the east side as they had on the town's west side. Rather, daily summer rain turned pounded dirt into thick slush, slowing horses, seizing wagon wheels. Wired street lamps lagged years, even decades, behind improvements on the west side.

By the end of the first decade of the century, new arrivals more than doubled the population, bringing all of Bartow to roughly four thousand people. But the very separateness of the black community, its irrelevance to whites, allowed Bartow's east side to flourish, to remain a hamlet within the town, a small thorp mitigating the harshness of Jim Crow, which birthed a middle class. The Sweets were among its most prominent members.

B y sunrise every Sunday the aromas of grits, bacon, fried white potatoes, frogs' legs, and sizzling pork chops filled the nostrils of waking children. It was the Sabbath and Dora Sweet was fixing breakfast. Later in the day she attended church with family and friends. She usually started preparing on Saturday by slaughtering hens, most likely a Rhode Island Red, from their own chicken coop. When her sister Sally brought the family from Clermont, she would prepare beef or pork to go with the fried chickens. If her husband had been working during the week, he tried to return in time to walk his children to church and welcome his friends from Homeland, Gardenville, or Primrose. These guests left their rigs hitched in their yard while they went to church. Later they would walk back to the Sweets', where they spread out their own baskets with muffins, cornbread, and ribs. Sabbath rules meant children were not permitted to wander. From the porch came sounds of youngsters stacking dominoes, throwing jacks, or placing the marbles of Chinese checkers. Adults sat inside—eight made a perfect fit around a big rosewood table in the dining room— talking about news of the day. When the topic turned to race troubles, caution muffled their tones. Before darkness settled, they would return to the St. James AME Church for the evening service.

Every few years Dora Sweet prepared for the arrival of another baby. Henry and Dora chose names evoking classical images for some of them—Parthenia Izola and Vessius—perhaps derived from her passion for Greek myths. She chose another from her equally powerful passion for the opera. When a baby girl was born in 1905 she called her Nordica after the internationally prominent soprano Lillian Nordica. And they gave Henry Junior the middle name of Wadsworth. It must have pleased Dora that lore assigned the derivation of Ossian's name to a third-century Gaelic poet whose reputation became fashionable in literary circles after 1805, when, supposedly, his poems were reissued.

Fervent about music and literature, Dora wanted her children to master both. Ossian and his brothers grew up studying violin. The girls, like their mother, played piano. Everybody sang in the choir—Dora for the church, the children at school wearing the clothes their mother had made them. Dora's talents as a seamstress were widely sought but she used them only for her own family. For the children's undergarments she bleached and washed flour and sugar sacks. After she sketched the design, she would size the garment with a muslin sample she made. From one bolt of cloth from the dry goods store, she could make each girl a dress. For each boy, it was a waist-length, buttoned jacket to go over the coveralls. These matching outfits showed to the world a family cohesion and the manifest unity Henry and Dora Sweet expected of their children. Yet even parents as protective and careful as they were could not guarantee safe harbor in the South.

No town in Florida has a better or more law-abiding colored population than Bartow," extolled the *Courier-Informant* on the occasion of the first day of school in 1909. "[W]e honestly believe this excellent school is largely responsible for it."

If education promoted public order, Bartow promoted public education. Polk County began supporting education for black students by endowing the local Baptist church with a two-story school and a gift of $500 in 1889. The gesture probably came from the kinship between cattle ranchers and the first generation of freedmen. By the time the Sweet children were going to school, the AME Church replaced the Baptists as leading educators. When Henry Sweet became a member of the school's board of directors, the Union Academy was enrolling more than two hundred students through the eighth grade. Boarders from Orlando and Key West lived with local families and paid the regular fees—ten cents in the upper grades, five cents in the lower grades—for monthly supplies. When his friend C. C. Johnson stepped down, Sweet replaced him as chairman of the board.

The Union Academy had earned quite a reputation and solid local support for the way it polished its students. It does "good work for the colored people," wrote the editor of the *Courier-Informant,* "and therefore for all the people of Bartow." And with too many students shoehorned into a tiny building, the paper solicited patrons for something larger. The confidence led the Board of Public Instruction to authorize funds for repairs, initially up to $300, later adding another $100 in matching funds. By then Henry Sweet chaired the advisory board, and he accepted the challenge to raise the funds on behalf of his own children and those of his neighbors.

Union Academy stopped at the eighth grade. Whatever advantages an eighth-grade education offered to Henry Sweet's generation, born in the shadow of slavery, it would not suffice for his own children. They would need learning, in addition to hard work and culture, to prepare them for the American dream. The social connections and personal references resulting from a good education were as important as the study of geography or moral philosophy, and Henry Sweet insisted his children have access to all of education's promise.

Owing to the family's church involvement, it makes sense that he consulted a figure no less influential than the Reverend Charles Sumner Long, from Florida's first family of AME ministers. Long urged Henry to send his oldest son to Ohio, to Wilberforce Academy, where the church had been nurturing promising youngsters since before the Civil War.

The name spoke for itself. Wiliam Wilberforce was a British abolitionist serving in Parliament when evangelism swept England at the end of the seventeenth and the beginning of the eighteenth century. When Bishop Daniel Payne founded the school in the 1850s, he named it after this hero. Since then it had become the main ingredient of a pious education. Southern planters loved Wilberforce, even if they had no idea who its namesake was or what he stood for. About sixty miles north of Cincinnati, it was one of the few schools educating children born of planter fathers and slave mothers, and masters sent their children for an education the South denied them.

Ossian's access to the American dream would be much improved if he attended the most prominent school preparing blacks for a high school diploma. The Sweet family was told a scholarship was available to help pay for his living expenses, thus making it all but guaranteed that he would attend. Once it was agreed he should go, all he had to do was get there safely.

CHAPTER 2

The
Education of
Ossian Sweet

W e can only imagine what dreams Henry Sweet held for
his oldest child, a lean, athletic sixteen-year-old with ears
sticking out like butterfly wings, when Ossian left Bartow to attend high school at Wilberforce Academy in Xenia, Ohio. It
was the summer of 1910, a time of the year when perspiration soaks
through a collar and leaves puddles behind the backs of your knees.
Starting out with his father, it took Ossian six hours to reach Jacksonville, where, in the evening, they visited with the Reverend Charles
Sumner Long. Years later Long would describe it as the occasion for
bringing Ossian Sweet into the African Methodist Episcopal Church.
The next day Sweet would continue his journey alone.

Did Henry offer wisdom, whisper advice as he purchased a ticket on
the Atlantic Coast Line's Number 32 train? It would be another day and
a half before Sweet reached his destination and could ignore the dangers
of travel in the South. Someone who witnessed a lynching when he was
not even seven years old probably did not need to be reminded to keep

his gaze lowered. It is unlikely that his father said very much before the train pulled away from Jacksonville at eight o'clock in the evening.

Jim Crow codes defined travel in all coaches, first and second class, plainly violating the equal protection clause of the Fourteenth Amendment. When traveling by train, blacks were not served food on board, and vendors ignored them at depots. After use and age destroyed the comfort and luxury of the old wooden cars, railway companies replaced them with slick, steel coaches, but everybody knew the new cars belonged to the white passengers. The downgraded cars were allowed to deteriorate even further when they were put into service for black travelers. Coal dust drifted across the aisles, into the corners, covering the air-dried spittle mounding the floor of a drafty coach. One toilet sufficed for men, women, and children. Ripening fruit was stored in the back of the car, giving off a thick, sickly smell, attracting bugs, vermin, and flies.

In these Jim Crow cars, a black passenger knew enough of local custom to avoid eye contact with a white, even a prisoner shackled to a sheriff with his ankle chains clanging together while they shuffled for a seat. When a white man used a "JC" car as a smoking coach, the foul air lingered long after he left the seats he had lounged across while black passengers sat stiff-backed, shoulder-to-shoulder on splintering benches. Like the mayor of a small town, a conductor controlled all services for Jim Crow cars, and public outcry from a black press did little to alter his behavior.

Ossian Sweet would have boarded one of these cars for the first leg of his twenty-five-hour trip, the part from Jacksonville to Cincinnati, Ohio. From there it would take another eight hours to get to the station at Xenia, and then twenty minutes by horse and buggy by way of a covered bridge to reach Wilberforce. The fastest route included four transfers in the middle of the night. In Tifton, Georgia, he had to wait one hour before connecting to the Georgia Southern, bound for Macon. Did his father remind him that Macon was the spot where, in recent memory, a man named Charles Lokie was lynched for allegedly making "insulting remarks to a white woman"? There Sweet would spend two hours before transferring to the Central of Georgia at 3:15 A.M. Three hours later the train would pull into Atlanta, Georgia, where he could watch the sun rise over the red-clay hills. For some, Atlanta may have evoked images of the dying hours of the Confederacy, the triumph of Union forces, the last great battle of the Civil War. For the black community, Atlanta was the site of racial slaughter, only five years earlier, when mob rule left twenty-five blacks and one white dead.

Could Ossian Sweet have traveled this train, sat in its filthy and decrepit coach, and not thought of his home in Bartow? At each meal, his father demanded a formal place setting, a freshly starched, white tablecloth. After each use, even for a snack, the cloth was carried to a three-legged iron kettle set outside in the yard over a wood fire. Ossian's parents would not permit unkempt children or uncouth manners, and Jim Crow accommodations would have been foreign.

Sweet was probably too young to realize how, when he left his family in Florida, the journey would propel his future. For now he had only one concern: How could he anchor himself to a routine at school that would not betray his parents and their dream for him to become the first member of his family to graduate from high school?

On the second Tuesday of September in 1910, Ohio schools opened their doors. That morning at Wilberforce, students lined up on a soggy lawn, under a warm and humid sky, outside the doors of Galloway Hall. They had come from as far away as Africa, Mexico, South America, and the West Indies. And from as near as Xenia. Students from Ohio, Kentucky, Illinois, and Indiana outnumbered all others. Florida sent three. Only Ossian Sweet hailed from Bartow.

The procession of speakers for Sweet's first day of school resembled a parade of peacocks. Bishops of the AME Church, members of the faculty, and prominent visitors graced the podium. President William Saunders Scarborough, among the more learned and imposing figures of his generation, ascended the stage in the light-filled, twelve-hundred person auditorium of Galloway Hall. His address about the need to "Do Something" was a meditation on public and personal conduct. The local paper said it made a "deep impression."

Wilberforce dated from the 1850s when the AME Church bought a fashionable resort at Tawawa Springs. Along with fifty-four acres, the purchase included a hotel with cottages and fine furnishings—beds, linens, and cutlery—resonant with the aspirations of its antebellum clientele. The church remodeled the buildings, turned the hotel into classrooms with a dormitory, the guest cottages into faculty homes. They were arranged in a horseshoe pattern, facing one another around a meadow. The rest of the campus consisted of natural springs and streams, "twisting through a valley . . . over and down a sloping hill which overlook[ed] the creek."

By the time Sweet enrolled in the high school, the acreage had grown by a factor of five. The original hotel had burned to the ground and been replaced. Other new buildings housed students, classes, and faculty offices. There was even a library, finished in 1907, built with a $15,000 donation from Andrew Carnegie.

No building on campus excited as much praise or symbolized the school's aspirations more fully than the Carnegie Library. With its brick and mortar construction, the facade had the look of scholarly asceticism, simple and unadorned, but the interior, with its stylized flourishes and electric-light chandeliers, denoted modernity. For the first time in the school's history, a public room, not an attic or the crawlspace under a faculty member's bed, housed books.

Students flocked to the library. The traffic was steady enough after three years to wear out the linoleum floor in the main entrance.

Ossian Sweet entered Wilberforce at a time of intense debate over the type of education most appropriate for black youth. The president, William Scarborough, led one faction, the group favoring the liberal arts for its ability to prepare thoughtful, committed, and inspired citizens. Scarborough was two years into his presidency of an institution with a high school academy and a college when Sweet arrived. Except for a brief interruption, he had spent his adult life at Wilberforce, where he started teaching Greek and Latin in 1876, at the age of twenty-four. Within five years he published *First Lessons in Greek* (1881). Another five years and his translation of Aristophanes' *Birds* (1886) appeared. He was debonair and well-traveled; and mutton-chop whiskers, which age had turned to white, scrolled his youthful, round face. At the age of fifty-six, this public intellectual who combined activism with scholarship became the sixth president of the oldest black college in America.

A portrait painter from Boston, Darius Cobb, once described Scarborough's face as having "strong character." Cobb called him dignified. Others would applaud his "quest for knowledge" and his "abounding optimism." Even his critics tucked their disapproval of his administrative weakness into compliments about his worldly travel, how it brought favorable publicity to a small black school in the middle of Ohio.

Scarborough had the unusual background of a slave mother and a free-black father before the Civil War, and the advantage of an academy education. He began higher education at Atlanta University, and after two years he transferred to Oberlin College, in Ohio, where he delighted in an atmosphere he considered gentle. Later he recalled, "I forgot I was a colored boy." When he was ready for his first teaching job, trustees of Atlanta University denied him a position because of color. He accepted an offer from Wilberforce, and initially he responded with enthusiasm. But it didn't take long for this "staid institution" to grate.

He found himself an outsider owing to his not being an alumnus of a denominational school in general, of Wilberforce in particular. Added to his isolation was a schedule layered with prayer from morning to night. Scarborough became claustrophobic. To combat the boredom of living on a campus three miles from town, seven miles down the road from Antioch College at Yellow Springs, he set out to find something to occupy his fast-firing mind. In a short while he discovered the world of "public life and its affairs" and threw himself into public speaking and magazine writing.

In his effort to demolish barriers to political and social equality, Scarborough wisely hired faculty manifest with mission. Theophilus Gould Steward, for one, had retired from the army before joining the Wilberforce faculty to teach history in 1907. Four years later he accompanied Scarborough to London for the First Universal Races Conference. Two years after that he contacted W. E. B. Du Bois, who was now the editor of *The Crisis,* a magazine published by the new National Association for the Advancement for Colored People. Steward hoped to start a local chapter on the campus. And at least fifty years before students called for Afro-centered history, Steward was teaching "History of African Peoples in the Western World," including a discussion of the controversial revolution in Haiti. Other Wilberforce courses fostered activism. A sociology class assigned Du Bois's annual reports, known as the Atlanta University Studies, which profiled the black experience in business, education, family, property ownership and the church. Students studying economics and social change discussed "trade unions, their justification and service to labor."

In substantial ways, the school matured beyond its original mission as a denominational outpost in the rolling hills of Ohio's antebellum free-soil, a place for black or mixed-race youth discarded by Southern educational policy. The college was beginning to resemble a modern institution of higher learning, and graduation requirements included the standard classes in the liberal arts: Latin, English, history, sociology, economics, laboratory science, foreign language—French and German—

and electives such as art and music. Part academic, part technical, part academy, part college, it had a normal school for training teachers and a graduate program, the Daniel Payne Divinity School, for seeding the AME Church. Eventually Scarborough would align the patchwork courses. In this he was no different from other college presidents, dusting cobwebs off their founders' legacies while they fashioned modern departments coalescing a curriculum dependent on courses scattered across subjects.

But, unfamiliar with running schools, the AME leadership practically buried Wilberforce in debt by allowing interest to pile up on notes, an oversight that depleted the school's finances. It had been more than two years since the trustees met the payroll. Along with the rest of the faculty, Scarborough was struggling financially, and insufficient funds crippled him both personally and professionally. He couldn't afford the $10 to pay his dues to the American Negro Academy and was forced to resign, but pride closed his lips and he never explained publicly why he left the organization he helped found. The state of Ohio was also refusing to accredit Wilberforce because it had not set aside $250,000 for an endowment. And fellowship aid, of the sort Sweet expected, was scarce. "Many of the students need a helping hand to enable them to continue their course; hundreds of letters imploring aid and opportunity for work . . . are annually received," lamented Scarborough in 1910, the initial phase of his fund-raising campaign.

The most serious threat facing Wilberforce, however, lay not in the financial deficits, the outmoded science labs, or the embryonic departments. Nor was it the evolution of a civic mandate that the founders would have called "repulsive sectarianism." The real danger, the serious crisis they all faced, was a growing racial prejudice that could easily girdle choices for black youth. Prejudice, Scarborough feared, "has increased to such an alarming extent that as a rule Negro students are not wanted in our white schools, and as a result they will sooner or later have to come to their own to get the knowledge." That was why

Wilberforce had to survive, had to thrive, to fulfill its mandate as "the Mecca not only of the AME Church but of the Negro people."

Conspicuously absent from Scarborough's inner circle was one of the nation's most well-known and celebrated black Americans, Booker T. Washington, nicknamed "Wizard" of Tuskegee. By the time Scarborough assumed his presidential duties at Wilberforce, a decade had hardened the differences between the two educators. The Scarborough faction included professors, intellectuals, and aspiring social critics who were known as the Talented Tenth. Under Washington's wing were small businessmen and entrepreneurs, known as the Tuskegee Machine. No major event ruptured their alliance. They were cordial, if not friends, but the factions competed for the same rewards, and they didn't need overt back-stabbing. There was enough innuendo to undermine confidence and guarantee a schism.

Washington's background could not have been more different from Scarborough's. Washington was about ten years old when Abraham Lincoln issued the Emancipation Proclamation, and unlike Scarborough he did not come from a class with the opportunity to prepare in an academy. He went to work in the West Virginia coal mines before a white woman employed him as a servant. After overhearing someone describe the Hampton Institute, in Virginia, which trained freedmen in practical skills, he decided his future lay in education. He was admitted to the school after demonstrating that he could sweep. "I swept the recitation-room three times. Then I got a dusting cloth and I dusted it four times." Unable to find any dirt, the headmistress had no choice but to admit him. In *Up from Slavery* (1901) he boasts, "The sweeping of that room was my college examination."

Washington founded the Tuskegee Institute in Alabama, along the Hampton model, in 1881. Students learned woodworking and carpentry, how to make bricks, set type, build buggies, carts, and wagons. They learned how to cook, beginning with how to prepare a fire. They were schooled in humility, deference, cleanliness, industry, and self-help. They were taught that white benefactors would guarantee their political gains. They were primed to make themselves indispensable to accommodate a Southern way of life, values and skills that would have been anathema to Wilberforce students.

Some date the fault line in the black community, especially the group of educators, from 1895, when Washington delivered a speech at the Atlantic Exposition that would forever be remembered. Washington was in his prime when his wife and three children accompanied him from Tuskegee to Atlanta. A big man with bulging gray eyes and a reddish tint to a full head of hair, he showed thickness around the neck and across his face. The intense Georgia heat of September nearly brought him down as he made his way to the hall where he would address the audience. Washington knew that the moment was unprecedented. At the same time he was nervous, appreciative, and thrilled. Perhaps he was humbled to be the only person selected to represent a nation's entire race numbering nearly ten million. Georgia's Governor Bullock introduced Washington, calling him a representative of "Negro enterprise and Negro civilization." It was far kinder than would be later introductions when speakers, including former President Cleveland, would make invidious comparisons to the "superior" white race, to the "slavery-bred imperfections and deficiencies" of blacks. For Washington the price of celebrity could be his dignity.

White Atlanta, at the turn of the century, was surely unaccustomed to filling a large hall to listen to a black orator. More than a few people probably drew a deep breath until, shortly into the well-rehearsed ten-minute speech, Washington assured them that "the wisest of my race understand that the agitation of questions of social equality is the extremist folly." The Wizard asked for black and white to work together to solve the South's color problems. The message was muted where it wasn't lost. What most people seized upon, what they remembered and what they talked about later, was principally the last line, which would boomerang. "In all things that are purely social we can be as separate as the fingers," Washington said, "yet one as the hand in all things essential to mutual progress."

The white press took note. The *Atlanta Constitution* called the talk "notable." The *Boston Transcript* claimed, "[T]he sensation that it has caused in the press has never been equaled." But historians judge him more harshly. His biographer, Louis R. Harlan, called it a "sweeping concession to the white South's desire for segregation," and John Hope Franklin has written that Washington "placated white supremacists by renouncing social equality." Perhaps David Levering Lewis said it best when he noted, "Neither black people nor white people were ever the same again."

The Wizard's success depended on pleasing whites, the politicians, ministers, and businessmen who exulted in his school's achievement. They could write one check, or several, to keep Tuskegee flush. Powerful capitalists, these were men of the maturing industrial age, and the New South took shape under their influence. William H. Baldwin was general manager of the Southern Railroad, Robert Ogden headed Wanamakers, and Andrew Carnegie was a titan-turned-philanthropist. Any one could influence the course of Washington's efforts. In their presence he was a minion, even at Tuskegee, to which visitors would come by the trainload to hear the choir or to join celebrations, and stay long enough to pose for pictures. If anybody could benefit from Washington's influence in training a generation of compliant workers, it was the Northern moneyed class.

Two years after addressing the Atlanta Exposition, Washington refused to attend a meeting at which the black intelligentsia would discuss forming the American Negro Academy. Modeled after the French Academy, it would limit membership to elite intellectuals, professors, writers, and artists—no more than forty in all. It appealed enormously to Scarborough, who came to Washington, D.C., along with W. E. B. Du Bois; poet Paul Laurence Dunbar; Kelly Miller, a philosopher and later dean at Howard University; Reverend Theophilus Steward, chaplain of the U.S. Twenty-fifth Infantry; and Reverend Francis J. Grimké, a minister and Howard University trustee. Alexander Crummell, an Episcopal cleric, put together the guest list, and Washington surprised nobody when he declined. Not only did the move seem serpentine, with a group consisting of his harshest critics, but it was not his style to build associations he could not control.

By the first decade of the new century, Washington's influence was ebbing. Black leaders who had initially accepted his ideal of vocational training now questioned relying on this strategy as the single panacea. Little by little, and threading through several years of upheaval, re-alignment, adjustment, and reconsideration, polarities had grown. It was more than a skepticism about the white philanthropists bankrolling Washington's Tuskegee Institute. It spoke to an apprehension, born of a stubborn dread, that the converts to Washington's approach might be, as Scarborough once remarked, "disposing of the Negro's preparation for the future." Whatever they called it, practical, industrial, or vocational, the black literati feared Washington's agenda would hasten a color line, marginalize them economically, politically, and socially, and block their own and their children's aspirations and opportunities. To many it seemed that Washington's reach was as bad as Jim Crow's creep.

"Among his own people," Du Bois wrote in 1903, "Mr. Washington has encountered the strongest and most lasting opposition." Du Bois offered a lamentation on Washington's vision when he said, "[T]here is among educated and thoughtful colored men a feeling of deep regret, sorrow, and apprehension at the wide currency and ascendancy which some of Mr. Washington's theories have gained." Citing a recurring paradox in the Wizard's positions, Du Bois noted, "He insists on thrift and self-respect, but at the same time counsels a silent submission to civic inferiority." While Du Bois was likely to plead steps promoting political action, Washington, incomprehensibly, sanctioned lynching, saying that "lynching really indicates progress. There can be no progress without friction." While the American Negro Academy advocated advancing education to promote the liberal arts, Washington was trumpeting vocational training.

Washington's adversaries could not decide whether he was a fool or a knave, but it mattered not at all because either way they didn't trust him. Working behind the scenes the way he liked to do raised suspicions and made him unaccountable. Had he not appropriated Du Bois's idea for developing an economic boost and claimed it as his own for the highly successful Negro Business League? Had he not refused to publicly join a lawsuit challenging Jim Crow sleeping Pullman cars at the turn of the century while privately, behind closed doors, he furiously wrote letters complaining to Tuskegee trustee William Baldwin, Jr.? He relied on similar tactics when it came to challenging residential segregation, fighting voting disfranchisement or defending those trapped by laws of peonage.

Nothing revealed the discrepant views of the two camps more boldly than the different curricula that determined choices, shaped a vision of how to live, what battles to fight, and how to prepare for civic involvement. Washington trained students to become blacksmiths, carpenters, house painters, and he endowed their aspirations with a group of skills to work in a white-controlled economy.

Of all of Washington's policies and programs undermining the kind of education Wilberforce parents, including Henry Sweet, wanted for their sons, none was more damaging than the Wizard's position as paid field agent of the Southern Education Board. The SEB was a Northern-moneyed philanthropy with a mission to underwrite education in the South. For white students, the SEB funded academic schools. For black students, it funded schools built on the model of Tuskegee. As field agent, Washington could recommend disbursements to the schools he visited, could use the prestige and influence of the organization to give a boost to one that was struggling. Or he could erase it by funding a competitor. By the end of the decade, the ruse was apparent. In a letter to the Jewish philanthropist Jacob Henry Schiff, Washington enumerated how a $3,000 donation should be disbursed: $1,000 to Tuskegee, $250 for Hampton, and $100 each for nine other schools. Somewhat disingenuously, he advised holding the balance, $850, in reserve for future applications or emergencies. Deliberately and conspicuously, the SEB tried to sabotage liberal arts education for blacks—especially at denominational schools like Lincoln, Morehouse, and Wilberforce. No wonder the intellectuals and scholars of the Talented Tenth often questioned his loyalties and did not trust him as one of their own. But neither did whites. William Henry Baldwin, Jr., a Tuskegee trustee, made it clear it "would not be wise, at least at present" to allow Washington to sit with the SEB. Baldwin decided that "inasmuch as Hampton and Tuskegee were represented by four members on the Board, more could be accomplished by keeping the Directors white."

While the debate about the preferred goal of education took place off-stage, the strife between the Tuskegee Machine and the Talented Tenth affected the education of all black youth including that of Ossian Sweet at Wilberforce. On fund-raising trips, President Scarborough discovered closed doors. "So much wealth and influence were being brought . . . to advance industrial education," he said. He feared "a higher culture was being thrown into the background." Funding patterns confirm this. Of the millions the SEB and its subsidiaries distributed (nearly $177 million before the Depression), only one million of it was funneled into black education prior to World War I.

Always the scholar, too much the diplomat, Scarborough never allowed the ideological divide with Washington to halt him. He kept open the dialogue with the Tuskegee Machine, even after it cost him an appointment as ambassador to Haiti and derailed financial aid that might have made the difference between a marginal existence and a confident future. In 1911, in what turned out to be a politically astute but perplexing move, he invited Washington to deliver the commencement address. Even the white-owned *Xenia Gazette* recognized that the moment was tense. "It is believed," began the story naively, "that the address of Dr. Washington will bring in closer union the two factions of negro educational thought, namely, the higher and industrial advocates." Indeed, when the Wizard died in 1915, Scarborough was chosen an honorary pallbearer. But the practical implications for students lingered well beyond Washington's death. For decades the educational experience of students like Ossian Sweet would ricochet somewhere between the poles of men with these fiercely competing visions of the duty and the privilege of education.

Whoever carried the rumor of a scholarship was undoubtedly earnest, perhaps enthusiastic, but he presented a wish for a fact and spoke without authority. Scholarship funds, which were already quite meager, had never been intended for one so young and so unproven. Discovering he was not the recipient of financial support was a tough way for Ossian Sweet to begin his education away from home.

Sweet's Florida family could be of limited help. Even had finances permitted, Henry Sweet endorsed the lessons of self-sufficiency and insisted that all his sons finance their own education as well as help their sisters. Thus Ossian Sweet needed to raise the money to pay his expenses, to become the first in his family to receive a high school diploma. He needed at least $150 a year to cover the costs of tuition, room, board, and heat. There were separate fees for the library, the laboratory, and violin lessons. He needed another $12 for a complete uniform for mandatory military service.

There was work enough to do on the Wilberforce campus. Shorter Hall, one of the boys' dormitories built after the Civil War, needed repair. The heating system was undependable and the wooden floors splintered. Students enrolled in elective courses teaching industrial and vocational skills—carpentry, plumbing and heating, or mechanical engineering—could be put into service. They had already designed and built President Scarborough's house, Galloway Hall, and Emery Hall. But Sweet's only class in the vocational curriculum, shoemaking, would never equip him with the skills to dent his expenses.

Help came from the administration, which found him a campus job sweeping snow from the walks and keeping the furnaces fired. Like his father, he must have been a good worker. While Scarborough was forced to turn down other students, he kept Ossian Sweet employed. And when the term ended, instead of enrolling in summer school, Sweet headed north to work in Detroit. There, Wilberforce alumni formed a protective community, finding jobs for students and opening their homes for temporary summer quarters while immigrants and other newcomers stretched the seams of America's fastest-growing city.

When Ossian Sweet started college, he had his heart set on becoming a violinist. After his father delivered a stiff message about the obligations he would face when he supported a family, and urged him to reconsider, Sweet changed directions. He traded his ambition for studying violin with preparing for medical school and geared his work toward Howard University's entrance requirements. He would need 120 hours in physics; 240 hours in chemistry, organic and inorganic; and 180 laboratory hours in biology plus the lectures. Howard demanded either French or German, which overlapped with Wilberforce graduation requirements. Conversational French *or* German was voluntary at both schools, but Ossian Sweet would finish college speaking and reading both. And before he graduated he would be employed as an assistant in the chemistry laboratory.

Sweet's relatives used to say, "You better have your facts straight," if you were going to debate him. More than facts drove his academic success. Hard work, coupled with an ability to put himself through school, fueled enough ambition that before he was eighteen he could purchase nine acres of grazing land adjacent to the railroad tracks just south of Bartow, for which he paid $475. And athletics absorbed him. He was vice president of the student athletic association and played tackle on the freshman year football team. If anything caused him problems it was his social nature. At the end of his freshman year, after already completing three years successfully in the academy, he was found in a situation that nearly cost him a place at Wilberforce College.

"I will admit I was in bad company," began his letter of apology to the president and the faculty committee on discipline. Ossian Sweet and two of his friends had been discovered in Xenia in a gigantic lie. The first part of their error was leaving campus unauthorized. Sweet may have been nineteen years old, and in other contexts need not ask for permission to go into town, but the unbending paternalistic rules of a denominational college stifled Wilberforce. "Bad company" could mean playing cards or shooting dice. Or it could have been listening to ragtime music, thought to corrupt the body and maim the soul, which was banned from campus. It could have been girls, and violating the prohibitions on unsupervised activities, notwithstanding the school's reputation as a "marriage school." And while the nation debated ratifying a constitutional amendment enforcing prohibition, few sins were thought to be as corrupting as the sin of alcohol.

"I'm a 'total Abstainer,'" Sweet declared unconditionally, professing never to become "a partaker of Intoxicants." Suspension resulted from less.

The faculty minutes of 1913–1914 are dense with student infractions, including suspension for playing hooky, missing train connections, returning late—meaning unsupervised—from vacation. Boys fought on the walkways; girls, more often, succumbed to the "habitual use of violent language." Improper posture or lax behavior during chapel earned miscreants a front-row seat. The college dismissed three young women after they "voluntarily" confessed to smoking.

The severe punishments meted to other students implies that the discipline committee let Sweet and his two friends off comparatively easy. Someone must have coached them, told them how to show contrition. Perhaps it was sufficient that they publicly confessed to the crime of bad company and owned their disgrace. They had already spent several weeks absent social privileges.

Whatever guided the decision of the discipline committee, with only a few weeks before the end of the term, the three boys—all members of the same ROTC division—were not dismissed. When the semester was over Sweet headed off to Detroit, as was his habit. He delivered himself to work, to the supervision of a Wilberforce alumnus, and to finding a job to continue financing his education.

His name does not appear on the official record again for any infraction.

There is a picture of eight Wilberforce students and one member of the faculty, the charter members of Kappa Alpha Psi in 1915. They look solemn, serious, perhaps even grave. No one smiles. They stand at an angle in two rows; they wear white shirts, jackets, and bow ties. Three are members of the baseball team; three are on the football team; one is the editor of the student yearbook, *Sodalian;* two are commissioned officers in the Cadet Corps; two plan to attend medical school, one of whom is Ossian Sweet.

These students organized a chapter of Kappa Alpha Psi, the fourth in the country but the first on an all-black campus. Joining these Greek-letter clubs resembled what their industrious, middle-class fathers were doing at home. Throughout the teens and twenties, they met in halls of the Elks, Odd Fellows, Masons, or Knights of Pythias—to name just a few of the dozens where they played cards, drank, and tended to their community's social needs. Most embraced a value, whether social service, ethnic pride, or even racial superiority. At roughly the same time Ossian Sweet and a dozen other students were practicing how to perfect the secret handshake for Kappa Alpha Psi, a man named William Simmons was trying to revive another secret society, the Knights of the Ku Klux Klan. The release of *Birth of a Nation* in 1915 provided the perfect opportunity to excite new followers.

Coinciding with the regeneration of the defunct Ku Klux Klan, the release of *Birth of a Nation* would become a moment as singular for the South as it would be for the future of movie history. Adapted from *The Clansman,* a book published in 1906, it was a melodrama about the love between a Southern belle (Elsie), a Northern beau (Ben), and a war they were able to transcend. But the peace threatened to divide them. The ambitious new director D. W. Griffith put Thomas Dixon's book to film with remarkable achievements, starting with length— twelve reels, or the equivalent of three hours. Griffith hired white actors in blackface to portray color-coded caricatures of good and evil. He represented the Klan as restoring gallantry and returning the South to antebellum stability. Ghostlike spectral figures rode horseback, draped in mask and cowl while leading people out of Reconstruction's belching chaos.

Their faces may have been hidden, but the film's message could not have been more transparent. The Klan would strictly regulate blacks and give lie to the promise of emancipation.

Advertising for the coming of this film was unprecedented. Griffith hired three publicists who plastered billboards at train stations and on highways from New York to Florida, spending as much as $40,000 a week. A live orchestra played Grieg, Liszt, and Beethoven with crescendos driving the audience to applaud, scream, and holler as if the actors could actually hear them urge Klansmen to splash through a river with their rifles held high. Griffith, the son of a Confederate army colonel and a native of Kentucky, knew how to unite whites in all regions and classes on behalf of racial solidarity.

In a culture unabashedly hardening lines of segregation, *Birth of a Nation* became as controversial as it was successful. Two weeks after the Los Angeles opening at Clune's Auditorium, the National Press Club offered a private viewing for five hundred dignitaries, including thirty-eight senators; the secretary of the navy, Josephus Daniels; and the Chief Justice of the United States, Edward D. White, a former Louisiana Klansman. President Woodrow Wilson, still mourning the death of his wife, received a private screening, after which he released a statement saying, "It was all so terribly true."

Wilson's remarks added to a controversy already taking shape. Progressive reformers Jane Addams and Rabbi Stephen Wise led critics in an appeal to the National Board of Censorship to suppress the film. In Washington, D.C., the NAACP student chapter at Howard University was in the forefront of the "stubborn" fight against the "photodrama." And in New York the national office of the NAACP filed lawsuits to censure the film's base theme. Critics asked for the removal of incendiary scenes portraying licentious black men lusting after white women, as well as a rape incident. But the board's mandate required monitoring obscenity in nickelodeons, not racial insults or provocations. In a divided opinion after three meetings, the board voted fifteen to eight to decline involving itself.

Griffith refused to voluntarily cut controversial scenes, but he did trim those that failed to evoke the audience response he expected. He would rise from his seat near the back of the theater and with light spilling from the projector, splice out scenes while the film rolled on. In this way, he cut 170 frames, citing his prerogative for artistic balance. As a result of such idiosyncratic editing, no two copies of the film were the same.

The embattled director defended his work by asserting that he paid "attention to those faithful Negroes who stayed with their former masters and were ready to give up their lives to protect their white friends." It was the "good Negroes whose devotion is so clearly shown" who received adulation, he maintained.

In cities where *Birth of a Nation* screened, theaters charged $2—anywhere from four to eight times the regular admission. New York City's Liberty Theater was clearing $2,000 a day in a short time, and more than 825,000 people saw the film before the first run closed. In Los Angeles *Birth of a Nation* screened for seven months. In rural America promoters trucked veterans from villages and hamlets to theaters in larger cities, and the continual showings wore down the twenty-four copies in nationwide use.

As the controversy rippled from the East Coast to the West, cities and states responded separately. A Massachusetts court and a New York City mayor jumped into the fray, asking Griffith to remove specific scenes. Pennsylvania and California demanded modifications. St. Louis, Missouri, declined to show it, explaining "tender" race relations. Iowa and Ohio forbade it from theaters in their states.

Ohio's decision to ban *Birth of a Nation* came after the attorney general fought the film all the way to the state supreme court. When the announcement came in July 1916, the black-owned *Cleveland Advocate* said it hoped that the movie would be restricted "for all time." The accord proved to be short-lived. One year later it became a campaign issue, and, wanting to see the film, voters tossed out of office the incumbent governor, Frank B. Willis. With America's entry into the First World War looking more and more likely, and the draft under way, black churches in Columbus cautioned that the government should not "insult any class of citizens." But it was too late. Ohio's board of censors voted again, this time reversing itself, and opened the door for *Birth of a Nation*.

None of the controversy that dogged the film in the West or Midwest incited the South. The *Augusta Chronicle* declared it was the "Greatest Picture Ever Produced." The *Houston Chronicle* called it "Gripping and Wonderful." *Atlanta Constitution* columnist Ned McIntosh compared Griffith to Homer. The advance work could not have been better or the coincidence more propitious for William Joseph Simmons, a man possessed of a dream.

For more than two decades Simmons had been hungering to resurrect the Ku Klux Klan, his father's defunct fraternity. His appetite grew while he followed reviews for *Birth of a Nation*.

Simmons hailed from Harpersville, Alabama. Thirty-five and un-married, he comforted himself with stories of his youth. Romantic yarns and fantastical accounts were embedded in memories of his father's short-lived connection to the original white caps. They started in Tennessee and aimed to wrest control of Reconstruction from Northern carpetbaggers, Yankee politicians, and emancipated slaves. But even if Simmons had not remembered boyhood stories, to live in the South in 1915 was to grow up with the fable and the fiction and, perhaps, some of the survivors. On the fiftieth anniversary of the end of the Civil War, anybody could have pointed to the white-haired veterans scattered around town, or heard someone limp with the dull thud of a man dragging a wooden leg onto a porch. Someone inevitably could have recalled Sherman's march to the sea, the burning of Atlanta, or the Klan's campaigns to subdue local black men in the name of a mythic Southern honor.

After an automobile accident laid Simmons up for three months, his imagination roamed freely. It wasn't a serious accident. It was hardly even an injury. But during the period of his self-imposed confinement, he followed reviews of the celebrated film with its eighteen thousand extras and three thousand horses, and the reenactment of the siege of Petersburg. And all the while he was recuperating, he doodled compulsively. He drew men on braying horses, clad in white, stampeding across the fields in their hooded costumes. He wrote a new language, words beginning with the letters "kl" including "kleagle," "klavern," "kligrapp." He created rituals, secret and mystical, for enlisting "gentile members of the Anglo-Saxon race."

Simmons's passionate desire to rejuvenate the defunct fraternity got a boost after 1915 when Leo Frank, a Jewish businessman convicted of a murder he didn't commit, was lynched outside Atlanta. Three months later Simmons gathered the lynch mob to plan for the resurrection of the Klan, and coordinated the announcement for the day in December when *Birth of a Nation* would premiere in Atlanta. An advertisement for the Klan appeared in the *Atlanta Journal* adjacent to the advertisement for the movie. Theatrics and frenzy accompanied the premiere, while sheet-draped men on horseback stormed Atlanta's Peachtree Street in front of the theater where viewers were lining up to buy tickets.

Until that moment Simmons's life was remarkably uneventful and inconsequential. After failing as a medical student, riding circuit as a Methodist minister, he sold burial insurance for Woodmen of the World, a fraternal organization, and he led regiments of its uniformed drill team. For this he insisted that the world salute him with the title colonel. The *Atlanta Journal*'s Ralph McGill wrote that he seemed equally at ease leading prayer or playing cards, and the mints and cloves he chewed to disguise the bourbon on his breath hardly fooled anyone. He was six feet, two inches tall, and flaming red hair topped his head as he walked around wearing stiff collars, conservative ties, and a diamond stickpin. With the charms from fraternal lodges clanging from his vest, you could hear him before you could see him moving through town, wearing holes into his shoes. While the nation focused on war in Europe, he was laying the groundwork to wage war for an evangelical campaign for racial supremacy at home, using the slogan "100 Per Cent American." And he fought it with a fervor equal to any soldier on foreign soil enacting a personal fantasy of patriotism.

Ossian Sweet, in the meantime, was finishing his studies at Wilberforce and preparing for his graduation in June 1917. After spending six years and nine months in Ohio, he had not only earned a high school diploma and a college degree, but set a precedent for his younger brothers and sisters, now numbering nine. The year he graduated, he was one of 455 black Americans to do so. The numbers would dip by about twenty-five percent during the Great War, and it would not be until 1921 that they reached that level again.

If attending college placed Sweet among the unusual, an admission to the medical school at Howard University, the ruby in the crown of higher education, practically installed him in the elite. In the fifty years since the Freedmen's Bureau founded a college on a one-hundred-acre knoll in Washington, D.C., it had attracted an urbane and talented faculty. It had schools of law, pharmacy, and dentistry, and the medical school received a top ranking when the Carnegie Corporation conducted a national study of medical education, the Flexner Report. Named after its author, Abraham Flexner, it was, in 1909, perhaps the most influential educational evaluation ever to determine a school's stature. The evaluation was inspired by the ostensible weaknesses of American medical education when compared to European teaching, and Flexner visited 155 schools, which he scored according to entrance requirements, faculty training, teaching methods, and course of study. Of the medical schools Flexner visited in 1909, one-third would fold within five years. For Howard University, Flexner's score was the equivalent of racial parity, an endorsement of standards and achievement for the next half century. Along with Meharry, it became the gold standard for training black doctors.

No parent could have wanted more for his son than to continue his education at Howard University's School of Medicine. No student could have distinguished himself more honorably. It left no doubt that Ossian Sweet was on the way to earning his place in the Talented Tenth.

CHAPTER 3

Moving Up

The United States entered the First World War in the spring of 1917. Nobody was really surprised when, on April 2, President Woodrow Wilson asked Congress for a declaration against the Central Powers—Germany, the Austro-Hungarian Empire, and the Ottoman Empire—a request that belied the campaign slogan "He kept us out of war." Within a month a military draft was registering soldiers, subjecting recruits to the army's new intelligence tests before shipping them off for segregated combat to fulfill Wilson's pledge to "make the world safe for democracy."

Of the two major impacts of a war for black America, one was intertwined with military service. Eventually four hundred thousand men would enlist. They would quickly discover that, with rare exceptions, uniformed prejudice ran as deep as civilian prejudice. Despite a segregated officer training camp, which opened in July in Des Moines, Iowa, and held the promise of training for leadership, black soldiers were expected to assist and not to guide. It was an expectation that would cause chagrin at home and embarrassment abroad, and that would become part of Germany's wartime propaganda machinery.

The other major consequence of the war for black Americans came when Northern factories enticed Southerners to replace workers who had enlisted. Conflict in Europe had already halted the steady supply of foreign labor, and now manpower shortages threatened an industrial output. Companies looked to the South, suffering its own economic crisis after the boll weevil nibbled the cotton industry into catastrophe two years in a row. Wearied by long days, little pay, and empty promises, southern workers idled their plows and tens of thousands abandoned a rural lifestyle starting in 1916. For the next ten years the lure of the North and the needs of the South forged a migration that became known as the Southern Exodus.

The trip North, by train or foot, that able-bodied black Americans made initially seemed no different from that made by other seekers of fortune, escaping poverty, speaking Greek, Polish, or Latvian. Southern blacks were fleeing a repression as harsh as any pogroms experienced by Jews or serfs at the hands of the czar, or a poverty as searing as any found in the hills of Calabria. And once it started, people could hardly contain their excitement. They talked about life in the North, of the advantages that would be theirs upon arrival. Conversations about better schools and housing, or the dignity of self-determination, crowded concern over thunder on Europe's battlefields, puny crops, or the boll weevil. They talked in barbershops. They talked leaving church, or chewing tobacco, or coming in from the fields. And those who feared talking openly because a white person might overhear the conversation and have them arrested could read about it anyway in the *Chicago Defender.*

The *Chicago Defender* was a weekly newspaper, a tabloid belonging to Robert Abbott, and, as the name implied, published out of Chicago. More than anything else, it became the emblem for the Southern Exodus and the unprecedented transit carrying more than one million people into cities such as Detroit. By the summer of 1917 editorials and letters published by the *Defender* reached a national audience and gave shape, form, and rhythm to people leaving the South.

Robert Abbott was the child of emancipated slaves who was raised in Georgia. He learned to admire the press, to respect its power, from his stepfather, the Reverend John H. H. Sengstacke. Sengstacke was of German descent. He had a white mother, a black father, and a family store three miles outside Savannah. In addition to his riveting belief in God, he believed in the power of the press to build a better world, and he founded a weekly newspaper in their hometown. There he taught his stepson how to set type, a skill Abbott improved with study at the Hampton Institute before moving to Chicago. At the age of thirty-five, and as a legacy to his late stepfather, he used the twenty-five cents in his pocket to launch the *Defender*.

In the early years Abbott managed the *Defender* with a combination of his own grit, help from family, and an editor whose miserly lifestyle was conducive to skimpy wages. He also depended on volunteers, the entertainers and Pullman porters who spent time on the road, visiting towns large and small, and on the way placing copies in restaurants, barbershops and theaters, and on the seats of Jim Crow trains. No town crier carried information to a national black community more effectively. In an age of tabloid journalism, Abbott enlivened copy with dramatic accounts of shootings, of young couples who surprised their parents and eloped, and of grisly fires. He carried news of social events outside of Chicago, politics, and mutilations, along with ads for hair straighteners and skin whiteners. Even error did not subdue him. The masthead, an outstretched eagle, resembled William Randolph Hearst's logo. Hearst asked him to change it, but he waited so long for a response that he had to threaten to sue before Abbott did. The *Defender* traded so heavily on rumor and gossip that it gave rise to the rumor that it actually belonged to Hearst. This only turned a spotlight onto a weekly newspaper that rejoiced over every controversy and all the gossip that could expand its circulation.

Part of the *Defender*'s cutting edge came from Abbott's pioneering use of the word "Race," as in "members of the Race," to replace words like "Negro" or the more common "colored." At its peak a national edition reached one and a half million people, and carrying it on the streets became a status symbol. Even illiterate people tucked a copy under their arms so others could see the paper, which was recognizable from its headlines, two inches high, inked in red, with pictures of fancy houses in Northern cities that made words irrelevant.

Readers wanted to believe Robert Abbott's claims that "justice and fairness" were widespread in the North compared to the "barbarous and wholesale lynching" in the South. They responded favorably when he bellowed that they should leave to escape a noose, when he said soothingly that they should leave with confidence. He urged Southern blacks to set their departures no later than May 15 "to become acclimated," he said, to cities like Detroit where the winter wind gathers force blowing across the lake and right through the seams of your overcoat.

Abbott thought a specific date was catchy, with just the right sound, perfect pitch for a season to move. But the trip North actually began without ceremony. With the exhortations of a prophet, Abbott infused readers with hope for a better life. What he could not do, alas, was make the dream come true. Success required education, ambition, and achievement, and even so, there were no guarantees.

Abbott was average in height and average in looks, and he was also quirky, stubborn, and controversial. When he posed for pictures, he wore a top hat, sometimes spats, creating an image of courtliness. He held a gold-headed cane. Nobody was surprised when he amassed a fortune, which made him the first black man in America to become a millionaire. But wealth and success did not unleash his emotions. Perhaps there was an inner warmth, maybe even a glow, but he is remembered as cold, aloof, and dictatorial. After twenty years he did not know his secretary's name, and his two wives never got beyond calling him "mister." He didn't smoke, drink, or swear, and according to his biographer, Roi Ottley, he smiled infrequently. Yet he sent associates to college, paid their tuition. And his memory was so sharp, it was said, that he never forgot a story assignment. A commitment to justice influenced his leadership. Scores accepted his guidance, and Kappa Alpha Psi, the fraternity Ossian Sweet pledged at Wilberforce, honored his achievements.

With the mettle of his newspaper, Abbott created a migration by ceaselessly castigating the increasing burdens of Jim Crow. The worst was turning the killing of black citizens into a new kind of sport. "Not Belgium—America" read the caption over the picture of the decapitated head of Ell Person,

> who was burned to death in Memphis, Tenn. This head was cut off the body, and is seen here with both ears severed, his nose and upper lip cut off. 'Twas not the work of the Germans, but the South—Memphis and its population that stood by and saw in broad daylight without any effort to stop the outrage.

Person had been accused of murdering a white girl—an accusation needing no more substantiation than his race for a lynch mob to justify its action. When Abbott compared Person's murder and the mutilation of his body to the way the Germans had massacred the Belgians during World War I, he evoked a modern benchmark for evil.

Once he decided, it didn't take Abbott long to open a corridor stretching from the South. Cities like Chicago, Pittsburgh, and Detroit were among the most popular of all destinations. So what if snow became dirty slush when cold spells swept the North? He had a folksy answer for that as for everything else. "To die from the bite of frost is far more glorious than at the hands of a mob," he opined. He sponsored travel clubs with special rates for groups of ten or more. Who would not be moved by reading the story of an idealized, happy workman in a Pullman factory earning twice what he made in Birmingham, Alabama? Readers responded as if Abbott had called them personally. "The colored people will leave if you will assist them," wrote a woman from Pensacola, Florida. And they did. Day after day, week after week, they went up North for work in the mills, the mines, and the factories.

Some were skilled mechanics or insurance salesmen, others were women who sewed or cleaned. There were men with wives but no children, men with wives and eleven children, some who taught school, others who couldn't read. One man who went to Detroit spent $50 for a new suit while another wore his overalls straight from the fields, still covered with Georgia's red dust. Journalist Ray Stannard Baker observed how a teamster would sit in his buggy, waiting to hear sounds of metal, faint at first, before the ground would tremble as the train drew close. When it was before him, in an instant, he would jump onto the train, leaving a braying horse. The car he boarded might have a message painted on the side: "Bound for the Promised Land." When the train crossed into the North, the conductor might stop just long enough to let passengers step onto the banks of the Ohio River, where they would fall to their knees and shout thanks to God, like their predecessors bound for Detroit on the Underground Railroad seventy years before.

The trip was easiest for the thousands with free tickets from companies such as Bessemer, which sent empty trains to carry workers into Pennsylvania's coal mines. The Illinois Central Railroad took them to Chicago's stockyards. Sharecroppers earning $15 a month went to Newark, where, it was rumored, factory jobs paid $2.75 a day, plus rent; to Pittsburgh where a man could earn $3 a day; to Detroit where $5 a day for auto workers seemed princely. From Savannah, Jacksonville, or Mobile, they left to escape lynching and perhaps to prosper.

Labor scouts helped. Employed by industry or hired by the railroads, they lived off the hopes of the desperate. Unscrupulous scouts demanded signed contracts from people who couldn't read. Or they made a profit by selling the same $2 ticket a company in the North was giving away. Or they took a finder's fee for a nonexistent job. A man who boarded a train intending to go to Detroit could end up in Flint if that was where the train that General Motors had sent wanted him to work. Even those with an eighth grade education could not fathom the standard contract. Just make an X on the line, they were told. It didn't matter if you couldn't read. Like carnival barkers, fanciful and fantastical, labor scouts shaped a new reality for those who were willing to believe. From Mississippi, 130,000 people fled, from South Carolina, 75,000; from Alabama, 60,000. And they swelled cities such as Pittsburgh, where the black population increased by nearly fifty percent, or New York City, by roughly sixty-six percent. But of all the cities where the population grew during the years of the Southern Exodus, none compared to Detroit, where the number of blacks increased by more than six hundred percent. Rumor, fantasy, and the desire for safety carried them North.

O f the million people who left the South before 1917, about ten thousand ended up in East St. Louis, Illinois. They had come in search of jobs. Some wanted to work badly enough that they came as strikebreakers. After the strike, they kept the jobs the white men thought were theirs.

Located across the Mississippi River from Missouri, East St. Louis rattled with the tracks of twenty-eight railroad lines tying East to West. Meat processors like Swift & Company, Armour & Company, and Morris & Company operated plants that ringed the city. It was home to the International Harvester Company, the Bon Bon Baking Powder Company, and the Aluminum Ore Company, which was worth more than $20 million. And it was a rough place with gamblers and prostitutes and 376 saloons—one for every 199 men, women, and children. Most of the town's revenue came from saloon licenses. Contemporaries described East St. Louis as a place to find plenty of coal and water to go with the cheap land and transportation. Life, too, was cheap, or so it seemed that summer.

The tensions had been building steadily since the previous year. Strikes at the aluminum ore and meat packing plants brought forty-five hundred workers to the picket lines. It could only mean trouble when a group of whites escaped indictment for a racial assault in May. A few weeks later, it would be too late.

It was warm on Sunday evening, the first of July, and still bright outside when white joy-riders drove along Market Street shooting into houses. In retaliation, black residents fired at the next car of whites to cruise by. It happened to be carrying plainclothes policemen, and bullets killed two of them.

The next day anarchy was loosed, as white set upon black. After clubbing one man into submission, a group of white men branded him between the eyes. White girls were playing games by running through the streets and kicking in the faces of black corpses lying here and there. One person used a butcher knife to cut off the head of a man before dumping his trunk over the Free Bridge. A mob nailed houses shut, then torched them while residents struggled to get out. Soldiers from Troop L of the Illinois militia watched a crowd torture seven drowning victims. Laughing, joking, they pelted men who were forced into the Cahokia Creek, where they were bobbing up and down. Local police shot off the arm of a cleaning woman standing with her nose against the window of her employer's house. Fires lit the city, and the awful smell of burned flesh hung in the air.

Initial reports estimated at least 75 people dead. By the end of the first week, when the fires had died down and a search was conducted through the rubble, smoking timber, and collapsed homes, the figure was nearer 250; another 6,000 people were left homeless; property damages exceeded $3 million (which would approximate $40 million in 2000).

Promises of more troops kept calm and pacified fears. Grand jury indictments followed. So, too, arrests. And the public response was varied: A select citizens' committee, including Abbott, petitioned Illinois governor Frank O. Lowden for an investigation. But their hopes gave way to cynicism when the investigations appeared to stall. From distant cities, readers sent letters expressing outrage. Ten thousand people marched on New York's Fifth Avenue to protest silently. Cleveland held an interracial forum to discuss the Exodus. Newspapers supplied their own explanations: a housing shortage, militant blacks, negligent police, labor unrest, national politics. In California, a columnist wondered whether a German conspiracy could be to blame.

Exactly one month later, on August 1, a delegation of black leaders visited Washington, imploring politicians and urging the federal government to respond. The group of savvy, Eastern leaders was headed by NAACP officials, joined by the Reverend Adam Clayton Powell, from New York's Abyssinian Baptist Church, and Fred Moore, editor of the *New York Age*. They called upon the president, whom they already distrusted, and their conviction was deepened when Wilson absented himself, sending his private secretary, Joseph P. Tumulty, to receive them and the petitions they carried. But he was no more than a messenger delivering what must have surely been depressing news, that the president had not yet decided whether the racial massacre "would justify federal action."

Congressional hearings convened in October to determine "whether the laws of interstate commerce were broken." After listening to a woman describe how she was forced to watch the mutilation of her husband and son before witnessing their execution, Wisconsin's Representative Henry A. Cooper expressed his horror when he said unabashedly, "Indians could have done no worse." The hearing's five thousand pages of testimony seemed pro forma. Long on talk, short on action, they were mute on race.

At a time when America was making the world "safe for democracy," who was making America safe for Americans? This was the question Robert Abbott asked, noting that the riot in East St. Louis erupted in the home state of Abraham Lincoln. Abbott wrote, "No country can long prosper unless steps are taken to remedy this evil internal strife." Despite the dangers of unrestrained racial violence, despite the shivers the words East St. Louis would henceforth invoke, Abbott continued to urge migration as the best solution to escape the oppression of Jim Crow. "Make your own destiny," he implored. In the early days of migration, threats seemed manageable in comparison to the state-sponsored segregation in the South. After East St. Louis, one couldn't be too sure.

The Harlem branch of the NAACP, still in its infancy, mounted a visible, organized response to East St. Louis, a demonstration on Saturday, July 27. On that morning the sun rose in a cloudless sky over New York City, where parades were synonymous with civic pride. The day would turn out to be a scorcher, breaking twenty-five-year-old heat records, and nurses and doctors set up first aid stations on Fifth Avenue while police on horseback cleared a path for the demonstrators. By 10 A.M. the streets of midtown Manhattan were closed to traffic.

With perspiration already beginning to moisten upper lips, ten thousand people converged to protest three riots—in Waco, Texas; Memphis, Tennessee; and East St. Louis—which left their brothers and sisters, cousins and parents dead. Young children headed the parade, eight hundred in all, dressed in white. Women followed, also in white. Then came the men, wearing mourners' black. They came from Harlem and they came from Brooklyn, and many of the spectators crowding onto the curbs had taken the day off. From Fifty-seventh Street they marched downtown neatly, in somber rows of twenty covering the black-topped streets. At Forty-sixth Street a young man stepped out to explain the procession to two white women. At Forty-third Street spectators applauded demonstrators carrying a banner, "Square Deal," Theodore Roosevelt's slogan. When the marchers reached Forty-second Street, red caps left their posts at Grand Central Station and pressed into the crowd, watching a slight breeze curl flags of Haiti and Liberia along with the red, white, and blue. The *New York Age* described it as "a sight as has never before been seen."

While the eyes of New York City washed over the Silent Negro Parade in Manhattan, for the second day a race riot raged in Chester, Pennsylvania. In addition to those who died in East St. Louis and

Chester, fifty people, including two whites, would be lynched, shot, or burned in 1917.

While workers flooded East St. Louis, other Northern cities, including Detroit and Washington, D.C., were being overrun by migrants who left the only homes they had ever known. What happened in East St. Louis was the first in a cluster of violent riots, and in days to come, the volatility of whites, the unpredictability of labor, and the power of xenophobia had to count among the risks of migrating North. Over the next several years, riots would erupt in northern cities like Duluth, Minnesota, Washington, D.C., and Abbott's own Chicago. They would ravage the South—Ocoee, Rosedale, Elaine, Tulsa. Each one, in whatever part of the country, must have tugged at Abbott's optimism, sobered his spirit, deflated his confidence. "Here we find civilization at its height and barbarism at its depth," he wrote, an awful dualism to ponder when deciding whether to encourage a departure or snuff a dream.

Two years later, when the 1919 riots broke out in Washington, D.C., Sweet was on summer vacation, between his second and third years of medical school. While he was far from East St. Louis, he was present in Washington, an eyewitness to the worst race riot in the nation's capital since the Civil War.

The year began happily with the local press praising the gallantry of the First Separate Battalion on behalf of the twenty-five black Washington men who were awarded the Croix de Guerre. But the goodwill did not last through the year, and by the summer, the city had become tense. A bomb exploded at the home of Attorney General A. Mitchell Palmer in June, unleashing a fear of Bolshevism that lingered in the halls of the Justice Department. Then the press ran sensationalist stories several days in a row, irresponsibly exaggerating rumors of assaults on white women. Unrestrained, the press accused black uniformed servicemen, fresh from Europe.

The clash began one Saturday night in July, almost exactly two years after East St. Louis, and its wild and frenzied pitch resembled elements of the Illinois pogrom. The press reported that whites hauled blacks from buses and cars, described how two hundred soldiers, sailors, and marines were "bent on lynching a Negro"; that trolley passengers shot indiscriminately into crowds, injuring civilians, police officers, and even one man on horseback. The riot occurred a few blocks from the Howard University campus on Fourth and N Streets, and reports spread that 150 blacks were attacking a streetcar. One of them was shot and taken to the hospital. To bring news back to campus, a junior member of the faculty, William Stuart Nelson, borrowed an army uniform and went to the scene to observe what he could and report back to the students. Ossian Sweet himself saw what the *New York Times* would later describe as "a band of soldiers and sailors" dragging a black man "from a street car on G Street, NW, between Ninth and Tenth."

True to form, President Wilson showed only casual interest in racial violence, and was heavily criticized for taking more than a week to declare martial law. Before he did, riots had broken out in Bisbee, Arizona, and Norfolk, Virginia. Meanwhile, the press responded with its own impressions. Before the Great War, "Negroes in Washington were well behaved," opined the *New York Times*. At one time, it said, "most of them admitted the superiority of the white race." But no more. The Great War changed all that, drawing workers away from their jobs, opening the door for replacements from the South. Like other Northern cities, Washington suffered from adjusting to the displacement, from the upheaval brought about by the presence of throngs of new people.

A few days later, while Washington still commanded headlines, Chicago would erupt, leaving several blacks dead, including a policeman who happened to be the cousin of Gladys Atkinson, the future Mrs. Sweet. But Detroit, where Sweet had been spending summers for nearly eight years, seemed different. Perhaps it would be a good city in which to make one's future.

CHAPTER 4

Getting Settled

I n 1911 when Ossian Sweet first went to Detroit for a summer job, the medley of local industries included pharmaceutical companies, employing more than twenty thousand people; manufacturers of cigars and cigar boxes; tanneries turning cow hide into leather goods; and shipyards serving the Great Lakes. But it was the ascending automobile industry, fiercely competitive, that was transforming this city with its growing population. Before the First World War, 270 manufacturers would produce four hundred different car models, and people such as Henry Ford, John Dodge, David Buick, Ransom Olds, and Walter Chrysler vied for prominence. Most competitors did not survive the decade, leaving an open field for Ford's Model T, called the "Runabout," which came out of the Highland Park factory, with the first assembly line, in 1905. With a sticker price of $390, the Model T cost half of what consumers had to pay for the Dodge Brothers' four-cylinder car. Both were beyond the reach of the typical worker, with an average wage of $2.74 a day. After Ford's revolutionary announcement of a $5-a-day wage in 1914, a steady supply of labor flocked to Detroit to work for companies making "the machine."

Detroit would change more in the first two decades of the twentieth century than in the three hundred years since the French built a fort near the river and Robert La Salle saw "vast meadows covered with vineyards, trees bearing good fruit, groves and forests." Ossian Sweet watched Detroit evolve from the sidelines, but its change was unmistakable. In 1910, with 466,000 people, it ranked as the ninth largest city in the nation. A decade later it had moved to fourth place with more than one million. Sweet couldn't work in the industries—most of which had color codes. But watchful Wilberforce alumni sheltered him and other students in summer jobs. He worked at the Fairfax Hotel as a bellhop, assisting tourists or businessmen coming to see Detroit's self-styled elegance; as a waiter for the D. & C. Navigation Company, which routinely hired black students for the sunset dinner cruise between Detroit and Cleveland. He worked on the segregated Bob Lo Island as a vendor selling soda pop to the whites. There a gentleman wore a stiffly starched white shirt under his black coat, had a lady on his arm, and strolled around the dance pavilion, built without electricity to discourage the turkey trot on this picture-perfect island.

One of the most profound areas of growth came from the black population. When Sweet first arrived, even by national standards the black community was small, with only fifty-four hundred people. By 1925 they would exceed eighty thousand people, and most came on the Exodus.

"During the past 12 months, the colored population of Detroit has increased by about 100 percent through migration," wrote Forrester B. Washington in 1917. Washington was head of a newly formed social agency, originally called the Associated Charities, later the Urban League, with a mission to help newcomers. And their needs were greater than anybody could have imagined. A youngster rode barefoot all the way from Tennessee with his feet sticking out of an open-air box car. By January, when he reached Detroit, his foot had frozen. The Receiving Hospital turned him away because he was not a resident. He stumbled into the offices of the Urban League. They contacted the Poor Commission. The Poor Commission sent him to Chicago, where he had family undergoing adjustment problems of their own. Other immigrants followed relatives who proceeded them. One woman sat for a week in the River Rouge post office where she had been writing to her sister in care of General Delivery; one brought her three-month-old baby, and together they spent four days sitting in the lobby of a different post office before her husband could arrive.

By early 1917 it was clear that the harshest of winters would not—could not—slow the traffic. Ten carloads left Selma, Alabama, in January. Soon after, the *Chicago Defender* reported eleven hundred people setting out for Pittsburgh and Detroit. Sixty followed from Macon and Bordel, Georgia. Two years later a similar pattern intensified. "There seems to be no let up on the part of colored people coming into Detroit," noted Urban League officials. Three years later the daily count was in the hundreds. One Sunday morning in May, 296 people arrived, a fraction of the 1,809 coming that week. By the end of the decade the black population had grown to forty thousand, more than seven times what it had been ten years earlier. In another five years it would double again.

Forrester Washington and the Urban League had a daunting responsibility. Was it possible to weave so many newcomers into the fabric of the existing community? Washington had never anticipated the magnitude with its resulting burden. In an article appearing in the July 14, 1917, issue of *The Survey,* a new magazine dedicated to the emerging profession of social workers, Washington described the migration to Detroit in the first part of a two-part story. It followed a description of the East St. Louis riot, aptly titled, "Welcoming Southern Negroes: East St. Louis and Detroit—a Contrast." The author of the portion on East St. Louis was a social worker from a local Jewish agency. He labeled the East St. Louis riot a "pogrom," calling forth images rife with symbolism and cautionary implications of the czar's campaigns to exterminate Russian Jews.

Washington said the purpose of his article was to help other communities facing problems similar to Detroit's. Suggestions sounded like textbook entries for how to intercede on behalf of displaced persons who needed jobs, housing, recreation, and information about "crime prevention." He emphasized that Southern pilgrims should maintain a sober, uplifting life, and he offered a formula for successful assimilation in the burgeoning industries of the North. It was the personal qualities—ambition, punctuality, cooperation—that would earn the system's reward, just as Booker T. Washington (no relation) identified personal qualities for surviving in a white world a generation earlier. Forrester Washington's advice could have applied to any of the Urban League's twenty-six member communities that helped their migrating Southern cousins.

What Washington did not say in *The Survey*, what he obscured for his colleagues who were mostly white and mostly women and whom historian Roy Lubove has called "professional altruists," was how much he feared that race mattered profoundly. Washington had heard what the larger community of black intellectuals, members of the Talented Tenth, were saying when the topic of race was discussed in public. "When the term 'Negro' is used in news matter," lamented the *Michigan Manual of Freedmen's Progress*, "it refers to the criminal Negro and not to that vast bulk of black people who are making good." Even for Washington, as a black social worker who received his education at Tufts University and Harvard College, race magnified the dilemma Exodusters brought to Detroit.

Like other members of the Urban League, a group whom sociologist E. Franklin Frazier would later call the "black bourgeoisie," Washington worked hard, carried civic burdens, and was inclined to judge Exodusters harshly if that is how he presumed his white counterparts did. Few traits caused them greater embarrassment than the rustic manners that recent arrivals, passengers on the Southern Exodus, displayed. These were the very traits that whites scorned. Washington worried about people who arrived "with no idea of where they were going to stop and entirely unfamiliar with conditions," he said. They had willingly traded the familiarity of agrarian rhythms, shaped by rural poverty, and edged by Jim Crow's boundaries, to gamble on a future in Detroit. Abandoning the only homes they had ever known, eschewing family and the aromas of a sweet spring dew, they straggled North to embrace a dream. No one imagined that urban poverty could be harsher than what they had left. That a man could not just walk into the woods and come out with a pocket full of huckleberries. That there were strategies and systems and lists for how to get jobs. That Jim Crow might still try to tell them where to live. Luck brought a few to a familiar face from home. Others searched for relatives of friends, or friends of relatives, people already settled, people who would, if they could, offer a meal or help finding a job. They might even suggest a place to live. But usually not.

Early on, Washington feared the increase in number would promote conflict along lines of class and race. "A great deal of discrimination has grown up," he reported to the board of directors, "on account of the loud, noisy, type of Negroes unused to city ways that are flocking to Detroit." Helping them manage involved more than pointing them toward food or housing, more than exhortations about moral uplift. It required intercepting new migrants, teaching them what to wear, how to speak, what not to say, where not to go.

Shortly after taking upon itself the obligation to help migrants, the Urban League had volunteers meeting trains. It sent them to the platforms so within minutes of hearing the sounds of metal on metal, they could weave in and out of the crowd, looking out for someone draped in a costume wearing the unmistakable signs of rural poverty. It could be a man in an undershirt and overalls, a woman in a calico dress—a "Mother Hubbard." Or someone who simply looked perplexed. And why not? Most had come from a town in which the station was little more than an open-air platform along a single track—a dramatic contrast to standing in a terminal about the size of a football field, with a ceiling ninety-eight feet above ground level covering a maze of steel rail. The Michigan Central Station was one of the nation's newest, grandest, most modern terminals, having opened in 1914. Public waiting rooms contained polished mahogany benches, glistening marble halls, gargantuan Doric columns, and delicate high arches. Luxurious restaurant dining required linen cloths; passengers sliding quickly through a meal would try the lunch counter. Commercial conveniences included a newsstand, a cigar shop, separate bathing facilities for men and women, and a barbershop with shoeshine stations. It offered more services than the cities most migrants had just left. And with 140 trains arriving daily, it was probably noisier, more congested, and busier, as well. But the train station was also the place where first impressions were made by the weary who had traveled anywhere from hours to days—changing trains, leapfrogging cities, leaving a wife or a child behind, if only temporarily, to seek a better life.

Volunteers from the Urban League met the trains thrice daily and a plainclothes policeman helped out, watching for trouble, protecting migrants from street predators. Police presence could also guarantee, as Washington put it, that Exodusters did "not make a nuisance of themselves by blockading sidewalks, [with] boisterous behavior and the like." Students from the Young Negro Progressive Association handed out printed cards with directions to Urban League Headquarters on St. Antoine Street, along with invitations to the Tuesday night dances at the YMCA.

The Reverend Robert Bradby often went down to the station to greet newcomers. Bradby was the minister at the Second Baptist Church, who viewed meeting the Exodusters as part of his calling. Years later many would remember the first time they saw this man with his fair skin, glasses shaped like silver dollars, and eyes that smiled even when his lips turned down. New arrivals must have noticed how he walked among the masses. It was the way, one imagines, an aristocrat might have. But he carried the social gospel to the streets, and the people he reached needed jobs and a roof over their heads as much as they did a tabernacle.

Bradby breathed zeal and the passion of the activist tradition of his church, dating from the nineteenth century when it hid runaway slaves. Founders were freedmen, impatient with the mainstream white Baptist Church because it refused to grant them equal voting rights in 1836. As insurgents, the congregation of the Second Baptist Church hosted abolitionist conventions, invited Frederick Douglass and John Brown. By Bradby's time, the church welcomed Exodusters. It organized picnics and boat trips to Sugar Island, one of the many islands in the Detroit River, one of the few available to blacks.

Soon after Bradby's arrival in 1910, the black power elite's orbit expanded. And it grew again the following year after Reverand Robert W. Bagnall became pastor of the elitist St. Matthew's Episcopal Church. This was Detroit's grand church of the nineteenth century, not a place for neighborhood parishioners, the people who came to pray on any given Sunday. It was where the upper-crust rented pews, where the self-appointed "blue book of colored society" sparkled, confirming what economist Thorstein Veblen once described as "conspicuous consumption." Here, elaborate displays of clothes, flowers, and other finery set the stage for lavish weddings. Black Detroiters would value St. Matthew's Episcopal Church as a place to find "pretty girls," those whose color was called "high yellow," meaning they might even pass for white.

Bagnall, the son of an Episcopalian minister from Virginia, was not primarily a society preacher. At St. Matthew's he was an activist who did away with pew rentals in the same way he challenged segregated schools in nearby Ypsilanti. He lectured widely throughout Michigan, opposing laws outlawing interracial marriage, organizing branch chapters of the NAACP throughout the midwest, including in Detroit where he called for its first meeting in the basement of his church. Bagnall served as treasurer for the Detroit chapter, among the earliest, while William Osby became its first president in 1911.

It had been only eight years since Osby arrived from Pennsylvania with a degree in engineering from a correspondence school. But already he was central, connecting the black community through his work managing apartment buildings, then hotels, along with his numerous charitable activities. As a power broker, he served on the boards of the Urban League and the Second Baptist Church, among others. Eventually he would raise money to organize the Dunbar Memorial Hospital, where as its executive director, he signed talented physicians, newcomers like doctors Edward A. Carter and Ossian H. Sweet.

The race riots that swept Chicago and Washington in 1919 spared Detroit despite the harshness of ghetto living. No matter what dream a person carried with him, without a job or means he usually ended up in Paradise Valley. This was one of Detroit's oldest and most decrepit neighborhoods, sometimes called Black Bottom. It spanned an area from the river to Gratiot Street between Beaubien Street and St. Aubin Avenue. That was before immigration swelled the district, forcing people to move north and east, beyond the downtown core, forming pie-shaped wedges in the surrounding white neighborhoods.

If you asked locals to describe Paradise Valley, they might talk about Long's all-night drugstore, or Brown Skinned Models, a revue at the Koppin Theater. Maybe they would mention dancing at the Graystone Ballroom at Adams and St. Antoine, where, after the whites left, they got started around midnight, stayed until dawn, and grabbed ham and eggs on the way out from "Cookies," at the corner, before going to work or home to sleep. The routine gave rise to the handle "breakfast dance." Those wanting a fancy meal could dine at the Lark Grill. If they wanted to watch a dinner show, the place to go was the Plantation Club in the basement of the Norwood Hotel. But they would have been hard-pressed to say there was much paradise in the housing on these narrow streets where aromas, sounds, and colors became one.

The story of Paradise Valley is a familiar one of changing tribes. It was a succession of peoples and cultures, losing some neighbors whose chatter was thick with a collision of consonants, gaining others who moved their words across an octave in lilting tones. Of course, plenty of people spoke English even if their Southern accent seemed foreign. Walking north on St. Antoine Street, they inhaled the aromas of Italian spaghetti dinners that Bagliotti's served up on Wednesday nights. If they turned right onto Gratiot Street, at the corner they might be draped by the fragrance of German rye bread baking. Another right turn onto Hastings Street and they would have stumbled upon a row of Jewish shops, with tailors and butchers and book dealers. But people of the old groups began to disappear from the streets they once shared with their black neighbors. And their departure left a ghetto that was poor because most blacks of means lived scattered throughout the city in homes they bought before 1920, before restrictive covenants legally shaped the racial contours of Detroit's neighborhoods.

Families lucky enough to find available housing near downtown stuffed themselves into the skeletons of nineteenth-century buildings that resembled "chicken coop style of architecture"—barns and stables, miserable alley dwellings where the wind blew cold. Others happened upon the "buffet flat," described as a "high class combination of a gambling parlor, a 'blind tiger' and an apartment of prostitution." It was said that they were "especially dangerous in a neighborhood camouflaged with private houses." Poor workers often shared rooms or beds—nineteen renters were discovered living in one of the attics—

with people who worked on the day shift alternating with those who worked at night. Some were happy to find an empty pool table for a few hours of sleep.

The Urban League's Forrester Washington described many of the worst situations in his housing report to the Detroit Associated Charities. He relied on the emerging methodology of visiting people at home, knocking on their doors, speaking directly, and making empirical observations. After spending months investigating the housing conditions of 440 black residents, Washington was not surprised that "not many Negro families in the city are well-housed."

Washington discovered that they paid higher rent for their homes, which were grossly inferior, than did white people. Their buildings and the construction were below par, and some needed substantial repair to make them minimally habitable. On Sherman Street, Washington saw a house where children were "stumbling over ice frozen on the floors." In another he watched rain "pour through the ceiling." In River Rouge several families who had no indoor plumbing were forced to use the village pump for water that would last them two or three days. "As a result," Washington wrote, "this water stands around unprotected and not boiled and offers a breeding-place for typhoid bacteria." Tenants recalled how frightened they were the first time the anger of a brawl threatened to burst through walls. Some had never used indoor plumbing. Even if there were acceptable vacancies, they were generally unaffordable. A family could spend $45 a month to rent a house, or $5 for each room of an apartment. After buying food, winter clothes, trolley fares, and medicines, that didn't leave much for the family, even of the wage earner who brought home $100 a month. And most black workers didn't come close to that. After the war, those who could afford the suburbs moved to Inkster at Eight Mile Road, or to River Rouge, thereby cutting down on the commute to the Ford plant, which could easily take up to two hours on the trolley.

If initial choices and inferior quality—even compared to the shacks some abandoned in rural Mississippi or Alabama—jolted the expectations of the poorest black migrants, they posed a staggering challenge for the Urban League. Its lists with names of landlords who had rooms to let, of industries that were hiring blacks were hardly sufficient. After Washington left, his replacement, John Dancy, appealed to James Couzens for help.

Couzens, son of a senator, was an original partner in the Ford Motor Company and the genius behind the $5-a-day wage bringing transplants to Detroit by the truckload. After harvesting his own fortune, Couzens left business for politics and was now Detroit's chief of police. Working with people like Couzens was a familiar experience for Dancy, who spent three years at Phillips-Exeter Academy before attending the University of Pennsylvania, from which he graduated in 1910. He had no difficulty telling Couzens, in his soft-spoken and urbane manner, that he wanted the city to do more for the Urban League than assign police to the Michigan Central Train Station. Not that the police presence wasn't important to greet newcomers. It was, and Dancy was grateful to have it. But it was insufficient for the people who arrived with so many needs. There had to be work.

Urban League research suggested that Packard Motor Car Company and Dodge Brothers were the best factories for blacks to find work. Dodge employed eleven hundred people. But the Ford Motor Company controlled nearly half of auto production, and blacks accounted for two hundred of the eighteen thousand workers at the Ford plant in Highland Park. River Rouge, which was built along a harbor on the southwest perimeter of Detroit, was just about the only automobile factory hiring blacks in all phases of production. There a worker might become a cog at an indoor assembly line where he would stamp, drill, punch, turn, press, and weld pins, bolts, and screws onto a moving chassis. Someone who was skilled had the best chance to become a cement finisher, an electric welder, an oven tender, a cone maker, a sand cutter, a machine molder, a press operator, a painter, or a sprayer. But industry called mostly for unskilled workers, and in the highly segregated workforce Exodusters were forced to settle for the dirty, greasy, and dangerous foundry jobs. Dancy appealed to Couzens for help in the automobile industry. He would have also accepted help in the pharmaceutical companies, tanneries, or textile companies, sewing garments, shipping, packing, and delivering. Could Couzens do anything?

Shortly after the end of the First World War, the economy softened and the Urban League panicked because more work went to women. Unemployed men began to leave Detroit. One hundred a day fanned out to Pittsburgh, Newark, New York, and Chicago. In October 1920 ten thousand were laid off in an economy that would continue to limp for at least one more year, with a depression and the consequent layoffs in the automobile industry. Some people made a U-turn and headed back South after their wages failed to keep them housed, clothed, and fed. We can hear despair in the voice of John Dancy when he reported that about one-third of Detroit's forty thousand black residents were on public relief in 1921. It was obvious, he said, "just what we are up against."

Class divisions roiled the black community as much as they did the white, and more so when blacks imagined themselves through white eyes. "There are, of course, untidy and uncouth white people, but white people are the judge and the colored people are being judged," Dancy wrote. And to deepen their despair, the women were ignorant about the use of the revolutionary new labor-saving devices that were being introduced rapidly into the home. Any woman who wanted day work had to be able to use machines for washing clothes, electric irons for pressing them, and electric sweepers—also called vacuums. In Detroit, home of the Eureka Vacuum Company employing 780 people, this was not a frivolous requirement. But the women had not brought that experience or knowledge from the South. And by 1921 urgency crept into the Urban League's vision. Dancy started reporting depleted relief funds, tired and overstretched volunteers, and the imbalance between job opportunities for women compared to the limited opportunities for black men. A rumor circulated, which was later denied, that the 1921 annual meeting of Detroit's Employers' Association recommended a hiring freeze on blacks and that its members agreed to fire blacks in some industries.

The downturn was so severe that it was beginning to affect even well-educated people, and Dancy wrote to college presidents heading schools in the South, warning that graduates would not have an easy time. Don't send them, he said. He feared that increased migration would "become a burden to the Northern communities and bring reproach and humiliation to thrifty colored citizens in communities where white people [had] not hitherto considered Negroes undesirables."

People who were part of the Exodus were later asked what it was like to come to Detroit. Understandably, their memories differed. Oscar Lee, who came by himself at the age of seventeen, remembered paying $50 to buy a new suit to make a good impression when he went to look for a job. The first hotel he found insisted he wash the suit to prevent the spread of lice. James E. Cummings, born in Alabama, moved to Detroit with his family when he was ten years old, and he remembered delivering newspapers, receiving one cent for every copy. Some months his family lived on his earnings, which could reach $50. Nathaniel Leach's first job after moving to Detroit from Tuscaloosa, Alabama, was cleaning spittoons in a barbershop next door to his house near Gratiot Street. He earned $1 a day. And Helen Nuttall remembers the family's return to Michigan after her father, Dr. Henry Nuttall, who had trained at the University of Michigan, was run out of his Alabama home because he was giving away railroad tickets for the trip up North. They moved into a house in Paradise Valley with a slate roof, a cork floor, and stained-glass windows. It was so fancy that it had central vacuuming. Sweet did not record his memories. But we know he discovered Detroit long before Robert Abbott called for the Southern Exodus, long before the Urban League tried to relieve its burdens, long before the increase in population displaced the black community.

It is estimated that ten percent of Southern blacks left in the first two years of the Exodus. By 1925 tens of thousands had passed through Detroit, leading to a siege mentality in which John Dancy, Forrester Washington, and Reverend Robert Bradby feared they would be stigmatized. It had happened before to other immigrants, to German Jews who looked askance at the behavior of their rural cousins, the Russian Jews. Like the poorest of the Exodusters, they wore conspicuous costumes and clung to their old-world customs and clothes that made them stand out. Despite the similarities of their bondage, differences that divided modern from traditional Jew also divided the black community.

Later Dancy would write about the "Old Detroiters"—blacks who were resident before the influx, blacks who had apparently assimilated—and the "New Detroiters," recently arriving Southerners. He would describe how their attempt to adapt to Detroit brought "a changed attitude on the part of the whites [and] caused a deterioration in the status of the older generation of black Detroiters, the "Old Detroiters." They recognized this, he said, and resented it. "The New Detroiters resented the attitude of the Old Detroiters . . . Little co-operation was secured between the two groups for political purposes, and for the advancement of the group as a whole . . . Because of his numbers and because of the fact that Negroes are treated usually as a race and not as individuals, the status of the Negro is low."

CHAPTER 5

"Detroit the Dynamic"

"I magine yourself in an aeroplane," began a story accompanying the picture of a 1920 overhead shot of Detroit. Taken from the plane, the photograph made Detroit look like a lace doily, folded in half in the shape of a semicircle. Along the doily's straight edge flowed the Detroit River. Woodward Avenue cut the semicircle in half. The view from above would have brought into focus Victorian turrets and steeples rising alongside tall buildings. The General Motors building, the largest office building in the world, was nearing completion. The Detroit Public Library, resembling a two-story, marble, Italian Renaissance villa, had opened a few months before. High from above, the once-grand Detroit Opera House, now streaked gunmetal gray by the flotsam of industry, looked like just another particle, a speck in any lens. Paradise Valley would have seemed but a smudge.

Detroit suffered no inferiority complex when it called itself "the shrine of the goddess 'Opportunity,' known to the wide world as 'Detroit the Dynamic.' " Detroit's local boosters considered theirs one of the more desirable, attractive cities in the world. They described Jefferson Avenue, a street dotted with the elegant as well as the ordinary, as one of the most glamorous streets, a rival to Fifth Avenue in New York City, Michigan Avenue in Chicago, Avenue de l'Opéra in Paris, and Königstrasse in Berlin. Biggest, best, most, first, finest, greatest—these were adjectives used to gild otherwise mundane observations. And Detroit liked to measure itself in numbers. Each volume of the *City Directory* contained pages and pages of numeric accomplishments, bubbling with civic pride, strung together for the curious and the proud. Detroit, which produced 40,000 tires a day, claimed the largest tire plant in America; 900 of the 1,100 miles of alleys were paved. Its city physicians made 1,709 visits and dispensed 24,370 compounds. The Belle Isle Aquarium exhibited 3,900 specimens, "denizens of both fresh water and salt," for 1,665,225 visitors. City comfort stations were visited by 18,623,750 people. Prohibition violations accounted for 7,391 arrests.

Of course, none of this was apparent from the plane above, although the naked eye might just be able to discern colorful floral arrangements patterned in Grand Circus Park, or see flowers on the ground spell, "In Detroit Life Is Worth Living." Many seemed to agree with this proclamation. By 1920 nearly one million people would crowd its boundaries.

After spending a decade as a summertime visitor, Ossian Sweet returned to Detroit in 1921, and this time he intended to stay. Like his father's decision to move to Bartow, his choice of Detroit was deliberate. It was a city that needed black professionals—doctors, lawyers, dentists, teachers, and insurance agents to serve and prosper in a community with an educated and vibrant middle class and a total population of forty thousand blacks. He had a group of friends from his summers, classmates from Howard University had settled there, as had his brother Otis, who had recently opened a dental practice after finishing Meharry Medical College. If that wasn't enough for a social world, the year before four Wilberforce alumni put together Detroit's chapter of Kappa Alpha Psi, which sponsored black-tie dinner-dances for couples and smokers for men only. With $200 in his pocket, a freshly acquired medical degree, and a bottle-brush mustache lending maturity to his boyish face, Ossian Haven Sweet approached his twenty-eighth birthday as an attractive eligible bachelor.

A city doctor could earn as much as $5,000 a year when Sweet began his professional life. He quickly figured out that most successful doctors supplemented their income from practicing medicine by owning a pharmacy. Dr. Alexander Turner operated two pharmacies, but he was among the most ambitious and certainly the most stylish physician in Detroit's black bourgeoisie. Turner also practiced out of two offices, employed a secretary, and had telephone service in each office.

Sweet didn't have enough money to open a drugstore, at least not right away. But he had enough to put together a favorable deal. He figured he could loan Cyrus Drozier, a pharmacist, money enough to open the Palace Drug Store at 1409 St. Aubin Avenue. Then Sweet could rent space at the back of Drozier's store. To reduce his costs he shared the office with a fraternity brother, a dentist named William Russell. For years their practices grew steadily. Sweet was happy with a $5 fee for setting a broken jaw when he began. The $100 he received one Christmas Eve for treating a patient injured in an automobile accident seemed like a gift. (In 2000, the equivalent would be about $1,000.)

Sweet was part of the avant-garde that learned as much about medicine from the bedside of a hospitalized patient as his predecessors had from textbooks and pictures. In his junior year of medical school, he was expected to know how to take a complete medical history, examine a patient, and propose a diagnosis. Because Freedmen's Hospital was one of the few admitting blacks south of the Mason-Dixon line, there was no shortage of patients for its three hundred beds, permitting faculty to stress "the value of ward and bedside instruction." This included knowledge about the full services a hospital offered for childbirth. Indeed one of the graduation requirements of students in Ossian Sweet's class would be to deliver a minimum of six babies.

After World War I, enthused and inspired to use science to cure disease, doctors viewed hospitals as "citadels of science and bureaucratic order." Sweet's generation had been trained to use X-rays and stethoscopes routinely, to take specimens for laboratory examination, to collaborate with experts, the burgeoning specialists whose knowledge, it was said, surpassed that of general practitioners. Doctors trained in the teens and twenties regarded hospitals enthusiastically, not the way their predecessors had, as putrid warehouses for the chronically ill or for incurables. Harvard's premier surgeon, Harvey Cushing, expressed his confidence when he wrote that hospitals were no longer "grievous and infected places." The author of a medical text on childbirth in the 1920s reluctantly conceded that hospitals could still carry a "stigmata acquired in pre-antiseptic days" but that, alas, was the wrong attitude. No longer an engine of contagion, the modern hospital brought "efficiency, comfort."

By the time Ossian Sweet planted himself in Detroit, the Southern Exodus had laid bare the need for hospitals specifically for black care and a group of black, middle-class professionals had built them. NEGROES BUILD HOSPITAL HERE announced the *Detroit Free Press* after the ribbon-cutting ceremony for the Dunbar Memorial Hospital in May 1919. The press celebrated achievements of the community leaders—John Dancy, Reverend Robert Bradby, and William Osby—who brought it about. Osby headed the fund-raising drive, collecting $6,000 from eighteen local black doctors, a few white philanthropists, and civic-minded groups, including parishioners from Reverend Bagnall's St. Matthew's Episcopal Church. The money enabled them to purchase a three-story brick house from a Jewish diamond merchant escaping Paradise Valley. The philanthropists spent one year renovating the grand home, turning it into a thirty-seven-bed hospital they named after the poet Paul Laurence Dunbar. Later they would add a school for training nurses. For the second time in two years, a hospital staffed by black physicians opened in Detroit.

Sweet's colleagues at the Dunbar Memorial Hospital were doing exactly what their white colleagues had already done. Whatever scientific mission intensified doctors' interest in building hospitals, an equally strong economic incentive drove consolidating resources while promoting their mutual social interests. Precedents abounded in the Jewish community, where physicians managed places called Mt. Sinai, Beth Israel, or Jewish Old Folks; among Catholics, it was St. Vincent's, St. Mary's, or St. Barnabas; for Protestants, hospitals were named Presbyterian, Methodist, or Lutheran.

Dunbar Memorial Hospital offered a system compatible with Sweet's training. Another hospital, St. Mary's, had opened for black patients the year before, but Dunbar was by far the better place for him to link up with the other doctors who saw themselves as scientists. They were men from the medical elite such as James Ames, appointed to Detroit's Board of Health, or specialists such as the surgeon Alexander Turner, active in the Urban League and the local NAACP. While these professionals were building civic organizations, their wives were pouring tea and raising money for the Detroit Study Club, the Scholarship Fund Club of Detroit, and the Detroit Women's Council. In the orbit of Dunbar Memorial Hospital, Ossian Sweet would spend his days among Detroit's most prominent physicians in the black bourgeoisie.

A few of the doctors also treated white patients or used white hospitals, but this could be cloaked in intrigue. Dr. George Bundy had to sneak in by the back door to attend the delivery of his patients at Women's Hopsital. And Dr. Albert Cleage had received guest privileges from Receiving Hospital, which the Poor Commission opened in

1915. But treating these patients was a dubious honor. To many it seemed little more than a frantically busy, grinding emergency room. A "clearing house for accident or injury cases" or a home for the "psychopathic ward," was how the *Detroit City Directory* described it the year Dunbar Memorial Hospital opened. Roughly 150 patients a day passed through this way station. The "worthy poor" could go to Grace Hospital free of charge. Others paid $14 a week.

Many of the worst problems arose among the Exodusters, said to be people from the "outside who come here and die." Pneumonia, tuberculosis, and malnutrition, all worsened by prison, poverty, or overcrowding in Paradise Valley, led the causes of death. The most serious cases were sent to Dunbar Memorial Hospital. Their treatments, often their demise, contributed falsely to the impression of epidemics in Paradise Valley. Some of this was misleading, based on larger numbers and not a greater incidence. While the black population steadily increased, doubling between 1920 and 1925 from forty thousand to more than eighty thousand people, the percentage of black deaths from tuberculosis held relatively steady at the high rate of nineteen percent. Yet the big numbers contributed to the impression that Dunbar's medical staff lacked skill when, in truth, their patients were deathly ill. It was a hard way to build confidence in the community.

To thrive, Dunbar Memorial Hospital had to build a clientele among the middle class, not just service for the poor. In the twenties, when marketing techniques became widespread, and advertising was deliberately calculated to influence the decisions people made, Dunbar Memorial had to teach patients to want diagnostic assessments in surgery. It had to promote beliefs that laboratory analysis of bloods revealed life-threatening microbes, that patients needed specialists or X-rays.

In 1920, when one-quarter of all babies were still delivered by midwives, the hospital needed to transform patients into consumers who embraced the creed that it was safer to deliver a baby in a tiled room with large lamps showering overhead light. It had to continue to wage war on midwives, to discredit them in the popular imagination and replace them with doctors wearing face masks, standing next to washstands, warding off more germs than in the traditional home environment. Obstetricians trained for hospital surgery could perform the Caesarean section, staging a comeback in popularity. For natural births, hospitals promised what consumers wanted, the analgesic "twilight sleep" to make labor pain-free. State-of-the art luxuries helped attract patients who thought of themselves as middle class.

Of all the subspecialists, surgical obstetricians had the most to gain by affiliating with a hospital. But Dunbar Memorial Hospital had opened without a maternity service. It would have been entirely within character for Ossian Sweet to carefully survey opportunities, take note of what was missing, identify gaps he might fill successfully. Delivering babies at Freedmen's Hospital in Washington, D.C., positioned him among the well-trained obstetricians in a hospital environment. Of the surgeons inducted into the army during the First World War, a survey conducted by the American Gynecological Soceity concluded that fewer than five percent had hospital affiliations.

In Detroit a black woman who wanted to deliver her baby in a hospital had to submit to a white doctor. The director of one maternity center, the Florence Crittendon Home, responded to criticism of this policy. "Whenever a colored patient has made application for admittance," she wrote, "the patient is informed that it will be necessary for her to enter under a white physician, usually our resident physician."

Sweet would have none of it. He came by his medical skill by hard work and application, and his pride would not yield to second-class treatment, to subordination to a white resident. One can almost hear his father's poised defiance, resisting employment under moneyed industrialists, retracting his family from the indignity of surveillance under Jim Crow codes. Ossian Sweet would become good, better than Detroit's best, the finest in his specialty. He would rise to the top of his profession, but to do this he would have to travel abroad, eventually to Paris, to study in the best medical training centers in the world.

Marie Curie's visit to America in 1921 probably helped refine Ossian Sweet's interest in a career as a gynecologist-obstetrician, including a plan for future training. The press spun her story, embellishing her traits, dwelling on her accomplishments. The accounts captured Ossian Sweet's interest, filled his fantasy in that interim between finishing his training in Washington, D.C., and settling in Detroit.

It was May when Curie arrived, and the exuberance surrounding her visit can only be compared to what the press usually reserved for prime ministers or actresses. Curie's trip had been planned for several months, and vast crowds, ranging from feminists to Girl Scouts, waited for the arrival of the *Olympia* in New York City. Slightly built with delicate features, in her fifties, the first woman of science wore black always. But it didn't much matter what the unprecedented two-time recipient of the Nobel Prize wore, because her intellect towered even when her hosts treated her as the standby widow and partner of Pierre Curie. The first of her prizes was awarded for their joint work in physics, for the discovery of radium, a metallic element found in uranium ores. The second was hers alone for work in chemistry. Never before had anybody received the prize twice. Nor had it been granted to any other woman even once.

Curie arrived just in time for her to travel the college commencement speaking circuit. Over the next six weeks she gave ten speeches, received as many honorary degrees, toured the Grand Canyon and Niagara Falls, visited a radium factory in Pittsburgh, attended a Polish reception in Chicago, met with President Harding in the White House, and attended a ceremony in her honor at Carnegie Hall. Her exhaustion by the end of the trip was attributed to the hectic pace. Actually, it was the result of radium poisoning, which, unbeknownst to her, slowly caused cancer and anemia. After two decades of exposure, an insidious depletion left her wanting. When her visit ended, she carried home a gift of one gram of radium probably mined from "Paradox Valley," the expansive fields in Colorado and Utah. It was valued between $120,000 and $150,000.

Radium had been Marie Curie's all-consuming interest since 1898 when she and Pierre first discovered it. Two years later they displayed radioactivity at the International Congress of Physics in Paris. Now, more than two decades later, the world shared her eagerness for its potential to cure cancer. The results were promising enough that hospitals across the United States and Europe were equipping their treatment centers with radium. To be sure, some of the press cautioned that "radium is still in the infancy period of investigation." But the more flamboyant promised that she would "end cancer," a statement she had to repudiate.

Qualifications or retractions did little to extinguish public interest in her work at the Radium Institute in Paris, a hybrid administration located within the Sorbonne. She headed the departments of chemistry and physics. A six-month course laying the foundation for treating cancerous conditions with radium therapy was available to foreign doctors. Sweet intended to be one of them.

Some of the most important forces shaping Detroit in the fall of 1921, when Sweet opened an office on St. Aubin Avenue, could not be seen from an aerial view, measured by a skyscraper's stories, or commemorated at ribbon-cutting ceremonies. They were taking place on the ground, activities on the streets, oddly intense and experienced in subtle ways. It was how people looked at one another, sweeping their eyes sideways, resting here and there long enough to notice how a man approached another leaving a church, or going into the Masonic Lodge, or standing in line to buy tickets for a Tigers game. And wondering who among them had joined the Ku Klux Klan.

The same summer Ossian Sweet arrived, C. H. Norton, the Midwest organizer for the Ku Klux Klan, moved to Detroit. He had come to monitor and expand the Klan's membership in the Wolverine state, which numbered only three thousand, skimpy when compared to Norton's other states, Ohio and Indiana, where Klan membership was well ahead of Michigan. Within eighteen months of his arrival, however, Detroit would be on its way to becoming the city with the third largest membership, totaling thirty-five thousand people of the more than seventy-five thousand in all of Michigan.

Controversy surrounding another attempt to release the film *Birth of a Nation* preceded Norton's arrival. The movie offended James Couzens, now the reform mayor of Detroit. Race relations in Detroit had been sufficiently cordial to inspire the NAACP to host its Twelfth Annual Convention there in April, and Couzens personally endorsed the NAACP, even held membership. But he also wanted to promote tourism, to build Detroit's image and reputation as a convention center. Couzens threatened to revoke the license of the Detroit Opera House, where the film would screen, unless it eliminated scenes he considered "indecent and immoral."

The bigger controversy by far, however, arose from a sensational exposé of the Ku Klux Klan that appeared in the *Detroit Free Press,* one of eighteen newspapers across the nation to carry the syndicated series. It was an indictment not to ignore.

The exposé originally appeared in the *New York World* in September 1921, when one of its reporters, Rowland Thomas, tracked down a lapsed Klansman and persuaded him to divulge details about its secret chambers. The resulting stories implied the Klan's ultimate goal was nothing short of undermining the nation's civil and legal infrastructure. Details were abundant. Thomas disclosed names, places, and times of the nighttime meetings. He reported how Kluxers punished people considered guilty of what it termed "moral lapses." He seized an unprecedented opportunity to shine a light on the Klan's organized activities that had been terrorizing immigrants and blacks, and boldly challenging the law.

As with readers nationwide, people in Detroit waited anxiously for the paper to reach the newsstands and they did not hesitate to pay fifty cents, instead of the normal three cents, for a copy of the *Free Press* each day the series ran. They were as curious as people anywhere to hear about initiation rites, ostentatious lifestyles of the Klan leadership, and atrocities on city streets where hooded riders roamed unabated.

After 1920 the most spectacular growth of the Klan came in the North and the West when the self-appointed "Imperial Wizard," founder William Simmons, enlisted public relations people to expand his organization. Simmons hired an odd couple, Edward Young Clarke and his lover, Mrs. Elaine Tyler, partners in the Southern Publicity Association. They were public relations specialists in Atlanta, and the short list of their clients included the Anti-Saloon League and the Salvation Army.

A photo of Clarke shows a man of imposing posture, an angled jaw, and a dimpled chin. He brushed his thick, wavy hair back, framing an open face with an earnest expression. Steel-rimmed glasses added a serious mien, imparting confidence to a face someone described as that of a dreamer. Tyler presents a different, less worldly image. A picture of her shows a dark-haired woman, buxom in a dress with a plunging neckline and a hat that looked like a helmet.

Without the work of a flamboyant and imaginative photographer named Matty, Clarke and Tyler might not have succeeded so quickly, or even at all. In Atlanta, Matty's reputation as a whimsical character grew after he staged a farcical picture of a zookeeper pulling an elephant's tooth with obstetrical forceps. When it came to contriving a picture of the Klan, he set up a photo shoot using hirelings, twenty people whom he dressed in cowls, robes, and pointed white caps surrounding a fiery cross. He paid them twenty-five cents each. Had they not been wearing robes and masks, it would have been possible to determine whether, as rumor held, they were actually black. The first picture reconstructed the meeting at Stone Mountain five years earlier when Simmons summoned the mob that lynched Jewish businessman Leo Frank. To resurrect the Klan, Matty's other pictures portrayed Klansmen marching to open-air meetings under billowy flags, or a torch-lit parade. They were widely reprinted to appear as if they were candid shots, resembling the spontaneous, the benign, and the home-spun at marches, funerals, and baptisms.

With Matty's help, Tyler and Clarke approached their work with the enthusiasm of college freshmen preparing for fraternity rush. They used Simmons's bizarre, newly invented vocabulary to craft a product under the aegis of goblins (managers) and kleagles (salesmen), kludds (chaplains) and kligrapps (secretaries). They carved the country into nine regional markets, franchises of hate. By year's end, eleven hundred newly recruited kleagles drove local recruiting, bringing new members into klaverns, headed by an "exalted" cyclops. They often spoke in code: "AYAK?"—Are you a klansman?—could be answered, "AKIA"—A klansman I am. The Atlanta-based Klan's Gate City Manufacturing Company sold official Klan robes for $6.50, netting more than $5 per item. Kluxers published a newspaper, *The Fiery Cross,* and Detroit editions carried advertising from local insurance salesmen and auto mechanics. Dry cleaners promised to "Klean Klansmens Klothes." Meanwhile, Simmons, Clarke, and Tyler profited handsomely from the proceeds, in addition to reimbursement of living expenses, salaries, and the upkeep of the "Imperial Palace."

The Klan left an obvious trail that the syndicated *New York World* series pounded. The *World's* series described beatings, lynching, and humiliation, with victims left to chance, run out of town, or covered with tar and rolled in feathers. It unearthed recruitment strategies; uncovered the identities of influential Klansmen; named judges, lawyers, and police—it was widely believed Detroit's Chief of Police Inches was a Klansman—who had sworn fidelity to the secret order. The newspaper listed kleagles and king kleagles by name, state, and hometown. Now any reader of the newspaper could thumb down the list to see whether his neighbor, his boss, or perhaps his cousin was a cloaked official in the secret Ku Klux Klan.

Amid mounting publicity and the ensuing controversy, Congress was forced to call for hearings to be held the next month. Politicians recognized that the right of association did not sanction violence, which might unravel social stability and result in anarchy. They recognized that the Klan's mocking of Catholic ritual with imitative, pompous titles, ecclesiastic garb, and an elaborate cleansing ritual called "naturalization" could provoke retaliation and result in riot. Despite disgust over the leaders' opulence and their abuse of tax-free education—Simmons bought a university—the only issue that brought the hearings under congressional jurisdiction was whether the Klan had committed fraud in its use of the United States Postal Service. In a few weeks, the public could judge for itself.

Never before had the numbers of clamoring spectators, including fifty reporters and one hundred congressmen, forced a hearing to move into the House Caucus Room, the largest assembly hall on Capitol Hill. As a result of the surge of public interest resulting from the newspaper coverage of the Klan, that is what happened in October 1921, when the Congressional Committee on Rules opened its hearings. The committee scheduled Simmons's appearance for the second day, following the testimony of Congressman Leonidas Dyer, whose district in Missouri bordered East St. Louis, the site of the riot in 1917. Dyer was the author of an antilynching bill that would soon be called out of committee. By far the most important witness was C. Anderson Wright, the whistle-blower, the *World's* key informant, the man who revealed the Klan's secrets. Much of Wright's testimony painted Simmons as earnest but naive, a man whose mission had been usurped by the scheming, clever Mrs. Tyler, executive of an organization excluding women.

As a prelude to Simmons's testimony, witnesses described a frightening medley of Klan abuses. There were accusations of the Klan branding and mutilating its opponents, descriptions of an election day massacre in Florida, allegations that it kidnapped a street vendor who dared to sell "wieners to Negroes," as well as assertions that "vigilante committees" cleaned up "fast and loose females" in a town on the Western frontier. Simmons was present to hear Monroe Trotter, Boston editor of *The Guardian,* argue that Congress should outlaw all secret societies built on white supremacy. If any of the testimony brought him discomfort, he kept it well hidden. He would get his turn.

Simmons had been waiting in the hearing room of the House of Representatives since early morning. On that Wednesday, October 12, an impatient press corps greeted him. They were still smarting from the night before when he had tricked them by coming into Washington by car and avoided the train station where they had been waiting. But he appeased their anger and rewarded their diligence when he arrived shortly after ten o'clock. With the assurance and the confidence of a celebrity, he strode into the hall and waved reporters to a quiet spot where he posed for their pictures. Cameras started clicking, lights started flashing, and he slowly turned his face from side to side. He tilted his chin and boldly looked into the lens, claiming the moment.

It would be afternoon before Simmons took the witness stand. But when he did, he was in charge. He began by reading a prepared statement listing his ailments, telling how he suffered from bronchitis, tonsillitis, pneumonia, and laryngitis. These infirmities kept him bedridden the previous two weeks. "I am a sick man," he said, and cautioned that spontaneous vomiting might interrupt his testimony.

His vitality returned, however, as soon as he described the Klan's philanthropy, its gift of $1,000 to the widow of an electrician who died on the job in Houston, and another $500 for the black victims of an explosion in Tennessee. Absorbed by his self-righteousness, Simmons was giddy by the time he described contributing to a "Christmas celebration of the old slaves in Atlanta." Calling them "darkies," he sent regrets because he was unable to go.

Simmons cleverly ducked direct questions about violence. And the committee did not persist. He avoided forthright answers about hooded costumes, and his answers were allowed to stand. He claimed memory loss when asked how the funds were spent, and his assertion went unchecked. And yet he admitted, actually he boasted, that the Klan had never paid income taxes on more than $1.4 million it had collected in six years.

After two days on the witness stand, it dawned on him suddenly, the same way one realizes that a mosquito has been lunching on one's neck, that he had been set up as a patsy, superfluous, secondary to Clarke and Tyler. Suddenly, and red with rage, he blurted out, "Mrs. Tyler is not my boss. I am not a figurehead." Then in a husky voice, he added rather solemnly, "I am sorry I am suffering as I am, but I cannot help it. Julius Caesar had his Brutus, Jesus Christ had his Judas, and our great and illustrious Washington had his Benedict Arnold." He turned to the audience and he asked forgiveness for those who persecuted the Klan. In a bizarre outburst he shouted, "Father, forgive them, for they know not what they do." He toppled over in his chair while the audience broke into wild applause, which the chairman's gavel pounded into silence. Had he designed the event with elaborate forethought, it could not have been more successful.

By collapsing into a heap before the committee, Simmons succeeded in transforming himself from a persecutor into a victim. When the hearings ended, despite testimony portraying the Klan's intimidating and violent rampages and hate-filled rhetoric, no one moved to censure Simmons or the Klan. Even the cynical H. L. Mencken said that the testimony hardly made the Klan seem any more anti-Semitic, anti-Catholic, or antiblack than any country club or most of the nation's best colleges.

By exposing the inner workings of the Ku Klux Klan, which began as a parochial Southern organization, Congress and the press unwittingly laid the foundation for accelerating its rapid national expansion. People clipped the application forms from their local papers and used them to apply for membership. They filled in answers to questions such as: "Are you a gentile or Jew?" "Are you of the white race or of the colored race?" "Were your parents born in the United States of America?" "Do you believe in White Supremacy?" Soon one thousand applications a day, containing $10 for a membership, flooded the national office.

Simmons was fond of saying, "Congress made us." The stampede to join after the hearings confirmed his hunch. By the end of May 1923 the largest memberships could be found in Indiana, Ohio, and Pennsylvania—nearly eight hundred thousand people. With the exception of Southern states, and California, all the rest had fewer than Michigan and New York, which each had seventy-five thousand members. Klansmen came from all walks of life, including high elected office. It was said that President Warren G. Harding was initiated in the White House. If an organization rich with ritual, promising fraternity in the service of secrecy and Americanism, could reach into the Oval Office, can it surprise that it also appealed to politicians, blue-collar workers, and tradesmen? Even a haberdasher from Independence, Missouri, put up $10 for membership. Harry S. Truman's biographer claims the future president demanded his money back after attending one meeting. That would have made him unusual.

Detroit's Norton was a clever kleagle who knew how to capitalize on the syndicated series in the *Free Press* to boost local interest. The Detroit chapter of the Klan enrolled twenty-two thousand people in less than two years. But Norton's boldness frightened too many, and the police rescinded a permit for a Thanksgiving Day parade. The Klan used other opportunities for building interest. On summer nights it would sponsor ceremonies. In 1923 one thousand men were inducted in an evening meeting on a farm in Royal Oak, just outside the city limits at Eight Mile Road. After turning off the highway, people were directed to the central stage, where the initiation would be held. Thousands had come to bear witness, some still wearing their office clothes, others already in Klan regalia by the time they arrived at sundown. They stood securely behind sentries with .45 caliber pistols strapped to their hips, beneath the American flag and in front of a fiery cross rising thirty feet in the air. Under the direction of the Great Goblin of the Great Lakes, they dropped to their knees and swore allegiance to the Ku Klux Klan. With the fervor and pleading of a camp meeting, the goblin pointed to the national flag waving overhead and shouted, "America for Americans." After the initiation the crowd, estimated at about ten thousand including students and faculty from the University of Michigan in Ann Arbor, stayed until midnight. It was a typical Klan event. People were eating hot dogs, drinking coffee, chatting.

Throughout the summer the scene repeated. In July five thousand Klansmen inducted eight hundred new members in the city of Detroit at Snyder and Seven Mile Road; the next month came another 792; ten days later, at the same spot, another three thousand joined. The summer's climax took place on Labor Day with two events. One was an all-day picnic at a field on John R at Fifteen Mile Road. The other took place in Highland Park, a town within and surrounded by Detroit, inhabited by local merchants and laborers from Henry Ford's assembly plant, which was located there. It marked the opening of the Michigan women's organization, and their initiation was more genteel, featuring a picnic with basket lunches.

The Klan's secrecy—its hoods and private language—terrified bystanders. At the height of these events in 1923, Michigan lawmakers passed the first law in the nation outlawing gatherings of masked men. The law was supposed to be a deterrent, but towns such as Cairo, Adrian, Unionville, Muskegon, Flint, and Ironwood flouted it. So, too, in Detroit, where Klansmen held late-night meetings, in front of the Wayne County Building, where they climbed to the rooftop to recite the Lord's Prayer and to hum "Nearer My God to Thee."

. . .

While the Klan organized white men in a city dominated by European immigrants coming from more than a dozen nations, and middle-class black professionals were securing hospitals and philanthropies for their community, Ossian Sweet was getting acquainted with colleagues. One of them, a fraternity brother and a physician, Dr. Charles Green, had invited him to an event of the Inter-Collegiate Alumni Association, an organization consisting of alumni of several colleges who gathered for luncheons, public lectures, and the opportunity to do business. Green was black but his tone was light enough that he was often mistaken for white. He had put together a table of ten for the luncheon at the Statler Hotel, and in addition to Sweet, Julian Perry, an attorney and a fraternity brother who dabbled in local politics, was part of the group. They had come to hear Judge Landis, the baseball commissioner, who was the announced speaker. After lunch, the plan was to continue on to Navin Field for a Detroit-Chicago baseball game. The stadium was one of the few places where black and white mixed. By now, however, legendary Ty Cobb was managing the Tigers as well as playing center field. While he brought pride to an ethnically diverse city like Detroit, his reputation as a racist was damaging in a different fashion. Except for a series of exhibition games against Cuba, he refused to play against blacks, including the Detroit Stars, a team with fabulous players that was part of the National Negro League. Whether or not he was actually a member of the Klan, suspicions persisted that Georgia-born Cobb shared their beliefs.

Had Ty Cobb's appearance at the luncheon been announced in advance, the ten men in Green's party might have stayed away. Unaware, however, they walked into a dining room and brought discomfort, "consternation when the colored party arrived at the table." Several years later Sweet would describe the event as if he fully remembered the indignation, trepidation, alarm, and agitation—the "consternation" that ensued because they were the only black table.

Later that evening, after his office hours, Sweet and Julian Perry went to a dance at the St. Antoine Y, where they tried to put the event behind them. Eligible bachelors could find women seeking husbands at these well-attended activities. The price of admission was ten cents, and couples could remain on the dance floor as long as they wanted, with live music, without having to stand in line, without waiting for whites to leave, without feeling debased in the process. By any standards, the dances were a great event and the Urban League could count them another of its successes.

Of all the pretty women Sweet saw that evening, it was Gladys Atkinson who caught his eye. She was finishing classes at the Detroit Teachers College, where she was enrolled in the elementary school program.

That night Gladys probably exuded the exotic quality which many would later describe. With her hair pulled behind the ears, secured by a velvet bow, she resembled women on the continent, in a fashion similar to what was regularly featured in the style section of Detroit's newspapers. Ossian and Gladys might have quickly discovered that they both loved music, and like their parents, they both played an instrument. For Gladys, it was the piano, and she had attended the Detroit Conservatory of Music before enrolling in the Detroit Teachers College. Her stepfather was a music teacher by day, a performer in the live orchestra at the Schubert Lafayette Theater by night.

After preliminary conversation, they probably discovered that when Ossian came to Detroit in the summers, he lived in a neighborhood near her home on Lamb Avenue (soon to be renamed Cairney). She still lived on that block with her mother, stepfather, and a cousin from Pennsylvania. Some would have called it a white neighborhood, south of Gratiot Street between Four Mile Road and Five Mile Road. Hers was one of two black families on the block. The other lived next door, a physician from Mississippi who would eventually join the staff of the Dunbar Memorial Hospital. Most of the white families were made up of motormen or street railway conductors, laborers working for an auto factory or a tanner turning leather hides into clothing or furniture. Most were born elsewhere, or their parents had been. Gladys's grandfather, her mother's father, came from Scotland.

After a courtship lasting barely eight months, and having just turned twenty-eight, Ossian Sweet ended his bachelor days when he married Gladys, twenty-one. Julian Perry honored his best friend as a witness. Later he would stand with the Sweets before a judge. Gladys's witness was Edna Butler, an interior decorator who would later measure the windows for curtains and the rooms for furnishings on the night they moved into their new house. Whatever else occupied their future, now before friends and family and shielded from the cacophony on the streets of Detroit, they stood before the Reverend E. W. Daniel at the St. Matthew's Episcopal Church, where they were married on December 20, 1922.

For the next eight months, Ossian and Gladys Sweet lived with her parents, Ben and Rosella Mitchell. They saved their money while they planned a grand trip, a honeymoon voyage on an ocean liner bringing them to Europe where they would remain for one year. Ossian would study in Austria, France, Germany, and England, and learn the most innovative procedures. In Vienna it would be the surgical techniques. In Paris, it would include the most up-to-date applications of radium to treat cancers in women. Upon return, he would possess superior skill and specialize in gynecology and obstetrics at the Dunbar Memorial Hospital.

CHAPTER 6

Two Cities:
Vienna and Paris

G ladys and Ossian sailed from New York City in October 1923, the height of the trans-Atlantic travel season when gossip filled society pages about the goings and comings of the Wanamakers, Millikens, and Harknesses, patricians whose names graced the entrances of hospitals and auditoriums. The weekend the Sweets planned to leave, the piers were unusually congested. The *Mauritania* carrying Britain's wartime prime minister, Lloyd George, had docked on Friday. Welcoming fans stretched from Battery Park to the Astoria Hotel, leaving a mess of balloons and streamers, which porters had to sidestep to haul mail sacks, steamer trunks, and provisions to sustain a week's worth of crisp linen service.

The National Weather Bureau had forecast fair skies and chilly weather in a season that did not require an act of bravery to cross the Atlantic. But even the roughest of climes would not have diminished the Sweets' excitement in boarding an ocean liner, distancing themselves from the racial belligerence stirred by Detroit's Ku Klux Klan earlier in the year.

Before reaching its final destination on the coast of France, their ship stopped at seaports in North Africa and the Mediterranean, where they went ashore as tourists, still honeymooners, before settling down to work. By late October they reached Austria by train, and eventually traveled to Vienna, where Dr. Ossian Sweet would begin study at the world-famous clinics of the general hospital, the Allgemeines Krankenhaus.

Study in Vienna in the 1920s brought dazzling prestige. In another twenty years there would be little difference between the training Sweet received in Europe's capitals and what would become standard for American medical education. It would entail hospital-based training, and it would incline toward specialties.

In the 1920s, however, doctors who chose to study abroad were typically older and more worldly than Sweet. His inspiration came from medical school instructors at Howard University, German-born professors Paul Bartsch and his sister, Anna Bartsch-Dunne. Bartsch taught histology and led international expeditions for the United States National Museum. By mid-career, he was already the author of 340 scientific publications. Bartsch's sister, Anna, a physician in the Washington, D.C., Women's Clinic, was an alumnus of Howard and taught gynecology at the medical school. The year of her divorce, she went to Vienna for retooling at the Allgemeines Krankenhaus, an experience that she meticulously described for the *Howard Medical News*. It may still be the best account in English of this remarkable adventure.

The Allgemeines Krankenhaus, the pinnacle of Enlightenment order, was built by Josef II in the eighteenth century. It was no less testimony to the accomplishment of the Hapsburg Empire than the Baroque churches that charmed this city on the Danube where Mozart premiered *The Magic Flute*. With twenty-six hundred beds and numerous clinics, the hospital was the heart of the medical school, and the medical school of the university.

A pilgrimage to one of Europe's medical meccas had to begin with a search within oneself for a standard of excellence in scientific and clinical detail. Then came a willingness to postpone the comforts of home and earnings. Most physicians could not meet the rigorous challenge. Some doctors, although they were small in number, aspired to this unparalleled training, and they became the profession's standard bearers, its pioneers and visionaries, certainly its teachers. Among America's pioneering physicians of the previous generation, those who founded hospitals and taught in research-based medical centers—Drs. Cushing, Halstead, Osler, and Welch—all spent time abroad. They went to Breslau to study pathology, to Strasbourg to learn anatomy, to Leipzig to understand nervous disorders, and to Vienna to improve skills in gynecology. After the First World War drew to an end, Vienna again became a favorite city for Americans.

In Vienna, Ossian and Gladys Sweet lived in the fashionable Landstrasse neighborhood, also called the Third District. Around the corner from their third-floor apartment, at Löwengasse 47, the Rotundenbrucke, a footbridge, carried pedestrians across the Donaukanal on their way into the Prater. Once the royal family had used the Prater for its hunting expeditions, but now it was a public park with a gigantic roller coaster. Half a block away, streets intersected at Marxergasse, a plaza where locals sat outside for afternoon *Kaffee* and *Strudel*. From the trolley stop at this intersection, Sweet would have been about thirty minutes from the university's Eiselsberg clinic, where he was acquiring the skills in diagnosis and surgery that inspired the trip.

No neighborhood in Detroit could compare to Vienna's Landstrasse, no street to Löwengasse, not even Jefferson Avenue, despite the enthusiasm of Detroit's most vivid boosters. Nineteenth-century aristocrats, including the statesman Metternich who crafted the enduring peace treaty of 1815, once lived in Landstrasse. He attracted ambassadors and aristocrats who built gated estates with gardens that bloomed at precisely the right time, and palatial halls in which to premiere newly commissioned music. Home to Gustav Mahler, Anton Bruckner, and Richard Strauss, Landstrasse throbbed with genius. The composer Anton von Webern once lived in the building next door to the Sweets on Löwengasse. A ten-minute walk from their front door put Gladys and Ossian Sweet at Ungergasse 5, where, a century earlier, Beethoven composed the Ninth Symphony.

Splendor surrounded the Sweets, who lived in an architecturally controversial apartment building named the Palais des Beaux Arts completed in 1909. Some thought its busy facade too cluttered with turrets, nymphs, cherubs, two enormous globes, perforated balconies, and a watch-tower with a clock. While the Palais was compatible with the older buildings of this commercial and residential neighborhood, massive structures bulging with articulated floral patterns, nudes, seminudes, and molded details accentuating window ornaments, critics sneered. The Palais des Beaux Arts, claimed some, was an insult to Art Nouveau's textured and slender restraint.

However much their Vienna experience was culturally enriched by living in Landstrasse, living on the opposite side of the city from the Allgemeines Krankenhaus also isolated Ossian and Gladys Sweet from visiting doctors as well as the resident medical community.

Vienna's postwar, inflationary, and constricted housing market usually forced visiting doctor-students to board in pensions within walking distance to the hospital. Both before and after the First World War, colonies of Americans chose Atlanta, Pohl, or Columbia, boarding houses which were popular with family-style atmosphere. Over meals, doctors revisited the day's lesson, traded insights about the nuances of medical care. They speculated about how their brand of doctoring would change, what might differ because of the training they received there. And while they were off in the clinics or lectures, their wives, if they came, prowled the streets, hunting bargains in the market for shawls or lace, or compacts studded with jewels. Evenings, if they were free, they toured Kaffeehauses, concerts, or nightclubs. Had these doctors never left the ethnocentric enclaves of small towns in America, they would have remained strangers. Instead they discovered one another, colleagues from South Dakota, upstate New York, or the Northampton Valley in Massachusetts met in the tourist haunts or soirees sponsored by the local branch of the American Medical Association.

Ossian and Gladys Sweet probably did not join the outings, or those organized by the Vienna branch of the AMA. Located across the street from the Allgemeines Krankenhaus, it had been comforting homesick physicians for nearly two decades. Its services included banking and money exchange, and a doctor could wander into the lounge between classes and at the end of the day while he waited for the mail, with letters and pictures from home. To guarantee that a doctor filled his social needs, the association organized parties and patriotic galas, such as the Thanksgiving Day banquet that drew Viennese doctors and university faculty who canceled classes to honor Americans, among the largest number of fee-paying students. The AMA also facilitated enrolling in clinics with renowned doctors who, in the words of one student, were "scientific investigators and teachers first, and then practitioners."

But it is unlikely that Ossian Sweet would have ingratiated himself in an organization in Vienna that would deny him membership in Detroit. Jim Crow influenced the AMA, the oldest professional association of doctors, as much as it had other social and professional aspects of life, and Sweet belonged instead to the National Medical Association, a group of black doctors.

Vienna may have been called the Imperial City, but it was neither a port nor an intercontinental trading center. Racial differences were practically unknown in the Austro-Hungarian Empire, which had not vied for colonial outposts or sent profiteers to exploit Africa. Despite the cosmopolitanism in the university—two-thirds of the medical students were foreign and half of the medical faculty were Jewish— Vienna was racially homogeneous. Whether black, brown, tan, or yellow, people of color were rare. Certainly Ossian and Gladys Sweet would have been conspicuous; singular may not be too strong.

After six months Ossian Sweet was ready to leave the Eiselsberg clinics and the Allgemeines Krankenhaus to continue his work at the Sorbonne in Paris. He would trade in Vienna, where the tempo of Strauss, father and son, patterned a waltz with egg-white stiffness, for Paris, where the tempo was spontaneous. In Paris, it was the Charleston; it was breathless, defiant, full-bodied. It was jazz and it was improvisational.

America's black soldiers introduced jazz when they reached France during World War I. By the twenties, the French showed their love of what would be known as America's own art form in Montmartre where musicians jammed, drawing crowds into dimly lit cabarets lining rue Pigatelle or rue la Bruyère. Jazz helped bridge the distance from home, and the French joined Americans crowding cafés to hear expressive music that had as much influence etching the profile of postwar Paris as any diplomat who redrew boundaries to form new nation-states.

"The French remind me more of colored folks," wrote Joel Rogers, columnist for the *New York Amsterdam News*, who compared Paris favorably to Harlem. "They are quite as noisy, excitable, light-hearted, pleasure loving, and take their own time about everything."

Americans adored Paris for its cosmopolitanism. A man could be "free to be merely a man," one black intellectual proclaimed. He could be free

> from the conflict within the Man-Negro dualism and the innumerable maneuvers in thought and behavior that it compels; free from the problem of the many obvious or subtle adjustments to a multitude of bans and taboos; free from special scorn, special tolerance, special condescension, and special commiseration.

Americans infused Paris that spring in sufficient numbers that one guide book described their presence as an "occupation" in the Latin Quarter. They conspicuously strolled wide boulevards, explored the narrow alleys, relaxed in Left Bank cafés, and flung their limbs about, dancing the Charleston at the Café Florida. It was the Paris of expatriates. Harlem Renaissance literati Langston Hughes and Alaine Locke met. Ernest Hemingway, F. Scott Fitzgerald, and Gertrude Stein lived and played while making their way to Sylvia Beach's lending library of English-language books, Shakespeare and Co. Kiosks and bookstands sold American newspapers and magazines. All of this led the dizzy heroine, Lorelei, from Anita Loos's *Gentlemen Prefer Blondes,* to proclaim, "Paris is Devine!"

Had Gladys and Ossian Sweet sipped beer at an outdoor café in Montparnasse on the Boulevard St. Germain, or sat down near the Pasteur Institute on rue Vaugirard, they most likely would have heard nattering Americans speaking, as one observer noted, "very slowly and deliberately." Somehow they believed "that spoken that way [English] must be understood by everybody."

While Americans revered Paris, the French revered Africa. In the spring of 1924, *l'arte negre* provided artifacts, carvings, and photography for magazine covers. African masks and mythology informed the artistic imaginations of Braque, Brancusi, Picasso, and Giacometti. The French automobile manufacturer Citröen organized a publicity stunt, a trans-African tour, and amassed pictures, photographs, posters, and artifacts for exhibits that would appear in the Paris Exposition the following year.

But the respect for black entertainers and intellectuals did not apply to all dark-skinned people from Africa, the Caribbean, or America. Disparaging racial images abounded. Even before Josephine Baker shocked the public with eccentric nudity in the satirical "Revue Negre" at the Champs Elysées Music Hall, advertisements used erotic cartoon images to deprecate race and define taboo. References to a "juvenile mind" appeared throughout the French press. While the Folies

Bergère had abandoned its disgraceful portrayal of blacks as cannibals in the 1870s, the revue still managed to stage a Southern plantation in the 1920s as if it were the norm. Racism abounded, and poet Langston Hughes wrote boldly about the rejection he met while hunting for jobs in 1924.

Ossian Sweet went to Paris at the end of April 1924 with enthusiasm to study medicine, not to sample culture. He came with the headiness of Vienna behind him and with an opportunity to now learn about what Madame Curie described in her campaign to inform the world about radiation therapies. In Paris he expected to focus his attention at the Radium Institute. It was part of the University of Paris and the Sorbonne, and jointly supervised by Madame Curie and Dr. Claude Regaud. Visiting physicians learned a great deal from treating charity patients who allowed doctors to experiment with new therapies for the benefit of their own understanding as well as for enhancing science in this eighteen-bed hospital. Only seven Americans would complete the six-month course between 1922 and 1927. Like the training one received in Vienna, work in Madame Curie's laboratory became the envy of many.

The season Ossian and Gladys reached Paris, the American Hospital was in the final stages of its campaign to raise funds and expand its services for Americans in Paris. Sweet donated 300 francs, about $15 in American money. Located in Neuilly, a suburb of Paris, the hospital expected to increase from thirty-two to more than one hundred beds. Completion was scheduled for Thanksgiving. It promised to "provide adequate facilities for taking care of Americans who become ill while traveling in Europe," and offered a sunny exposure in every room, just like the Mt. Sinai Hospital in New York City. They were still $300,000 short of their goal, and they mounted a huge public relations campaign.

Gladys Sweet was due to deliver their first child in Paris soon after they arrived that spring. After leaving Vienna at the end of April, they had about a month to get themselves ready for the birth. Just as hospitals had come to dominate obstetrics in America, for the *petit bourgeoisie* they were growing in popularity on the continent.

When her labor began, Ossian and Gladys headed toward Neuilly. It may not have occurred to the wealthy who endowed rooms, people such as Mrs. L. V. Harkness, or Jay Gould, or Percy Peixotto, the president of the American Club in Paris, to ask what the American Hospital might mean to a black family living in Paris. Nor would it to Myron T. Herrick, the American ambassador to France; or Dr. Edmund Gros, chief of the medical staff; or Dr. Charles Mayo, one of America's most highly visible physicians, cofounder of the Minnesota clinic that still bears his name, who inspected the new facility when he attended the garden party to celebrate its dedication. It is likely that no one questioned whether someone like Gladys Sweet might need or want the American Hospital's services.

Whoever was on duty when Ossian and Gladys arrived for the maternity service decided that the mandate of the American Hospital did not include them and refused to admit Gladys Sweet. Although she was in labor, she was sent away. Even in Detroit it would not have happened that way.

In the words of the American ambassador, the American Hospital was the "spirit of America." If one were to ask Gladys and Ossian Sweet about that spirit, they would have probably said that it followed the tradition of Jim Crow.

Until now Ossian Sweet had reached all his goals. He had attended the right schools, achieved prominence with a medical degree that was likely to guarantee financial and social contentment. He found what seemed to be the right city in which to open a medical practice, married an educated woman from a good, even a musical family. He had money in the bank and had just finished studying with the world's most es-

timable surgeons. None of it, however, protected him from the opprobrium of racism.

Ossian Sweet did not need rejection from the American Hospital to
teach him the lessons of Jim Crow's malevolence. He was, after all, a son
of the South. No matter how detestable the indignities of racial politics,
its previous application had been broadly impersonal. The American
Hospital changed that. It was different from the endemic, anonymous
racism he witnessed growing up, or that occurred in the nation's capital
or at home in Michigan. This time it carried a personal name tag as if
Jim Crow had searched for him, sought him out to deliver a blow tar-
geted to his sense of masculinity—he would later use the term "manli-
ness"—and to his ability to protect his wife and unborn child.

Historians have called the spring of 1924 the best of times for blacks
to enjoy Paris. Yet for all the pleasures one could imagine, for Ossian
Sweet, it was the worst of times.

When Ossian and Gladys Sweet's daughter, Marguerite Iva, was
only days old, they all boarded the S.S. *Paris* leaving from
LeHavre on June 21. For now, at least, Sweet had to cast aside his expectations and defer dreams of further study in England and Germany.
In the meantime, while Gladys remained within the postpartum period when new mothers were advised to remain "quiet and free from
visitors," they came home.

After eight days at sea, the thirty-five-ton S.S. *Paris* pulled into Pier
57 at Fifteenth Street in New York City with a crew of six hundred
outnumbering the passengers. According to ship records, three-week-
old Marguerite Iva Sweet was the youngest. A few toddlers and one
six-month-old baby also made the trip.

Just as their departure from New York City took place on the
fringes of a nationally compelling event, the arrival of Lloyd George,
their return at the end of June did, too. The Democratic Party had

gathered at Madison Square Garden in New York City to put together a platform for a candidate to challenge incumbent President Calvin Coolidge. The convention was long and contentious and the summer was hot and steamy. Before it ended, tombstones would cap the careers of prominent presidential aspirants, including William McAdoo, William Jennings Bryan, and Al Smith, each with a different reason for feeling accomplished but each with a serious liability according to the constituents. Whatever high hopes with which delegates to the Democractic convention arrived in New York, to choose a candidate from a crowded field, they seemed bent on a self-destructive course. After tolerating one another for nine days, they pulled off one fistfight and 103 ballots before nominating John W. Davis, a corporate lawyer whose greatest asset seems to have been offending the fewest number of delegates.

The other contest erupting from the divergent opinions during that contentious convention was framed by debate over the Ku Klux Klan. After days of discussing whether to censure the Klan, denounce its purpose and secrecy, a vote came during that last week in June 1924. By the slimmest of margins, a fraction of one delegate's vote, the nation's Democrats refused to condemn these vendors of hate.

When the S.S. *Paris* tied up on June 29, and the Sweets left their first-class stateroom, this news greeted their arrival.

CHAPTER 7

2905 Garland Avenue

S ince returning from France, the Sweets had been living with Gladys's parents. Early in the spring of 1925, they started looking for a place of their own. Detroit's fast-paced housing market was in the third year of a bubble, surpassing previous record-breaking streaks. Construction of new housing and industrial plants on Detroit's east side consumed farms and the surrounding woods and extend the city boundaries outward, about a half mile a year, beyond where corn and wheat fields once stood. Developers were trimming and taming manicured residential enclaves beyond Eight Mile Road, making suburbia.

Despite the unprecedented growth, it had become more difficult for middle-class black professionals to find decent housing. Homes built after 1920 in Detroit often carried restrictive deeds promoting segregated ghettos based on race: whites in one neighborhood; blacks elsewhere. The Detroit Real Estate Board reinforced housing segregation with a stipulation in its "code of ethics" discouraging agents from selling to any family "whose presence will be detrimental to property values in that neighborhood."

Most of Sweet's colleagues lived scattered throughout the city, as they always had, next door and across the street from their established white neighbors in older homes and solid neighborhoods. Dr. Peyton Johnson, a Harvard graduate and founding member of Dunbar Memorial Hospital, was the only black man on Rhode Island Avenue in Highland Park, where he and his wife had lived since 1916. It was a neighborhood with artisans, merchants, and Russian immigrants, interspersed with workers from the Ford factory a few blocks north. A prominent Wilberforce alumnus, lawyer Robert Barnes, lived several blocks away on Josephine Avenue, a tiny street south of Highland Park. And for many years William Osby's was the only black family on West Hancock Avenue until Charles Mahoney bought a house across the street. Among their friends, they were all considered comfortable, if not well-to-do.

Some realtors promoted neighborhoods with one or two black families among many whites as satisfactory because the scarcity of available housing forced affluent blacks to pay premium prices. But when more than one or two black families lived in close proximity, many realtors and neighbors feared property would depreciate.

It was May when a realtor directed Ossian and Gladys to the Waterworks Park area on Detroit's east side, a few blocks beyond Four Mile Road. Its name came from a slender water tower rising 185 feet, which observers thought made it look like an "ancient Oriental Mosque." A postcard favorite, it bordered a park with 110 acres, next to a lagoon that emptied into the Detroit River. About three blocks away from the park, a bungalow had come onto the market at 2905 Garland Avenue, at the corner of Charlevoix Avenue.

An interracial couple, Ed and Marie Smith, was selling the house in which they had lived for two years. It was a two-story, brick-faced home with dormer windows, a front porch, and a three-car garage. A

German couple, a piano tuner and his wife, lived next door. Across Garland Avenue were two-family flats, a grocery store, and an empty lot. The Charlevoix side of the house faced a two-story apartment building. Kitty-corner was an elementary school. A streetcar stopped at the intersection.

The seller, Ed Smith, was light-skinned, and most of the neighbors did not know or did not believe the rumors that he was black. It had been only a few months since November, when Klansmen almost elected their candidate in the mayoral election. Had technicalities about write-in ballots not thwarted their success, Klan favorite Charles Bowles would have been elected instead of Catholic John Smith. Someone with Sweet's learning and background, a person who had seen lynching and ridden the insults of race, knew to act cautiously, to ask questions. Was the Klan active on these streets? Sweet asked the Smiths. No, they said, the neighbors are foreigners.

Ossian and Gladys Sweet liked what they saw. Friends suggested that he use a white proxy to purchase the house, or that he send Gladys to buy it alone. She had skin the color of wheat, and might pass unnoticed. But passing as white was not in his character or in hers. Just the opposite. He visited the neighborhood several times and made himself entirely conspicuous while he assessed its suitability; he sat on the front porch and walked through the streets. They were four blocks from his friend Julian Perry, equidistant from Gladwin Park at Jefferson Avenue, and a few minutes from the baseball stadium Mack Park, where fans of the Detroit Stars and the Negro National League filled the bleachers several times a week.

What Gladys especially liked about the house was the amount of space it provided for Iva to spend in the fresh air, outside in their front corner yard. It was the kind of neighborhood where children met at the school on summer evenings to play baseball or hopscotch. Most families did not own cars, but those who did parked them in a garage, back in the alley, not on the streets. Others took the trolley to work, returned home for dinner by five, and then sat outside reading the newspaper and watching fireflies on their front porches, especially on the hot and humid nights between June and September.

The first week of June, the Sweets and the Smiths agreed on the inflated price of $18,500, definitely in the upper reaches of what other black professionals were spending to purchase a house. They signed a contract, with a $3,500 down payment, and $150 a month. The Sweets were part of a seasonal ritual, people shopping for new homes, making payments on modern ice boxes, selecting pedestal washbasins made of marble for their bathrooms. They would move in August.

Buying their own home meant more space than they'd had at Gladys's parents' cramped house on Cairney Avenue. Ossian's brother Otis had been living with the Mitchells, too, and he intended to follow Ossian and Gladys when they moved into their house on Garland Avenue. He had opened his dental office at Columbia near St. Antoine Street in the heart of Paradise Valley. To afford the office, he spent a year working for the Wabash Railroad, saving his money. But when it came to finding a place to live, he was confined by the same shortage of apartments and houses that beset other black professionals. Soon Henry Sweet, an even younger brother, would come to Detroit for summer work between his junior and senior years at Wilberforce. That summer a friend, John Latting, came with him, and they, too, lived with the Mitchells, waiting for Ossian and Gladys to move.

Ossian was doing for Henry what other Wilberforce alums had done for him—providing shelter and security during the summer. Actually, Ossian was doing a lot more, helping his brother financially and emotionally. It is easy to imagine that Ossian Sweet felt triumphant the winter he and Gladys went to Xenia, Ohio, to watch Henry play football. Returning to his college campus after his trip abroad must have given him an added sense of achievement as he showed off his lovely wife and saw Dr. Gilbert Jones, his former professor and adviser to Kappa Alpha Psi, now president of Wilberforce.

Once Henry arrived in Detroit, it would be a full house at the Mitchells. As they had done before, they would make room, throw another mattress onto the floor until moving day. In the meantime, Gladys started planning her flower garden.

Two weeks after Gladys and Ossian signed a contract for their home, Sweet's colleague Dr. Alexander Turner moved into his new house on Spokane Avenue. The Spokane location, on Detroit's northwest, was an affluent neighborhood, suitable, it would seem, for the city's most prominent black physician. On moving day, June 23, Turner's van pulled into the driveway of his new house barely five minutes after the former owners left. He brought with him a crew of handymen and painters and put them to work right away.

Soon the Turners had company. About two hundred angry neighbors—they called themselves the Tireman Avenue Improvement Association—gathered in front of his house and began bombarding workmen with garbage, chunks of food, rock-size potatoes. They threw bricks through the windows. The police arrived, made one arrest, but did nothing to extinguish the fervor, to disband the crowd, which, by early evening, had taken over. Then two white men knocked on Turner's door, saying they represented the mayor's office. They shoved their way inside, pointed a gun at Turner's head, placed a deed to the property on the table, and demanded that he sign the house over to them. Although his wife wanted to hold out, he complied quickly. After the ink dried, the police escorted Dr. and Mrs. Turner, and her mother, outside, along with the two white intruders who threatened them. The mob loaded his furniture onto a van parked in the driveway. Turner's family got into his chauffeur-driven Lincoln, which pulled away from the curb under a shower of rocks shattering the car's windshield, shards of glass cutting Turner's face.

When they forced the doctor from his home, Turner's assailants also destroyed hope for peaceful race relations on Spokane Avenue, revealing an implacable tension that the press and public could no longer ignore. Some people who were not on the premises, who did not have a gun pointed toward their heads, who had not seen the police protect the intruders, or the mob, would later question Turner's decision. They would cast doubt on his fortitude, perhaps even his moral fiber, accusing him of fawning, submissive, and obsequious behavior before whites. Some went so far as to say later that his actions actually encouraged "mobbism against colored property owners."

Whether Turner's response was prudent or cowardly, similar attacks came to pass shortly. Two weeks later, on July 7, an undertaker named Vollington Bristol moved into a house he owned one block east of what was generally regarded as the "colored district." He had built the house on his own vacant lot, where, he said, he knew he would be the only black resident on the street.

Hints of trouble had been apparent since the first week in June, soon after he finished construction on the two-story apartment building. It started with an anonymous phone call demanding that Bristol rent the entire building to white people. He said his asking price was $50 for the upstairs, $60 for the downstairs. The caller responded by saying that it was too much. Forty was a better price, he said. Bristol disagreed and ran ads seeking black tenants. He received harassing phone calls. When black applicants arrived to look at the apartment, neighbors threatened them. He let things slide for a few weeks, but at the end of the month he placed another ad in a local paper. On July 4 he interviewed four black families. About two dozen whites showed up, determined to intimidate him. Rather than confront them directly, he gave up and moved into the downstairs apartment himself on July 6 in the hopes of avoiding further trouble. Then calm collapsed.

For the next two days and nights, a menacing group took over the streets. The police arrived, a crowd gathered and, from his window, Bristol saw a woman telling the crowd that if "they did not get the nigger off the street, she would do it herself. She wouldn't have her children brought up among them." The crowd cheered, the police moved people along, then bricks and stones came flying, an officer sounded a warning shot, and then he, too, was stoned, along with the house.

The next night, on July 10, a black man named John Fletcher similarly attempted to move into a house he had purchased the week before. Just as he was sitting down to dinner with his wife and two children, a neighbor walked by yelling, "Niggers live in there. Niggers live in there." Fletcher immediately called the police. When they arrived he was dismayed that they appeared to be cozy with the crowd. Another call brought more police, by which time an estimated four thousand people surrounded the home, yelling for lynching. Some noticed that five tons of coke had been dumped onto the ground, a delivery for the next-door neighbor. People in the crowd picked up the pieces and started hurling them toward the house. Some broke through windows, landing inside. Two shots were fired from an upstairs window, and one of them ripped through the thigh of a teenage boy. After living there for two days, Fletcher grabbed his family, collected his furniture, and fled the house, which did not have a single intact window. For the shooting, he was charged with "grievous bodily harm" and spent one night in jail.

That evening the Ku Klux Klan held a mass rally where an estimated ten thousand people gathered before a burning cross at West Fort Street. A Tennessee Klansman urged the crowd to demand laws compelling blacks to live within specified areas of the city amounting to a segregated ghetto.

STOP RIOTING, SMITH PLEADS WITH CITIZENS read the headline of the Sunday edition of the *Detroit Free Press*. Mayor John Smith, the liberal Catholic who squeaked into office narrowly defeating a Klansman in the last election, responded quickly to the outbursts. Smith delivered different messages to different audiences while appealing for all citizens to end damaging outbursts in a city portraying itself as the "Goddess of Opportunity."

Smith disparaged "the moving of colored persons into neighborhoods in which their presence would cause disturbances." He denounced "any colored person who endangers life and property simply to gratify his personal pride." This type of person, said Smith, was "an enemy of his race" because he incited "murder and riot."

But Smith's concern about appearances, how Detroit might look to the outside world, could not be minimized. Detroit was one of the few Northern metropolitan cities of any size that had not been blemished by racial conflict and slaughter. Politicians and business leaders were desperately hoping to avoid a "lasting stain." Smith would do what he could to avoid escalating the racial conflict, to prevent the anarchy and bloody streets seen in Chicago, East St. Louis, and Washington, D.C. "The persons either white or colored who attempt to urge their fellows on to disorder and crime are guilty of the most serious offense upon the statute books," he said, implicating whites whether Klansmen or sympathizers. He called upon the police to prosecute provocateurs.

The article in the *Detroit Free Press* reporting Smith's pleas to stop rioting concluded with news of a meeting called for Tuesday night, July 14. It would be sponsored by a new organization, the Waterworks Improvement Association, an offshoot of the vigilante Tireman Association, which proudly claimed credit for organizing Turner's departure, terrifying Bristol, assaulting Fletcher. Most people, save the organizers, had never heard of the Waterworks Improvement Association, which planned to gather at a school on the southeast corner of Garland and Charlevoix, kitty-corner from the house Ossian and Gladys had just purchased.

Tuesday night's meeting would discuss "the high standard of the residential district." At least seven hundred people read between the lines when they saw the other, announced, discussion topic: "Do you want to maintain the existing good health, conditions and environment for your little children?" It was paradoxical that the *Free Press* article describing

Smith's indictment of mobs should end by inviting the neighborhood to a meeting that was likely to contribute to another riot.

A hot and humid auditorium cramped the overflow crowd of the debut meeting of the Waterworks Improvement Association on that Tuesday evening. Many had trouble hearing. They moved to the outside yard at the Howe School where they could listen to speeches. They heard a neighbor, a realtor who lived on St. Claire, and a guest, someone from Tennessee, spew invective about black neighbors, integrated neighborhoods, the value of property. It is unlikely that many in the crowd noted the irony of listening to speeches invoking violence to keep out black families at a school that was named after the nineteenth-century abolitionist Julia Ward Howe, who wrote the "Battle Hymn of the Republic." Everybody knew that the black family they had in mind was named Sweet.

After a period of stagnation, new energy infused the Detroit branch of the NAACP in the spring of 1925. The accomplishment was more conspicuous because notable white leaders supported it. Judge Ira Jayne, who started his career as a social worker helping the Urban League, was now an NAACP board member, and he helped raise funds, including $200 from automobile scion Edsel Ford. And he raised $75 from the German-Jewish businessman Fred Butzel. After a campaign in the summer, Detroit's NAACP was again muscular, with 556 paid-up members, making it one of the country's larger chapters. With the black population in Detroit exceeding eighty thousand, it had the potential to grow even more.

Relations were strained between the local NAACP chapter and New York's national headquarters because of disagreements about member dues and conflicts during a drive to organize junior members. Despite those tensions, they shared a vision tinged with alarm as they watched the Ku Klux Klan expand in the nation's fourth largest city.

The local branch of the NAACP kept the New York office apprised of the street violence by which residential segregation was maintained in

Detroit. Reverend Robert Bradby, local president, expressed dismay as he accused the police department of being "friendly to the mob spirit." He had little doubt Detroit's police harbored "prejudice to our group." After reading Mayor Smith's ambiguous statements, he reported that the mayor was unreliable, the press onesided. To make matters worse, Bradby reported the outbreak of hostilities on the streets of Highland Park.

None of this surprised the national headquarters. Director of Branches Robert Bagnall came to his job after leaving his ministry in Detroit's St. Matthew's Episcopal Church. He could fill in gaps in the report with his own local insights. Bagnall responded to Bradby at the end of July, outlining a strategy to contain the violence and expose the lawless mobs attempting to "oust colored homeholders, to threaten their peace and safety, or to assault their homes." Knowing Detroit as well as he did, he feared the uneasy social tensions "will probably result in a disgraceful race riot."

Bradby was apprehensive, and quite protective of his jurisdiction in Detroit. But he was also grateful to the national headquarters for its support. He invited the executive secretary of the NAACP, James Weldon Johnson, to speak at a series of special lectures in Detroit churches to bolster local resolve. Johnson promised to come in September, as soon as he got back from vacation.

Ossian and Gladys carefully planned the details of moving into their new home. They were mindful of the string of racial incidents in the month since they signed a contract to buy the house. Sweet must have wrestled with himself all summer, every time someone mentioned one of the people who had been attacked. Fervently independent, with a family heritage steering him away from pursuing the rewards of white society, Ossian Sweet was now menaced by those whose approbation and companionship he had never wanted, had never sought.

Nobody doubted the copycat Waterworks Improvement Association was a shallow disguise for the Ku Klux Klan, invidious in mission yet powerful in ambition. After Gladys and Ossian tried to back out of the sale, but were unable to, they hoped to outsmart any mob that might take to the streets. They had no intention of concealing themselves, but their move would require planning if they were to avoid the troubles that beset others. They knew some people had been denied gas and electrical hookups. The day they bumped into Vollington Bristol, who continued to enjoy police protection, he encouraged them to call upon the police for their move. But they were suspicious of the police, whom Gladys believed "aided the mobbers instead of protecting life and property."

The Sweets were mindful that Detroit's police had a reputation for excessive force and impulsive actions. A local black paper that Gladys and Ossian read, *The Independent,* regularly reported on police incidents such as the shooting of a pregnant woman, Mrs. Lillie Smith, who had come to Detroit as part of the Southern Exodus. In February 1925 she died from a gunshot to the neck. Her baby, delivered at Receiving Hospital, lived. It was common knowledge that the jury deliberated for five minutes before finding the police officer "not guilty." There were fast-flying rumors about another murder, of George Sims, who was about the same age as Sweet. Sims worked in the River Rouge Ford plant, was a member of the St. John's Methodist Church. He was a nine-year resident of Detroit, working his second job, which was delivering coal, when police presumed the thermos bottle under his arm was a weapon and shot him, claiming self-defense. Detroit police had already killed twenty-five blacks in their custody in 1925, eight times the number killed that year in New York City, whose black population was at least twice as large.

For all these reasons, Sweet took precautions. He told Bristol that he was postponing the move until September. Guarded but optimistic, Ossian and Gladys hoped to diminish the problems by timing the move for the day after Labor Day. With the neighborhood made up of workers, foreigners they were told, the Sweets presumed nobody would want to lose a day's wage to gawk at them. Gladys reasoned that "an employee must be on the job the next day [after Labor Day] or lose pay for both days." Naively, they thought the logic of economic self-interest would trump hate.

One summer day, a group of doctors found themselves talking in an office at the Dunbar Memorial Hospital. Drs. Sweet, Edward Carter and Herbert Simms, along with William Osby, the general manager, were listening to Dr. Turner describe his ordeal. A telephone call from Mrs. Marie Smith pulled Sweet away. She had just been threatened, she said, because she was selling her house to him. The aggressors told her they would get Sweet too. After hanging up the phone, Sweet returned to the conversation about the Turner incident and raised his own concerns about himself. He told his colleagues he wasn't going to run away.

"We're not going to look for any trouble," he said, "but we're going to protect ourselves if trouble arises."

Years later Osby described the advice he gave to Sweet two days before the move. If he were in Sweet's situation, Osby said, he would send his wife and son out of town. But he would also get his revolver, shotgun, and ammunition. About four hundred rounds sounded right to him. He wouldn't attack first, but he would not hesitate after the first person attacked him.

After speaking with Osby, Ossian Sweet purchased guns and ammunition to protect himself and his family in the event of trouble.

Gladys and Ossian expected moving day would be hectic. They left Iva, fourteen months and just old enough to get into everything, with Gladys's mother. They rented a small moving van and got help from Henry and his Wilberforce buddy John Latting, both of whom expected to return to Ohio for the beginning of the fall semester and their senior year. Morris Murray, a handyman who did assorted errands, and Joe Mack, Sweet's chauffeur, followed in Sweet's Buick.

Between ten and ten-thirty in the morning, Police Sergeant Clayton Williams stopped by the house and chatted with the Smiths, on their way out the door. When the Sweets arrived, he introduced himself and told them he was there "to protect your property on orders of the inspector." Residential segregation enforced by mob rule had apparently become so commonplace that police procedures assumed its occurrence.

It took two trips to move their belongings from Gladys's mother's home. They had little—they would shop the next day—but there was a card table and chairs, a bedroom set, extra mattresses, and clothes, along with valises, one of which still bore tags from the *Paris,* the ship they sailed from LeHavre. Having heard that the grocer on Charlevoix, barely one hundred feet from their front door, would not sell to them, they packed enough food to stock a pantry. Once everything was unloaded, they set to cleaning the cupboards and turning their new house into a home.

Later that night, friends visited. Edward Carter, a doctor and the former polemarch from Kappa Alpha Psi, brought them a set of new dishes. Interior decorators came to measure the rooms, advise Gladys on color schemes, and plant ideas she would employ the next day when she and Ossian went shopping for new furniture. But these women, Serena Rochelle and Edna Butler, saw distressing signs when they tried to leave the house that night. People had begun to mass on the streets, a dozen on one sidewalk, several beyond a curb, and women with children stood gawking, staring at the corner house that was Gladys and Ossian's new home.

Afraid to leave, Rochelle and Butler remained all night. But they didn't get much sleep. Nobody did. When they boarded the Charlevoix Avenue streetcar the next morning, they overheard a passenger tell the conductor that a black family had moved in, but reassured him that the crowd would take care of them later that night.

After thinking about it for most of the day, trying to decide whether it was too worrisome to convey, Rochelle called Gladys to tell her what she heard on the trolley. This was not the only warning the

Sweets received that day. When John Latting and Joe Mack went out, someone warned them, saying, "[T]he fellows had a meeting last night in the confectionery store. [Y]ou fellows better watch yourselves, they say they are going to get you out of here tonight."

That morning Sweet went to his medical office to see patients before meeting Gladys downtown, where they shopped for furniture. They picked out a walnut dining room set and a bedroom set, and scheduled delivery for the following day. At three o'clock Sweet met with insurance agents from whom he had bought a new policy. Apprehensive about the warnings he received, he invited the three men to come to his house. Although nothing overt had happened, Sweet was anxious that nothing should.

Ossian and Gladys got home at five o'clock. Henry had spent time during that warm and humid afternoon relaxing on a front-porch swing; and now, while people mingled on the street, Ossian sent him to pick up Mack and Murray. Gladys headed into the kitchen to cook dinner—ham, sweet potatoes, and green vegetables. The kitchen faced the next-door neighbor's house to the north, and she could not see what was happening on the streets. But anybody sitting in a room in the front of the house, which looked onto Garland and Charlevoix, could see policemen at the intersection, the sun glinting off their gold buttons, along with a steady flow of people walking back and forth.

About six o'clock Henry returned home with Mack and Murray and half an hour later, Ossian's friends Hewitt Watson, Leonard Morris, and Charles Washington, agents from the Liberty Life Insurance Company, arrived. They scooped up a leather bag with a grip, as well as a bundle, wrapped in newspaper, measuring about three and a half feet long and six inches around. Henry went outside to open the garage door.

Meanwhile Ossian waited for his brother Otis to return with William Davis, a friend of Ossian's from Washington, D.C., a pharmacist he met at Freedmen's Hospital. He had fought at the French Battle of Argonne. After the war ended, Davis had changed careers.

He returned to the United States and became a narcotics agent. No city in the country offered greater challenge tracking bootleggers during prohibition than Detroit, the nation's epicenter for the entry of illegal liquor. Davis arrived that summer, and he intended to live in Ossian's new house, to share a room with Otis. They were now on their way home, most likely from a baseball game at Mack Park between the hometown Detroit Stars and the formidable Cuban team.

While they waited for Otis and Davis, Ossian and his friends sat down for a game of bridge. Henry and Latting, who had been sitting on the front porch, came inside to help Gladys with dinner. Their job was to churn the ice cream. In the meantime the sun was dropping and they turned on the lights inside, giving themselves privacy, walling themselves in. They would not notice, until later, that the crowd was growing thick. Nor would they hear the sounds until something crashed into the wall. The first rumble may have come from a rock tumbling down the sloping roof. But the thunder became louder. It came again and again and again. Someone looked out the window. For the first time it was clear just how many people had been walking toward the corner of Garland and Charlevoix. There were a couple of hundred at the Howe School; some were coming and going from the grocery store. "Something's going to happen pretty soon," a guest blurted anxiously.

Ossian went looking for Gladys. He searched the kitchen, opened the back door, heard a stranger, someone from the mob shouting directions. A vigilante screamed that he would go to the back of the house. He ordered others to swarm in front of Sweet's house. Ossian locked the door. He turned off the lights, ran upstairs, and grabbed a gun. Then he went to a closet and fumbled for ammunition. He rushed to the upstairs bedroom at the front of the house. He lay down flat on the bed, facing Garland, and he carefully looked through a narrow crack in the curtains. His eyes swept up and down Garland Avenue where he could see policemen. They stood at the intersection of Garland and Charlevoix, directly in front of his house, moving people along. Up Garland and Charlevoix, groups of men got out of taxis, and the barrage of rocks continued to rain down on the house. Then a rock came through the window, shattering the glass, spraying shards throughout the bedroom and on him.

A taxicab stopped in front of the house. Through a crack in the curtain Ossian saw Otis get out. Davis followed. Ossian darted downstairs and opened the front door, permitting them to run directly into the house without getting trapped between the car and the entrance. As it was, they ran for cover under a shower of rocks and slurs. "Niggers, Niggers, get the Niggers," the crowd chanted. As Ossian stood at the landing, watching the mob, memory swept over him, fear seized him, and the hate-filled faces seemed too familiar, like images of mobs and lynchings he had seen before.

Henry grabbed his rifle. Later he would describe how he was shivering when he knelt down on the floor, how he opened a window overlooking the street, how he saw men clustering on curbs and women and children spilling over the neighboring porches, how he picked up a rifle and took aim.

Washington and Watson pulled out their revolvers. They walked outside to the back porch. Bullets exploded. The two ran in opposite directions. An instant of calm followed. Then there were several more shots, crashing glass, and a fusillade of stones thundering down the roof. Then it was silent.

Just at that moment of silence, a large man in uniform knocked on the door and identified himself as Inspector Schuknecht. "For Christ's sake, what the hell are you fellows shooting about?" he asked after Sweet opened the door to let him in.

"They are ruining my property," Sweet replied.

"What have they done?" Schuknecht asked. "I haven't seen a man throwing stones, and I haven't heard any commotion or anything else."

Schuknecht, who had never met Sweet before, told him that he was in charge that night. Inspector McPherson had been there the night before, but now it was Schuknecht, and he said the house was surrounded by police. There would be no more shooting, Sweet said, and placated Schuknecht, who left.

Within a few minutes the inspector returned, flanked by five officers. They herded the occupants into the living room and handcuffed them. Police turned on the lights throughout the house, leaving everybody in full view. Their profiles were apparent, visible to people on the street, the same people who had been taunting them all evening. One of the officers, Lieutenant Hayes, sensed risk and ordered the shades dropped to cover the windows, to protect the Sweets and their guests. In the meantime the police searched the house and confiscated guns, automatic pistols, rifles, the diamond-studded blue-steel revolver belonging to Otis's roommate, the narcotics agent William Davis. Police searched upstairs. One officer saw broken glass and a stone on the floor of an upstairs bedroom.

The eleven occupants remained handcuffed, standing in the middle of the room, while police readied them for a trip to headquarters. Lieutenant Hayes pulled Sweet aside and uncuffed him while they spoke for several minutes. Then the men were escorted to a van. Gladys was taken in a separate vehicle to police headquarters. They were separated and interrogated individually. Nobody was permitted an attorney. Most refused to talk. Those who did told entirely different stories. Joe Mack denied hearing anything. He was taking a bath, he said. Henry confessed that he shot, but said it was over the heads of the people lining the street. Ossian Sweet said he was resting upstairs in an attempt to calm his nerves and he denied having guns in the house. The police had already uncovered the lie. Sweet had dumped the contents of his pockets—ammunition and his house keys—into a cuspidor next to the chair in which he was sitting at the police station. Lieutenant Johnson and a young prosecuting attorney, Edward Kennedy, inadvertently discovered this when they picked up the cuspidor to move it out of the way.

Meanwhile, Gladys's mother contacted Ossian Sweet's friend, attorney Julian Perry, to represent the Sweets. The Liberty Life Insurance Company called lawyers Charles Mahoney and Cecil Rowlette to represent the three agents. They went out to Sweet's house late that evening and saw stones littering the front lawn, policemen standing at the corners. The lawyers went to the jail to speak to their clients about eleven o'clock but were denied access to them. After they filed writs of habeas corpus, chief prosecutor Robert Toms permitted the lawyers a visit.

While the Sweets were taken to headquarters, thousands of neighbors emptied onto the streets. The Waterworks Improvement Association held a meeting at Amity Hall, which was "called in the interest of a Mr. Callahan, a political aspirant for some office."

About three o'clock in the morning, the defendants learned that Eric Hogsburg had been shot in the leg and taken to the hospital. And that Leon Breiner had died as a result of a wound he received that night.

A hearing was scheduled for Saturday in Judge John Faust's court.

CHAPTER 8

James Weldon Johnson
and the NAACP

James Weldon Johnson had just returned from vacation when news of Ossian Sweet's arrest traveled through the community more like a tremor than an earthquake. It was not unusual for him to reach his office in the early morning and find a news report, or an overnight cable, asking for help. It could be a request to investigate a lynching, to help a suspect in police custody, to provide legal advice about an upcoming trial. Johnson's correspondence with the local Detroit branch earlier that summer put him on alert that streets were rife with racial conflict. On this slow day in September, when his eye caught an article about Sweet in the morning's newspaper, he had no way of knowing in which ways the situation differed from Detroit's other disturbances that summer. As he had done dozens of times before, he wired for updated information.

It had been nine years since the NAACP hired Johnson, five since they made him the executive secretary. During these years the association had worked for many homeowners who needed help defending their rights to occupy a house because vigilantes used violence to maintain segregation. At that moment the NAACP was working with a New York family on Staten Island, but similar problems afflicted citizens in more than a dozen cities that fall of 1925. Until black and white received the same rights, enjoyed the same guarantees, and were protected by the same laws, Johnson remained watchful for new crises where the NAACP's intervention might lead to a landmark consequence. That had happened once before, in 1917, after the United States Supreme Court ruled in their favor in a case involving housing discrimination, *Buchanan v. Warley*, in Louisville, Kentucky.

The Court ruled that Kentucky's law unconstitutionally prevented William Warley from building a house on land he bought from Charles Buchanan. Johnson was new to the association when the Louisville decision was handed down, and the Supreme Court's decision left him breathless, perhaps unduly optimistic. It had taken the NAACP years to move this case through lower courts, which kept affirming Kentucky's restrictive law. This was typical of the NAACP's strategy, still in its formative stages, to find a lawsuit that could represent a deeper grievance, preferably one bordering on constitutional infringements, and move it through the courts by relying on lightning legal minds. Moorfield Storey, NAACP president and Boston Brahmin, shepherded *Buchanan v. Warley* through the Supreme Court. The unanimous decision, including the opinion of Chief Justice Edward White, a former Klansman from Louisiana, was a momentous achievement.

Johnson voiced the NAACP's enthusiasm when he penned his column for the *New York Age* in 1917. "If the NAACP never did anything else," he said, "this victory in the Supreme Court by which segregation was killed, alone would justify all of the money and effort which has been put into the organization." But no amount of hyperbole could equate the Court's judgment with the death of segregation, and if he was rightfully enthusiastic he was also naive in failing to anticipate just how easy it would be for Southern states to undermine the decision. Perhaps the idealism that came from his training—Johnson was the first black admitted to the Florida bar although he never practiced—blinded him to the likelihood that affected states would begin rewriting laws and replacing the outlawed prohibitions almost immediately with new and more subtle clauses. Residential segregation was hardly dead.

Like Sweet, Johnson hailed from Florida. He grew up a few blocks from the Argretts, the maternal side of Sweet's family, in Jacksonville. In a segregated, isolated Southern town, even if they did not belong to the same church, it is inconceivable that the families were unacquainted. At the turn of the century Johnson headed the Florida State Teachers Association, when one of Sweet's uncles, George Devaughn, was teaching school in Orlando. Even had it taken Johnson a while to figure out the likely connections, the name Ossian must have brought to mind the name of the legendary governor Ossian Hart, after whom Sweet was named. As a youngster Johnson played on Hart's vacant lot, picked berries from his garden, which was next door to the Stanton School where Johnson began his career as teacher and principal in the 1890s.

Under any circumstance, the attack on Ossian Sweet's home certainly justified the NAACP's immediate attention. Johnson set out to find what had happened.

The poet and literary critic William Stanley Braithwaite once observed that James Weldon Johnson was born with creative talent but had to make himself into a race leader. Johnson had not aspired to such leadership, but it grew on him, slowly at first, later more confidently. He began to realize that he had an ability to persuade, that he could bridge worlds that were not color-coded, arenas of culture, literary and musical talents, and spheres of influence including philanthropy. But in 1916 he was struggling when he backed into working for the NAACP.

James Weldon Johnson might not have taken the association's job as field organizer had Justice Charles Evans Hughes beaten President Woodrow Wilson in the election of 1916. Johnson's respect for Hughes's record as a Supreme Court justice—Hughes was the author of the de-

cision to overturn an Oklahoma law linking literacy to voting rights—
was as strong as his antipathy to Woodrow Wilson. Feelings about Wilson were personal, more than the axiomatic rejection of a Southern president's expansion of racist policies segregating Washington, D.C., and more than his dislike of Wilson's stand on *Birth of a Nation*. Johnson had been personally wounded when Wilson assumed office in 1912 and sent Secretary of State William Jennings Bryan as his personal emissary to dismiss Johnson from the Department of State. He loved the eight years he spent as a consul in Nicaragua and Venezuela, appointed by Teddy Roosevelt with help from Bookerites, who recognized his value as a leader within New York's budding Republican Party. But nothing was more anathema in Wilson's Washington than erudite, accomplished black men linked to the opposing party.

After his dismissal, Johnson had written for the *New York Age* while he tried to resurrect a successful career as a composer and songwriter. Whatever inspiration led him to compose over two hundred tunes for Broadway with his brother, Rosamond, had dwindled. He never returned to the stage, nor did he resume managing the national and international performances for the team, Johnson and Cole. And as a writer, he remained an unknown quantity because his first novel, *Autobiography of an Ex-Colored Man,* had been published anonymously.

But he also had not relinquished his love of the exotic and the genteel, and he hoped a Hughes victory might restore his diplomatic career. He spent election eve, November 1916, at campaign headquarters in New York's Astor Hotel, and when the tremendous lead in the East made Hughes's victory seem all but guaranteed, a near-euphoric Johnson retired to the offices of the *New York Age* to craft his remarks. "We say 'Thank God!' from the bottom of our heart," rejoiced the editorial congratulating Hughes. Johnson called Wilson a hypocrite and a coward, and he flayed the Democratic administration with its entrenched Southern bias. "The re-election of Woodrow Wilson would have meant the continuance of the policies and practices which have for their end nothing less than the total elimination of the colored American from all part and participation in the government," he wrote. Johnson believed the defeat of Wilson was synonymous with the death of Jim Crow, and he called the election "a day of Thanksgiving for us as a people."

After carefully choosing his words—as he was also a poet—Johnson dropped off his editorial at the offices of the *New York Age* on West Forty-sixth Street and then turned toward home. Speeding up to Harlem in the underground subway, his imagination, no doubt, wrapped the globe, stopping in the Azores—a destination former President Taft had picked for him—or perhaps Haiti or Nice, assignments he had requested. He could see himself standing on the deck of an ocean liner that was pulling away from New York's harbor, with his wife, Grace, at his side. Whatever his dreams, they were shattered. When he climbed upstairs in the early morning hours from the subway station at 135th Street and Lenox Avenue, he heard shouts of "Extra." It was the breaking news that Wilson would be reelected. In the meantime, it was too late to change his editorial. Soon the *New York Age* would be on the streets with Johnson's irrelevant exultation under the banner headline HUGHES WINS IN A CLOSE RACE.

Before the week was out, Johnson had accepted an offer to work for the NAACP.

When Johnson accepted the new position of field secretary in December 1916 he became only the second black man, following W. E. B. Du Bois, on the payroll. Gradually but systematically he began to expand the NAACP's membership to bring the voices of black Americans into the movement, and he persuaded the board to let him recruit in the South. This departed from the NAACP's earlier strategy of relying on wealthy, well-meaning, but paternalistic white support in Northern ghettos of liberal thought. The trip would take place in the wake of two violent incidents earlier that year. One occurred in Waco, Texas, where a mentally retarded teenager was strung up and burned alive as entertainment for fifteen thousand spectators. The other was in Gainesville,

Florida, when three men and two women were murdered after a fight with a white man about a pig. Southern volatility could be measured by the pattern of its lynchings. Yet, into this region, which black residents were beginning to abandon for the Southern Exodus, Johnson, a native son, pleaded to go alone, visiting twenty cities from Richmond to Tampa where Jim Crow laws blanketed all custom and manner of life.

Johnson would later say, "the ultimate and vital part of the work would have to be done by black America itself." In a stunning display of talent and charisma, he showed how the NAACP could expand the constituency with a cadre who would become the nucleus of the organization, people who were eager to do what was necessary, to do the "work that must be done." Early in his campaign thirteen new branches were added, bringing the total to eighty-one. Twelve months later 165 branches with nearly forty-four thousand members swelled the association. It doubled again the next year, with about one-third of the 310 branches located in the South and a membership approaching one hundred thousand by the end of the decade.

In Atlanta Johnson met a twenty-five-year-old volunteer named Walter White. There was something special, something different about this young man, and later Johnson would say it was his energy, his focus. It may have also been his impassioned drive to stop Atlanta officials from diverting public funds from black schools to white. Whatever it was, shortly after returning to New York, he offered White a job as his assistant. Learning of the offer, White's mother feared the rumored life in New York City would tempt her son. Friends tried to discourage him, saying financial security was more important than a hopeless cause. Only his father understood the call, which White eagerly accepted with an annual salary of $1,200, less than he was earning in an Atlanta insurance office. Ironically, it was also less than what was paid to the white clerical staff of the NAACP.

Johnson had a quick student in White. And in Johnson, the young White had a counselor, a mentor, an amiable sophisticate, who was well placed through marriage—Johnson's wife was the daughter of real estate tycoon John Nail, who drove Harlem's transition from a Jewish to a black ghetto. James Weldon and Grace Nail Johnson lived a few blocks from the epicenter of Harlem's burgeoning vitality, near the Lafayette Theater, which drew black audiences for black performers, freeing each, as Johnson later said, from the taboos of whites. During the evening the Johnsons could walk to LeRoy's Café, popular for its southern fried chicken, where patrons came to listen to Willie "The Lion" Smith bang out stride on the piano—heavy tempo from the left hand, melody from the right. Through Johnson, White was exposed to a world of belles lettres, to writers who became friends, and friends who became editors, and editors who became partisans of the NAACP in those heady years when, as one historian has written, "Harlem was in vogue."

But the chemistry of White and Johnson's friendship may have depended as much on the color line in the offices of the NAACP as it did on the relationship of a dutiful student and a dapper, avuncular sage. White had light skin, blue eyes, and blond hair—he was seven-eighths white. In his soul he was uncompromising as a proud black man. Southern upbringings most likely initially fashioned a bond between these two alumni of Atlanta University. Each could detect sounds that peel silence, like the vapor inhaled by sniffing bloodhounds or boots crackling on a carpet of dry leaves. Neither would have been naive enough to step into closed chambers behind a door with the local police and a judge who disparaged the NAACP, challenged its right to organize a branch in his Texas town. Johnson and White each understood Southern customs.

But Johnson's boss, a young, white social worker from Westchester County, New York, didn't know any better when he met with officials in Austin, Texas. He was invited to a private conversation that became an inquisition about the NAACP's local activities. When he left, officials followed him out to the street and nearly beat him to death. The Texas governor applauded the work of these vigilantes, and the judge and the constable were later implicated in the battering. John Shalliday never completely recovered, and two years later he resigned.

Of all the people the NAACP employed, White was the only one likely to understand what Johnson was feeling when the association turned to less experienced white men for the top spot, not just once, but twice. After Shalliday's resignation in 1919, the NAACP searched for six months before offering Johnson the job, first as "acting" secretary, finally naming him to the post of executive secretary in 1920.

On-the-job training hurtled Johnson into the brink of horrors, first in East St. Louis, later during the "Red Summer" of 1919 when two hundred sharecroppers were slaughtered in Elaine, Arkansas, as they were trapped in a burning church where they had been organizing. In Tulsa, Oklahoma, two years later, white citizens massacred a prosperous black middle-class and dumped the corpses into mass graves. Enraged, Johnson felt compelled to speak out, determined to organize the multiple sources of energy that could be harnessed for NAACP battles. He took to the road, traveling on Pullman sleeping cars, racing between cities, spending nights in dilapidated hotels with creaky metal-framed beds, fluctuating between the fatigue of insomnia and his longing for home and for his delicate Grace. Yet he could not slacken his pace, diminish his goal. Sometimes he spoke as many as four times a day on behalf of the NAACP, to arouse what he called "the conscience of the nation against the 'Shame of America.' "

Nowhere was Johnson more engaged than in the campaign to end lynching. It had been nearly twenty years since his own escape from a lynching, and he had not forgotten the hours of panic and the lingering terror after armed soldiers had seized him in a park for only one reason: he was in the company of a woman whom his persecutors *thought* was white. By 1920 lynching had become pandemic, as American homespun as Betsy Ross's flag, to which Southern pride and states' rights clutched feverishly. No insult cut him more deeply than the nation's toleration of the lawlessness that a lynch mob arrogated in the name of justice.

By 1920 some of the skills the critic Braithwaite saw earlier in Johnson had coalesced when he organized mass meetings, lobbied politicians, and fought to challenge Southern lawmakers for whom racial justice was an oxymoron. Impotent governors announced with hearty alacrity their inability to control mobs or the sheriffs who collaborated with them. Added to that regional brutality was the federal indifference as Washington winked at the slaughter. Congressional investigations unabashedly subordinated the loss of life to the interruption of interstate commerce. The daily confluence of brutality and indifference became more than Johnson and the NAACP could tolerate any longer.

Condemning lynching did not create a legal basis on which to ground its prohibition. As a result, Johnson spent most of 1921 and 1922 commuting between New York and Washington, D.C., to lobby for passage of an antilynch bill that was introduced by Congressman Leonidas Dyer, whose Missouri district bordered East St. Louis. It would protect all Americans by making lynching a federal crime, and no longer tolerated by the caprice of legal authority.

Johnson's passion and knowledge dazzled legislators. And soon they came to rely on him, asking that he supply statistics on the number of lynchings of women, or in what states they happened most often. North or South? Were there statistics for the West? And under what conditions was a lynching likely to occur?

Like a missionary on foreign soil, he distributed a booklet the NAACP had written, *Thirty Years of Lynching*, wherever he went. Walter White had compiled the list of 3,224 confirmed lynchings—an average of two each week—for thirty years through 1918, listing the name, location, and "official" reason given for the lynching. Of the victims, 2,522 were black; 50 were women; 2,834 occurred in the South. Georgia ranked first with 386 people, followed by Mississippi with 373, and Texas with 335. The facts rolled off his tongue like a preacher citing chapter and verse.

Simultaneous with the NAACP's efforts to pass the Dyer antilynching bill in the fall of 1921 were the syndicated columns from *New York World* and the congressional hearings exposing the Ku Klux Klan. In a different political climate the exposé might have, should have, provided independent confirmation that the nation needed a federal antilynching law. But it did not. In the midst of this bizarre twist, the NAACP had to redouble its efforts. In November, after numerous postponements nearly sabotaged the Dyer bill, Johnson warned the Republican leadership that further delay would constitute a betrayal. Political maneuvering nonetheless prevented a vote in the House of Representatives until 1922, after the Christmas recess.

It was momentous for the seven hundred spectators who left their homes on January 25, a frigid day in the nation's capital, to bear witness to the House of Representatives debate lynching. It was not common for blacks and whites to sit together in the public halls of Congress, and black visitors were sent upstairs to the segregated galleries. Representative Blanton from Texas blasted the Dyer bill and announced that even if enacted "we will lynch Negroes just the same." His rhetoric inflamed an already explosive situation where congressmen trembled with suppressed emotion. The staged decorum framing the debate exploded after Representative Sisson of Mississippi thundered justifications for lynching "black rascals." Whatever Congress chose to do, Wisconsin's Cooper screamed back in outrage that this was the first time he had heard lynching justified in Congress. "Then the colored people in the galleries rose up and cheered," Johnson said. The next day the House passed the Dyer antilynch bill, 230 to 119. Johnson would later write that "Thanksgiving and jubilation swept the colored people of the country."

Next stop was the Senate Judiciary Committee. Members locked themselves in place like migrating birds in flight formation. Several were lawyers, all were born before the Civil War, and four came from

the South. Most doubted the constitutionality of the bill. Any potential for compromise was hardened by the acrimony still lingering from
their debate over the controversial Treaty of Versailles following World
War I. The NAACP's mission seemed impossible. The association
launched a major drive to patch together a compromise. Johnson went
to Washington at the end of August, again in September, only to have
the Senate table a vote until after the fall recess. During the delay the
association used the time to orchestrate strategies that would eventually become its template.

To pass the Dyer bill, the NAACP launched an unprecedented campaign to appeal to black voters in cities showing strong local membership,
an innovation in the twenties, when the party system was still weak at the
national level. The Seventeenth Amendment permitting the direct election of senators was new, and the NAACP applied voter pressure to a
group of officials who had never had to worry about appealing to a popular constituency. It organized letter-writing campaigns and newspaper
ads and probably startled senators facing reelection. Never before had
they been asked to respond to the people who could decide whether to
perpetuate their careers. If the association had ever wondered about the
value of Johnson's earlier efforts to organize new chapters, to fortify
branches with black voices, the grassroots activities local chapters waged
should have laid that doubt to rest.

While Johnson organized the lobbying, Walter White planned the
press strategy, deciding which of the magazines or newspapers was most
influential. With the joy of discovery that sounded almost childlike,
White calculated that an ad in the *New York Times* was eight times more
likely to reach a national audience than an ad in the local paper. Johnson
preferred advertising in the *New York World,* thinking it the more influential paper. White then figured that for $250 the association could
reach about one hundred thousand people based on *The Nation's* circulation of thirty-one thousand. When Congress convened again, full-
page ads appeared in *The Nation,* the *New York Times,* and six other daily
papers. An open letter denouncing lynching was signed by twenty-four

governors, thirty-nine mayors, twenty-nine lawyers, nineteen judges, and the American Bar Association and, by all accounts, grabbed attention. But it is unclear how much influence it carried.

Pressure on the white community remained a priority, but the NAACP needed also to mend fissures in the black community. Although his popularity was cresting, militant separatist Marcus Garvey openly criticized the bill, perversely saying making lynching a federal crime was no substitute for black self-determination, his passionate goal. Garvey even met with the Klan's Imperial Wizard to discuss support for his "Back to Africa" movement. Applying pressure on the other flank, the Negro Press Association condemned the NAACP, complaining that money spent to purchase ads in the white press should have been spent on the black press. Then a meeting between President Harding and William Monroe Trotter, editor of the militant *Boston Guardian,* triggered Walter White's fear that the NAACP might be eclipsed. After seven months of diligent work, White wasn't about to let Trotter steal the association's moment of glory, and he began planning a star-studded photo opportunity followed by a victory celebration to upstage dissidents. "We should set up now the control of the ceremony when President Harding signs the Bill," he told Johnson in October. White imagined focusing the eyes of the nation on friends whose help had been essential, including Congressmen Dyer, Mondell, Fess, and Burton, and Senators Lodge and Watson. These men would surround President Harding and James Weldon Johnson. The press would be invited, there would be a magnificent photo opportunity, and White predicted "a big publicity scoop for the Association." He planned to have Trotter out of the picture.

One month later, however, the picture looked different. Congress expired before the bill could be voted, and President Harding had to call a lame-duck session over the Christmas holidays. By the time Congress reconvened, Johnson worried that the Republicans were too disorganized to break the Southern Democrats' filibuster. Still Johnson did not give ground. "If we can only prevent the Republicans abandoning the bill on the terms laid down by the Rebels, we still have a chance," he told White late in the process.

But it was too late. The Democrats were prepared to talk the bill to death and to stall the nation's business with a two-month filibuster. When Congress reconvened after March 4, it would tend to new business. Alabama's Senator Underwood made explicit this common knowledge when he candidly threatened Republicans not to even try to break Southern Democratic control.

The realistic prospects for success probably never matched the energy Johnson exerted. The judiciary committee was intent on strangling the bill, and the Republicans were afraid to halt the filibuster. The combination killed the antilynching momentum, including the success of any legislation during that session. Johnson considered the committee's lapse, its unwillingness to vote on the bill, a personal betrayal and a national humiliation. His conviction that the full Senate would probably have passed the bill that was stalled in committee was no consolation. It would be hard to exaggerate how defeat of the Dyer bill sapped Johnson's vitality.

Although Johnson never gave up on the campaign to end lynching, it ceased to be an exclusive preoccupation after December 1922. In the months that followed, the frenzied pace caught up with him. He grew concerned, perhaps obsessed with his health, and worried about nutrition. He started to read diet books. Judging from what he told Grace, he decided to cut back on red meat and milk. He advocated eating only whole wheat bread and bran muffins. His marching in the campaign for civil rights seemed to falter. Platitudes and generalities flattened his prose. He spoke about using Congress as a forum to publicize lynching and wondered whether the failed vote on the Dyer bill contributed to the drop from sixty-one murders in 1922 to twenty-eight in 1923. Who could say? But phrases like "continuing the struggle" or injunctions about how much more they had to learn sounded listless when they came from the author of catchy show tunes, lyrical verse, and piercing editorials.

The association, in the meantime, languished. Income diminished and activity dwindled by the end of 1923. The next year the Internal Revenue Service started badgering the NAACP about its not-for-profit fund-raising status. They demanded documentation of contributions. For Johnson this was pure and simple irritation. "If the societies for [prevention] of cruelty to children and to animals are entitled to exemption," he said, "a society for the prevention of cruelty to adults ought to be entitled to exemption."

Meanwhile, restrictive housing ordinances continued to frustrate local chapters of the NAACP. In Detroit board member Ira Jayne wanted to test the local housing laws by selling "to some colored people." While waiting for this challenge, a seemingly better opportunity for a test case arose in Washington, D.C., where local courts enforced restrictive covenants barring the sale of houses to blacks. A challenge to *Corrigan v. Buckley* in the District of Columbia would permit a new opportunity for the NAACP, which, if successful, might serve them broadly, the way the Louisville segregation case had.

Elsewhere, problems cascaded. The state of Louisiana imposed residential segregation in cities with more than twenty-five thousand residents. Then in August Klansmen visited Washington, D.C., climbing the Capitol steps in full costume. They had gathered for a march, forty thousand strong down Pennsylvania Avenue, where they walked confidently, brazenly displaying their strength in front of the White House. The excitement that Johnson imparted a decade before now seemed mangled and NAACP membership was stagnant. By the summer of 1925 sagging hope and two bouts of illness dampened his spirits.

One place where Johnson was harvesting satisfaction was in the vitality of his own writing and in the robust Harlem Renaissance. Publisher Harcourt, Brace and Company brought out an anthology in 1922, *The Book of American Negro Poetry,* with his introduction. And with his brother, Rosamond, he wrote arrangements for *The Book of*

American Negro Spirituals. Reviewing the galleys in 1925 stalled his departure for a summer vacation in the Berkshire Hills of Massachusetts, where he and Grace had recently bought a barn in need of renovation near a stream, six miles from Great Barrington. There birdsong replaced the metal clang of subways. Invigorating air replaced the perfume of Broadway. In the abandon of the country, Johnson could deliver himself to solitude. Guests remembered his elegant desk, brightened by pots of flowers and bowls of apples, where he would write the poetry and verse that secured for him a pivotal role for an entire generation of poets, novelists, and critics.

Johnson was anxious to stretch out his time with Grace, away from the burdens of the office. When the weather turned sunny in August, he did not want to be cheated out of a single day. They took sun-warmed walks in the woods. "The weather is perfect here now, and I want to get the fullest benefit and results possible," he told his secretary one week before he returned. Still preoccupied by his own health he noted, "I am feeling splendid today but my condition fluctuates. Some days I go up and other days slip back."

The pace would quicken once Johnson returned to the office after Labor Day. Raising enough money for the plethora of cases the NAACP was defending was what worried him most in the fall of 1925. The association had four cases of great importance on its agenda. One was the six-year-old defense of World War I black soldiers on trial for murder in Houston. Another attacked segregated schools in Philadelphia. Two cases were pending in the United States Supreme Court. One challenged El Paso, Texas, which was trying to stop blacks from voting in the state's primary elections. The other aimed to overturn *Corrigan v. Buckley,* in Washington, D.C. How could he not worry? He figured he would need at least $50,000 from an impecunious membership of roughly 110,000 people. Mostly, he knew he would need another success, another flash point to ignite the association's enthusiasm.

Then he read about Dr. Ossian Sweet in Detroit.

. . .

O ne can only imagine what the first meeting between James Weldon Johnson and Ossian Sweet entailed. Did they acknowledge overlapping experience growing up in Florida? Whom they knew from Jacksonville? From Orlando? Or even from Ocoee, Florida, a town outside Orlando where black voters were massacred after one of them, Mose Norman, ignored warnings for blacks to keep away and tried to vote on election day in November 1920. The barbaric incident terrified Sweet's little cousins every time they drove to Orlando to visit their grandfather. They would roll onto the floor of the car and stay there like potato bugs until Ocoee was far behind and out of sight. It was an event Johnson knew well, having testified before a congressional committee that it exemplified how "voting rights were being murdered."

It is easy to see how Sweet's predicament reignited Johnson's fighting spirit. It had been a long time since he had harnessed his passions to organize teachers or to enlist new NAACP members. Almost three years had passed since he had walked the halls of a recalcitrant Congress, beseeching its members to end their tacit approval of lynching. Now at fifty-five, he had slowed his pace. Bespectacled and mannerly in bow ties and suspenders, he was soft-spoken. He had more time for his favorite pleasures—a game of bridge, a good cigar, an evening at the theater with Grace and their friends. But no amount of social gaiety or personal reward could disguise aging, how each year flattened his boyish-round cheeks. After years of toil, his gray eyes sagged. But reading about Sweet sparked the fury of his youth.

Neither Johnson nor Sweet recorded his first encounter or impressions. But it is likely that one reason Johnson wrapped himself, and the NAACP, in what came to be called "the Detroit case" had something to do with the fact that, in the trials of Ossian Sweet, James Weldon Johnson could trace so many of his own footsteps.

CHAPTER 9

Send Walter White

The days following Ossian Sweet's arrest looked dismal. Initially the local branch of the NAACP declined James Weldon Johnson's offer to help. Detroit could handle it alone. After the Sweets were arraigned in court, however, Detroit's branch officers saw how truly grim the circumstances were and they changed their minds.

The arraignment took place on Saturday morning, September 12, in Judge John Faust's courtroom, and the prosecution built its case with police witnesses. The undisputed facts included police testimony that eight officers had been assigned to patrol the streets as soon as the Sweets arrived with their moving van on Tuesday. Police remained throughout that night and the next day. At three o'clock in the afternoon, when the shift changed, replacements came from headquarters and watched the comings and goings of local residents along with guests of the Sweet family. On the afternoon and evening of the second day, police also blocked off local streets to divert traffic. Later that evening officers ringed the corner, including the alley behind the house, and three plainclothes men mingled with the crowd.

Then the testimony became more subjective and interpretive, setting the prosecution's scene. The police testified that while car and pedestrian traffic appeared heavier than usual, it did not create undue agitation. Police maintained that nothing on the streets endangered the occupants or threatened the house. They described the gathering as peaceful. When bullets sprayed from the house at 2905 Garland Avenue, the alleged calmness broke down. In response to the shooting, people left their homes and wandered the streets, police reinforcements arrived, and the Sweets were escorted out the back door. Searching the home, police discovered guns, rifles, and ammunition. Spent cartridges and cigar butts mounded the windowsills. Mattresses had been set up under windows in otherwise bare rooms.

Incontrovertible was the death of Leon Breiner. Some described him as an innocent bystander at the time he was shot and killed. Immediately before his death on that humid night, witnesses said he had been relaxing on his front porch, smoking a pipe in the company of his wife, two teenage daughters, and neighbors. Another neighbor who had been shot in the leg remained hospitalized in stable condition.

The avalanche of police evidence against Ossian Sweet and his guests led Judge Faust to order the eleven defendants held for trial. He denied a request to release them on bail. They were remanded to jail, charged with conspiracy, "malice aforethought," and murder in the first degree, implying intent to kill. If convicted, they could be sentenced to life in prison. Trial date was set for October 13.

After keeping Gladys Sweet in solitary confinement for two days, the state moved her into the Wayne County Jail. All the defendants had been denied access to counsel until their arraignment.

The testimony against the Sweets stunned board members of the NAACP who attended the arraignment. Mose Walker, vice president of the Detroit branch, and W. Hayes McKinney, a board member who was also a lawyer, left the courtroom greatly shaken by the state's accusations. While Reverend Robert Bradby was out of town, they reversed his decision to handle the situation independently and called James Weldon Johnson.

In 1925 a phone call from Detroit to New York required operator assistance to complete the connection, but Johnson was nowhere to be found. It took Walker until the next day, Sunday afternoon, to locate him just as he was about to tee off on the seventh green of a New Jersey golf course. Relieved to finally hear Johnson's voice on the phone, Walker made a request as simple as his pursuit was complicated: Send Walter White.

White's reputation, his knowledge of the violence that engulfed blacks in the 1920s, surpassed that of all others in the association. Several years earlier he had investigated racially inspired lynchings and riots. He had collected the stories and circumstances behind the nearly four thousand people for publication in the NAACP's booklet *Thirty Years of Lynching*. For personal reasons, however, it was a bad time for him to leave New York. Spirited writers, poets, and musicians were breathing life into Harlem. White was attempting to expand his sphere of influence based on the publication of his first novel, *Fire in the Flint*. It had been out for a year and was still receiving favorable publicity. But he wanted a broader role for himself, and this coincided with pressure from his editor, Blanche Knopf, who was anxious for him to deliver the next book. The manuscript was nearly complete. He was just as anxious as she was to meet the deadline, one month away, and receive a $400 advance, which would permit him to enroll his daughter in the Ethical Culture Society School without asking for financial aid. But his work for the NAACP came first and drew him out of New York City, away from his writing.

White prepared to leave for Detroit on Monday evening's overnight train, the Wolverine. He knew the bare outline of the situation well enough to describe it to a friend, and on the way out the door he wrote:

> [A] group of some five thousand Nordic gentlemen have been demonstrating their biological and mental superiority by attacking the home of a colored physician who was too prosperous "for a Negro." The po-

lice force kept their hands off and the mob got the surprise of its life when the colored doctor opened fire on the mob, killing one of the Neroes and wounding another.

White could not have encountered a more familiar story. It came not from a particular crisis he had researched, but from the book he published the year before. Had the timing been reversed, White could have been accused of lifting the details for his protagonist in *Fire in the Flint*, Dr. Kenneth Harper, who bore an uncanny resemblance to Dr. Ossian Sweet. Both were doctors with superior training. Each had grown up in the South, had been educated in the North, had studied in France, had been harassed by Klansmen. And each had a father who told him the best way to get along with whites was to "stay away from them and let them alone." The biggest difference came at the end of the story, with the lynching of Harper. For White there must have been a bizarre sense of déjà vu as he unraveled the threads to Sweet's story.

In many ways Detroit was about as well known to the NAACP as any city in America. White left knowing he could rely on the NAACP's director of branches, Robert Bagnall, to point him toward the people in Detroit who could help him gather the information he would need. Even without Bagnall's connections, White and the NAACP had their own independent relationship with Detroit's larger community of middle-class leaders after the success of the association's twelfth annual convention in 1921, which drew a respectable four thousand people. With his background and his knowledge of the summer's violence, White could plan his moves before pulling into the Michigan Central Terminal early Tuesday morning, September 15.

Without delay, White set out on a fact-finding mission. He spoke to the defendants, consulted with Detroit's NAACP executive board, and met with the three attorneys who were already working on the case. White was dismayed to discover how quickly the press had turned public opinion against the Sweets. On the morning after their arrest, citizens woke up to front-page *Detroit News* headlines shouting

SLAYING LEADS TO NIGHT RIOT. The press implied that the mob followed the shooting rather than provoking it. "Within 10 minutes after
the shooting, 2,000 men jammed the street and the entire detail from
the McClellan Station, the riot squad from the Central Station and a
dozen motorcycle officers were called to preserve order," read the story.
Another article claimed that "Sweet bought the house Tuesday and
immediately moved in." The *Detroit Free Press* reported that a crowd of
five thousand poured onto the streets in the presence of an armored
car. The crime scene was described as "lighted only in the upper windows." The *Detroit News* repeated, without corroborating, the police
account that "no threats were made and no missiles were thrown." The
house was described as having no furniture yet stocked with a lot of
food, as if the occupants were preparing for a siege.

It took White barely one day to realize how the press reports had
complicated his job. His investigation required speaking to as many
people as possible, to get beneath the newspaper's bias to learn what
really happened on Wednesday night, to build a case from the facts.
Among the NAACP's friends, opinion was divided. White liberals rebuked the Sweets because they fired guns. Many in the black community expressed ambivalence, with some convinced that the Sweets
should have permitted a more prolonged attack on their home, perhaps fifteen or twenty minutes longer, before they fired their weapons.

The NAACP believed that if handled properly, the Sweets' case
might focus the nation's attention on residential segregation. Gladys
and Ossian were an attractive couple, dignified, educated, steeped in
culture and accomplishment. Their experience could personify otherwise dry legal principles involving deeds and covenants and abstract
constitutional guarantees.

Most people excluded by discriminatory housing laws did not challenge them. Or if they did, it did not lead to the death of one man and
the injury of another. The association's next best case was unraveling
because Samuel Browne, a postal worker whose house on Staten Island
was trashed by the Klan, was negotiating independently for a favorable

financial deal to sell his home and settle his grievance. He didn't fit the association's needs.

The Sweets' predicament differed and should stir the proper passions. Theirs was a story of self-defense in the face of malicious racial violence in a Northern city styling itself as urbane and cosmopolitan. If a mob could deny Ossian Sweet's family the rights to live in a house he could afford to buy, what guarantees existed for anybody else? It was a question that would reverberate.

To capitalize on the case fully, the NAACP had to begin its work before rival groups diminished outrage or contaminated the purity of the message. And it had to move quickly because Reverend Bradby didn't like sharing power. Many considered Bradby temperamental, if not an unrestrained egotist. White was working against time to lay the groundwork for the NAACP's strategy, alternating between influencing public opinion and developing a defense plan. The two objectives were combined and made more difficult by White's goal, the NAACP's desire to hire the most prominent white attorney in Detroit. Choosing the right lawyer was central to the NAACP's pursuit, to influence public opinion.

White learned, however, that Ossian Sweet had hired his own attorneys. They were men of local prominence with offices in Paradise Valley and leadership responsibilities in civic organizations, including the local NAACP. As recently as July, they had successfully defended a woman arrested on a weapons charge. Their success in that case brought gratitude and accolades. One of the lawyers, Julian Perry, was Ossian Sweet's best friend and fraternity brother. Another lawyer, Cecil Rowlette, was Perry's partner and one of two who went to look over the house on the night of the shooting. He was accompanied by Charles Mahoney, another black attorney whom the Liberty Life Insurance Company hired to defend the three insurance agents. White learned that after surveying the house following the Sweets' arrest, they had been denied access to the defendants for several days.

Despite these lawyers' local status, White thought they lacked the polish, style, and finesse essential for so important and visible a case.

And none had experience litigating capital crimes. Still, they were not willing to defer to a white attorney. Rowlette argued that a white attorney could never understand black psychology. White said he was more interested in understanding whites, the people who were most likely to make up the jury. Their fear of declining property values made them vulnerable to incitement. If these so-called improvement groups, such as the Waterworks Improvement Association, could maintain racial purity in a neighborhood, they could keep the schools segregated, too. Whatever one might think of their beliefs, they would sit in judgment of the Sweets and the rest of the defendants. The judge would surely be white; a white lawyer would seem more compatible to a jury that probably had more in common with the neighbors on Garland and Charlevoix than with the Sweets and their black lawyer. Walter White was convinced it was the whites, not the blacks, whom the defense needed to understand and to persuade if the defendants were to receive a fair hearing.

White attempted to handle the attorneys, as he said, with "delicacy." He explained the NAACP's ambition of turning this case into a looking glass for the average citizen from Dubuque to San Francisco, people who could empathize with how Dr. Sweet, his friends, and his family had been treated by their neighbors, how they had been violated by the police, abandoned by the courts. But Cecil Rowlette, Julian Perry, and Charles Mahoney disdained the strategy.

Rowlette, spokesman for the three, threatened to withdraw. But for his fear of a public relations backlash, White would probably have gladly accepted the offer. But he couldn't afford to antagonize the local black community. Even so, Walter White was horrified by Rowlette's performance before Judge Frank Murphy, which White characterized as "blustery, noisy, pompous." Still, on behalf of the NAACP, White tried to persuade Rowlette to work with white lawyers in defending Sweet.

While White was trying to negotiate with the attorneys, other issues erupted. Raising money for a defense fund provoked dissension and created splinter groups. Reverend Joseph Gomez, Ossian's classmate from Wilberforce, led one faction. Bradby led the other. Even UNIA—Marcus Garvey's separatist organization, the Universal Negro Improvement Association—vied for influence. But none was willing to maintain the records, documenting all contributions and disbursements, that White and Johnson thought essential. The only goal everybody shared was finding an attorney who had the best chance of successfully defending the Sweets. It was a question of how.

Before the NAACP could proceed, White insisted that the defendants sign an agreement, basically a contract vesting authority in the NAACP's national officers and headquarters to hire the lawyers and to pay them. Such an agreement might untangle competing claims for leadership. Scrupulous record keeping and control of fund-raising was the only way the NAACP in New York imagined it could prevent rumors or innuendo from tarnishing their motives or reputation.

After speaking with the defendants and reaching an agreement, the association compiled a list of white attorneys who might qualify as candidates for the highly visible responsibility. Two friends, Judge Ira Jayne and Judge Alfred Murphy, helped collect names and screen candidates, thus permitting an exhausted Walter White to return to New York.

White was happy to be home again. He had promised to give Blanche Knopf his new manuscript by October 15. In the meantime Mark Van Doren, editor of the *Century*, asked White to write a book review that was due shortly after the novel. But Detroit was never far from his thoughts while tending to the stack of papers that had accumulated.

Back in New York, White learned that in his absence, fissures threatened the arrangements he had negotiated with the defendants before leaving Detroit. Reverend Gomez had moved aggressively to gain more control. And Reverend Bradby had ignored White's effort to consolidate fiscal responsibility in the NAACP's headquarters. In addition, Rowlette, Perry, and Mahoney continued their criticism, openly disdaining the NAACP's strategy to hire a white attorney as lead counsel. In response, White told Walker, "If things get rough, threaten to go public of the various things which these lawyers have said and done . . . By all means hold these lawyers in check. They have got to know that we are doing the employing." White did not disguise his discouragement: "It is a tragedy in a case so touching as this," he said, "that our greatest difficulties are coming from our own people."

Meanwhile the defendants were languishing. Visitors, mostly family, brought letters and home-cooked meals. Gladys's mother and step-father, and the wives of other defendants, came to the jail. So did "Papa" Sweet. It is hard to imagine what emotions accompanied his trip from Florida to Michigan, where he would find three sons and a daughter-in-law in jail, his first grandchild, now sixteen months old, living with her other grandparents.

According to family legend, Papa Sweet's first visit to see his sons in jail required him to speak to them through barred windows on separate cell blocks. And despite what Dr. Sweet told reporters about friends' confidence propping his spirits, or his opportunity to de-nounce the "theory of Ku Klanism," he was deeply troubled. Papa Sweet could see his oldest son only by standing on his tiptoes, peering through steel bars. And his son poured out his heart. He regretted having let down the family and his parents, and having disappointed his father. But Papa Sweet would hear none of it. "Ain't nothing in the woods that run off from your family but a rabbit," he told his oldest child. "All you were doing was fighting for your family."

Before he returned to Bartow, Mr. Sweet spoke at an evening church service to raise defense funds. And even though it temporarily cheered them, his visit could not lift the pall hanging over his sons or the other defendants behind bars on Ward 5 of the Wayne County Jail. There was no lead lawyer and no income to pay any lawyer. And even if the Sweets were not living in the house, they had to make mortgage payments. Ossian's brothers Otis and Henry had separate concerns.

Otis's dental practice stopped, and Henry's education was interrupted during his last year of Wilberforce, perhaps forever. The same was true for John Latting, his college roommate, who had come to Detroit for summer work and stayed to help the Sweets move. One of Ossian's employees, Morris Murray, had a wife; the other, Joe Mack, had different financial burdens. And despite having issued a statement affirming their faith in William Davis's innocence, the federal government refused to help with the defense. The three insurance agents brought additional complication because their employer, the Liberty Life Insurance Company, had hired Charles Mahoney, which empowered Mahoney to work a separate defense strategy and trial.

By the end of September the defendants had begun to quarrel. Since the night of their arrest they had been held four to a cell. Gladys was locked in with three other women, who were charged with murder, jumping bail, and violating prohibition. She missed her daughter. She missed her husband. And she admired him tremendously.

At least four of the defendants—Otis Sweet, the federal narcotics agent William Davis, and the insurance agents Leonard Morris and Charles Washington—were frustrated by the apparent lack of progress, and they urged Rowlette, Perry, and Mahoney to allow the NAACP to take charge. They wrote a similar letter to board member Hayes McKinney, affirming, "It is a case that boldly challenges the liberties, the hopes, and the aspirations of fifteen million colored Americans." A favorable verdict could repel residential segregation. A failure invited calamity and they expected the consequences would be so great that "none of us can now predict." Mistaking W. E. B. Du Bois for the NAACP, they explained their restiveness, saying this was not the time "to permit the sordid efforts of narrow self-seekers for material gain or personal glory."

Ossian Sweet's name is not on any of these letters. His confidence in the attorneys, based on his personal friendship and loyalty to Julian Perry, seemed as generous as it was misplaced.

The NAACP's failure to quickly find a suitable white attorney undermined its position and the Sweet defense. Two of the finalists, one the former president of the local bar association and the other a former judge, declined. The local branch objected to a third because he was too closely associated with bootleggers. But the most discouraging news White heard three weeks after he thought all the details were final was that the defendants had not yet signed the agreement. Ossian hesitated, waiting for a clause protecting his lawyers.

The good news White heard was that Judge Frank Murphy had agreed to bail for Gladys Sweet. He set bond at $10,000.

With the opening date for trial only a week away, on October 13, White was dismayed. Black powerbrokers grew increasingly intolerant of the local lawyers. "The question as to who should take the lead in the trial and all such minor questions, should be forgotten in the biggest issue ever before our group in Michigan," said one prominent lawyer and friend of the association. The eleven are "on trial for their lives and self interest should be subordinated to the best thing possible to save the defendants," he told White.

Yet White was paralyzed. For the first time since early September pessimism edged his vision. "The case is hard enough without these complications. With them it is formidable."

Clarence Darrow thought long and hard before accepting another case—even one as attractive as this would be. One week had passed since the NAACP's delegation found him at Arthur Garfield Hays's home and implored him to take the case. At the age of sixty-nine, did he really need another trial to deplete his energies? He had repeatedly tackled and succeeded defending some of the most thorny legal issues challenging society—cases for the disadvantaged, cases of national importance. He was an icon among those who shared the moral and philosophical principles he promoted. His abhorrence of the death penalty weighed heavy in the closing arguments of the defense of confessed killers, socialites Leopold and Loeb, who murdered a youngster for sport, and his ability to win prison sentences instead of

Henry W. Sweet,
circa 1890. (Courtesy of
Sherman Sweet)

Dora Devaughn Sweet,
circa 1890. (Courtesy
of Sherman Sweet)

Train depot in Bartow, Florida, from which Ossian Sweet left for Wilberforce Academy in Xenia, Ohio, in 1910. (Courtesy Polk County Historical Association)

Post office on the campus of Wilberforce University, circa 1915. (From W. A. Joiner, *A Half Century of Freedom of the Negro in Ohio,* 1915)

The founding members of Wilberforce University's Delta Chapter of Kappa Alpha Psi in 1915. Ossian Sweet is in the second row, first on the left. (Courtesy Kappa Alpha Psi Fraternity)

Michigan Central Station opened in 1913, shortly before the Southern Exodus started flooding Detroit. Built in the Beaux-Arts style, it was designed by two architectural firms, Warren & Wetmore and Reed & Stern, the same firms responsible for Grand Central Station in New York City. (Author's collection)

Police shot Mineola McGee while she stood looking out the window of her employer's house during the 1917 massacre in East St. Louis. Her right arm was amputated as a result. (Crisis Magazine)

July 1917: Negro Silent Parade marched down New York City's Fifth Avenue to protest massacres in East St. Louis, Illinois; Waco, Texas; and Memphis, Tennessee. (Crisis Magazine)

Fifteen doctors raised six thousand dollars to purchase this Victorian house in Paradise Valley and renovate it for a hospital to serve Detroit's black community. Dunbar Memorial Hospital, with thirty-seven beds, opened in 1919. (Detroit News)

Staff physicians pose on the steps of Dunbar Memorial Hospital three years after it opened. (Detroit News)

The Detroit Waterworks Tower was located at Gladwin Park, a few blocks from Ossian and Gladys Sweet's house. It bordered Jefferson Avenue and the Detroit River, and boat service from the park ferried visitors to the popular Belle Isle Park. (Author's collection)

Docks where tourists boarded ships for leisure cruises on the Detroit River.
(Author's collection)

Start of a Ku Klux Klan parade at the Michigan State Fairgrounds, Seven and a Half Mile Road and Woodward, 1924. (Walter P. Reuther Library, Wayne State University)

Imperial Wizard Col. William J. Simmons before testifying about the Ku Klux Klan, House Rules Committee, Washington, D.C., October 12, 1921. (Library of Congress)

August 7, 1925, one month before Ossian Sweet moved into his house, the Ku Klux Klan visited Washington, D.C., and staged this march down Pennsylvania Avenue. They ended at the Washington Monument. (Copyright © Bettman/CORBIS)

Ossian and Gladys Sweet's house at 2905 Garland Avenue. On the witness stand, Sweet said: "I had hoped to have a home for my baby—a place where she could attend school and her environments would be healthy and helpful. It was for her sake that my wife and I determined to sacrifice many things in life so that our little one would have the best advantages possible." (Crisis Magazine)

Occupants of the house arrested on the night of September 9, 1925; in addition, Iva Sweet, who was in her grandmother's care at the time. TOP ROW, LEFT TO RIGHT: *Henry Sweet, Dr. Ossian H. Sweet, Leonard Morris (insurance agent);* CENTER: *Hewitt Watson (insurance agent), Joe Mack (employed by Sweet), Dr. Otis Sweet.* BOTTOM ROW: *Morris Murray (employed by Sweet), Charles Wasington (insurance agent), John Latting (Henry Sweet's Wilberforce classmate), and William E. Davis (federal narcotics agent and friend).* EXTREME RIGHT, *Gladys Sweet. (Chicago Defender)*

James Weldon Johnson, executive secretary, and Walter White, assistant secretary, led the NAACP's strategy for turning the Sweet's case into a broad campaign to fight residential segregation. White's light complexion enabled him to work behind the scenes where he was not known, gathering information about lynchings and violence, influencing the press and public opinion. (Johnson: Library of Congress; White: Yale Collection of American Literature, Beinecke Rare Book and Manuscript Library)

NAACP headquarters in New York City. LEFT TO RIGHT: *William Pickens, field organizer; Robert Bagnall, director of branches; James Weldon Johnson, executive secretary; Walter White, assistant secretary; Arthur J. Spingarn, president of the board of directors.* (Walter P. Reuther Library, Wayne State University)

Arthur Garfield Hays, one of Ossian Sweet's defense attorneys and co-counsel to Clarence Darrow. They had defended Thomas Scopes in the famed Tennessee trial earlier that summer. (Princeton University Library)

Clarence Darrow, defense attorney, 1925. (Walter P. Reuther Library, Wayne State University)

Robert Toms, chief prosecutor, who became a circuit court judge in 1929. (Walter P. Reuther Library, Wayne State University)

Robert Moll, who assisted Toms, also became a judge later in his career. (Walter P. Reuther Library, Wayne State University)

Judge Frank Murphy, Detroit Recorder's Court, circa 1920. Soon after the trial, Murphy was elected mayor of Detroit. (Walter P. Reuther Library, Wayne State University)

Henry Sweet with defense attorneys (LEFT TO RIGHT): *Julian Perry, Thomas Chawke, Clarence Darrow.* (Walter P. Reuther Library, Wayne State University)

Jurors in the trial of Henry Sweet. The foreman, George C. Small, stands third from the left in the front row. (Courtesy Burton Historical Collections, Detroit Public Library)

Dr. Ossian H. Sweet and Gladys Sweet. (Walter P. Reuther Library, Wayne State University)

Henry Sweet.
(University Library,
University of
Illinois at Chicago)

the electric chair brought acclaim as well as criticism. Earlier that summer crowds and the press flocked to Dayton, Tennessee, to see the Scopes trial, during which he took a beating. It was not so much because he did not win—that was not a surprise—but the American Civil Liberties Union did not want him to participate in appealing the decision. Darrow was used to controversy. But humiliating and trouncing William Jennings Bryan on the witness stand in Dayton seemed excessive. The untimely publicity surrounding Bryan's death—Bryan was the Democratic standard-bearer in 1896, as well as secretary of state under Wilson—fringed the spectacle all the more. It also confirmed the ACLU's apprehension that Darrow brought headlines even if he did not always seek them, even where they were not justified.

Years later Darrow's decision to enter the Sweet defense would be hailed as the passionate conviction of a man dedicated to the pursuit of social justice, the bold resolve of one person—a white person—speaking for an entire black race. His involvement would be portrayed as a natural conclusion to an illustrious career. But the facts indicated otherwise. While he was one of the century's greatest trial lawyers, he had never tried a major case involving racial conflict. Despite his humanitarianism, his genuine dislike of racial intolerance, the NAACP had to work very hard to secure his services in 1925. On October 13, five days after their meeting at Arthur Garfield Hays's house in New York City, James Weldon Johnson was still waiting to learn Darrow's decision. In the meantime White went to Chicago, hoping to pin him down to an agreement to represent the Sweets. Then, in a seemingly sudden turn of events, Darrow made himself available to Walter White. They spent eleven hours talking about the case, about Detroit, about the Sweets, and the events of the previous month.

"Did the defendants shoot into that mob?" Darrow asked White.

Caught off-guard, White hesitated. "I am not sure," he mumbled. Years later he recalled Darrow's irritation.

"Don't try to hedge," he said. "I know you were not there. But do you believe the defendants fired?"

"I believe they did fire," White said.

"Then I'll take the case. If they had not had the courage to shoot back in defense of their own lives, I wouldn't think they were worth defending."

Darrow prepared to leave the next day for Detroit, where he would ask for a delay in the case. Judge Frank Murphy of Detroit's Recorder's Court gave him two weeks.

The NAACP immediately announced that Clarence Darrow would take the case and that Arthur Garfield Hays would back him up as he had in the Scopes trial. They needed another white lawyer who lived in Detroit, and Darrow liked Walter Nelson, a man known for his favor to labor. A friend of Darrow's from Chicago, named Herbert Friedman, volunteered his help, and Darrow accepted. Rowlette, Perry, and Mahoney would have looked pretty silly if they declined to work with Clarence Darrow. They remained on the case under his lead.

Before the trial, the defense had to research the night of September 9. They needed to get to know the eleven people who occupied the house at the time of the shooting; they had to decide on a strategy, including whether to ask for separate trials or a joint trial for all eleven defendants. Two weeks was not hardly enough time.

Most of Detroit's judges feared an association with the case and did not want to have to hear it. Too political, they said, the kind of issue that could easily cripple careers. There was even talk of bringing in an outsider. Judge Frank Murphy, from Detroit Recorder's Court where criminal cases were tried, held a different view. At the age of thirty-five, Murphy was a slightly built, abstemious, Irish Catholic liberal. As early as his undergraduate days at the University of Michigan, he announced his devotion to the working man and proclaimed in a sociology paper his desire to do something "uplifting for the poor." Some considered him a "boy-politician" when he was elected to Recorder's Court after a short but successful shift in the prosecutor's office. Idealistic and politically ambitious, he began his second year on the bench that October of 1925. It was also his month of service as the rotating chief, a position that carried the responsibility of assigning cases to judges. Murphy was widely respected as the most astute judge on the court, and, mindful that race relations in Detroit had never seemed more explosive, he assigned *People v. Ossian Sweet* to himself.

Had the NAACP been given the power to name a judge, Frank Murphy would have been its choice. Mose Walker gloated when he wrote that Murphy's "positive stand against prejudice" would reveal itself as a tower of strength among blacks as well as the "better whites of Detroit." Rumors circulated that he was considering a bid for mayor. Consequently, the black community believed the Sweet case could help Murphy "win the Negro vote to put him over" when he ran for election sometime in the near future.

There can be no doubt that Murphy had a genuine interest in liberal race relations and wanted to imprint Detroit's future. But he also had his own personal reasons for wanting to preside over the case. He wanted to see Clarence Darrow, to observe the man many considered the greatest trial lawyer of his generation, someone renowned for a skill, humor, and passion that left jurors charmed and judges speechless, a jurist who argued cases with inventive persuasion, who used psychology, history, and moral truths in a way most lawyers had never considered. Darrow was a living legend, and Murphy told his friend Josephine Gomon over lunch one day that watching Clarence Darrow would be one of the greatest experiences of his life, "something never dreamed of."

It was too good to let go. There was no doubt that the case would begin in two weeks, on Friday, October 30, and not one day later than the end of Murphy's term as chief judge of the Recorder's Court because Murphy wanted it badly. As he told Gomon, "This is going to be a famous case."

CHAPTER 10

Clarence Darrow
Sets the Stage

A two-inch snowfall already quilted Detroit, and forecasters predicted another cold blast for the opening day of court Friday, October 30. That did not stop five hundred spectators from crowding the steps before dawn at the Wayne County Building. By the time Clarence Darrow arrived, the spectators filled the halls outside the courtroom of Recorder's Court, forcing Judge Frank Murphy to delay the trial until more police could arrive to keep the corridors quiet and calm.

Clarence Darrow brought more than crowds. He brought sparkle to the trial and relief to the NAACP. The black press loved Darrow's celebrity although not his attitude about religion, including his avowed agnosticism, which came out during the Scopes Monkey Trial on evolution. It had been only three months since Darrow occupied world attention while he reduced populist hero William Jennings Bryan to a Bible-thumping caricature. When Darrow walked through the halls that morning, reporters crowded him in a scene that publicists dream

of. RIOT TRIAL ON; DARROW HERE read one headline. RACE RIOT TRIAL
OPENS; DARROW AIDS 11 NEGROES shouted another.

On that Friday morning nothing was more important than selecting a jury.

Darrow knew that the defense was not about the facts of who shot
whom and when. It was about the psychology of crowds, the terror of
mobs, about the average person's sense of justice and compassion in an
unfair world. It was about reaching into a collective conscience, about
whether citizens, probably white, could empathize with black victims of
circumstances beyond their control. Darrow's most important task was
to guess who among the candidates might allow himself to remain open
to appeals for fairness, who could see the world as a black man might.

From the start, Darrow displayed his gifts for romancing jurors.
While interviewing prospective candidates, he paced in front of the
jury box looking thoughtful and deliberate. He tilted his head, bending
it slightly toward the person as though nothing in the world was more
important than the conversation they were having at that moment.

The press, as always, dwelt on his personality, preoccupied with his
gestures and clothes. They noted how he kept his hands in his pockets,
how nonchalant he looked when he locked his thumbs into the armholes of his vest. They were obsessed with every detail, the color of his
shirts, his wrinkled pants, his chiseled features and the gray locks of
hair falling over his forehead. They described how he poked the air
with his index finger to emphasize a point. The fascination stopped
just short of fetishism while spectators seemed almost to be straining
to hear him think.

Darrow asked candidates the obvious questions about their birth-
place, neighborhood, or street. He probed for their opinions about
owning property, delved into their friendships, past and present. He
wanted to know about their children, their social lives, their prejudices.
Who among them, he asked, employed a black maid? He paced back
and forth, pondering the answer to his question, "Do you believe in

equality of the law?" He wasted no time in getting to the heart of the case. "Do you believe a man in this free country should purchase property where he chooses and his means permit him?" He asked whether and how their lives overlapped with those of blacks. And he wanted them to say whether they thought black Americans have as much right as a white person to "shoot to protect their property."

Darrow excused prospective jurors who boasted prejudice or could not conceal bias. Eva Cox, a music teacher, was excused after she told Darrow she "had considered the possibility of the depreciation of the value of her own property if Negroes moved into the neighborhood." Presuming the prosecution would object to Henry P. Ward, the only black candidate in the jury pool, Darrow excused him. The wife of a policeman, Mrs. Cora Korte, was not seated. And Mrs. Jessie Dessert, whom both sides accepted, asked to be excused for reasons of her own.

Those who refused to answer questions about their own participation in secret societies were excused. The process was tedious and thorough. "Do you belong to any secret organization which you do not care to discuss here?" Darrow asked.

Fred Buell said yes, and he was discharged.

If a juror admitted he was intrigued by Darrow, his interest qualified as bias and the prosecution did not want that person. Mary Young told the court she "knew nothing about the case but was anxious to hear Darrow plead." And she was excused. William Cullum was excused for a similar reason.

The prosecutors quickly realized they needed to ask jurors if they were "likely to be affected by Darrow's record as a criminal lawyer." Did candidates react strongly to his most recent cases, including the trial of Leopold and Loeb in nearby Chicago? Did a prospective juror's religion influence his view of Darrow's performance in the Scopes evolution case in Dayton, Tennessee?

It was hard not to be captivated by Darrow. Even the judge was struck by the skill with which he educated jurors during the interrogation. "Every question sets up a chain reaction in the mind of every man in that box," Judge Murphy told his close friend Josephine Gomon over lunch one noon at Miss Lincoln's Dixieland Tea Room. He told her how he could see clues on the faces of the prospective jurors to what they were thinking. To Murphy it was obvious that, "They never thought about race prejudice in this way before."

Even Darrow's mistakes were instructive. After the preliminary questions in which a prospective juror described his social activities, family history, and attitudes about race and property, Darrow was in a jocular mood and feeling a little too relaxed, too confident. He let go of his restraint and asked, "What news sources do you consider the most reliable?"

"The Nation," replied the candidate. It would have been hard to select a more indentifiable marker of liberal thought, and prosecutor Robert Toms jumped up and excused the juror for cause.

"You have to know where to stop," Darrow told a friend. "You can lose a case by asking one question too many." This idea would become dogma for interrogating witnesses, and Darrow was clearly perturbed with himself for asking a question when he knew the answer would be more useful to the prosecution than to him.

While those in the courtroom respected the solemnity of the proceedings, loud and unruly spectators lining the halls did not. When a black spectator taunted a prospective juror and implied that she had lied about secret societies, the juror complained of harassment. Angry, Judge Murphy instructed the police to arrest anybody guilty of such misconduct. He summoned Walter White to the bench, later to his private chambers, and admonished him to monitor his partisan observers. The "case would be seriously damaged if any more of this took place," Murphy said.

On Monday morning Arthur Garfield Hays arrived from New York. Just as he had assisted Darrow in Tennessee for the Scopes trial, he would assist Darrow in Detroit for the Sweet trial. Jury selection came to a stop so defense attorney Walter Nelson could introduce Hays to Murphy. By the end of the day rumors were circulating that a prospective juror who professed prejudice could probably get the judge to dismiss him from the case, which was now expected to last for two or three weeks.

The original list of 150 potential jurors was exhausted. An emergency drawing of names brought forth another 65 people. But it still did not yield a jury. "The stage is set, but there is no trial," opined the *Chicago Defender*, adding that Detroit has been "unable to date to find 12 of its citizens free enough of race hatred to give [the defendants] a sporting chance in a death trial."

The mayoral election fell on the Tuesday of jury selection, and court was adjourned. It was inevitable that the election would be affected by the underlying racial antagonism that reached a crescendo that summer and was embedded with suspicions about the Ku Klux Klan.

Three candidates had vied to become mayor of Detroit in 1924. It was remarkable, and purely accidental, that the Klan candidate, Charles Bowles, lost this election. His misfortune was laid directly to more than fifteen thousand people who, showing more enthusiasm than skill, misspelled his name on their write-in ballots. Had their votes been counted as they intended, he would have won handily with a five-thousand-vote margin over John Smith. A third candidate made the election more unpredictable. But 1925 would be a more straightforward contest between Smith and Bowles, and Detroit's 350,000 voters would decide it that day.

During his one year in office Mayor Smith had showed himself to be an able leader despite equivocating statements after the summer's racial violence. After the death of Leon Breiner and the arrest of Ossian Sweet, Smith formed a committee, more cosmetic than effective, to study ways to improve race relations in Detroit. In reaction to Detroit's heavy immigrant and ethnic concentration, the Klan drew strength from the anti-Catholic and anti-Jewish xenophobes along with the antiblack homeowners' associations sprinkled throughout the city and its suburbs.

On several occasions Bowles denied that he was a Klansman. But nobody believed him. Twenty-five thousand people who attended a Klan rally in Dearborn the weekend before the election were invited to return to Klan headquarters on Hancock Street to pick up campaign literature that they would distribute.

Ira Stout, who had been a Boy Scout leader in Jackson, Ohio, before becoming Detroit's grand kleagle, made clear the contest when he said, "This year Smith forced us to get in line behind Bowles because of his charges that we were inciting race troubles."

We're going to defeat John Smith and we're going to do it right out in the open. We're going to put up an electric K.K.K. sign in front of our headquarters so people will know where we are, and we're going to let the newspaper reporters attend our meetings. We're going to have a clean, Christian American in public office.

Local papers endorsed Smith, applauding his fiscal policies and his capital improvements, such as the expansion of the transportation system, including new trolley tracks. His efforts to bring harmony to the racially tense city also received mention. The choice of candidates, said the business weekly *Detroit Saturday Night,* was a question of whether voters wanted "the present incumbent to continue his administration or prefer to be ruled by the kleagles and loppers who are behind Mr. Bowles." The *Defender,* obviously more attuned to the radical implications, said, "Detroiters of all races should realize that a Klan government . . . will not settle Detroit's race problem."

Early returns confirmed predictions of a record turnout. By the time they started to count votes, according to the November 4 edition of the *Detroit Times,* "the second, third and first floor corridors of the City Hall were jammed and uniformed men were turning away all comers."

Some 250,000 voters turned out, and, by a margin of 30,000, Smith was reelected. But the message of Bowles's 100,000 supporters who elected Klan-backed candidates to the city council had to trouble the defense.

Court resumed on Wednesday, the day after the election. Another eighty people joined the pool of prospective jurors. Darrow still had nearly three hundred peremptory challenges—those that needed no justification—out of his original allotment of thirty for each defendant. The court knew his reputation for using challenges to get the exact composition he wanted. His criteria specified people who were "alert, witty, emotional." He preferred members of the Catholic Church, or those "without religious faith whatever." He asked himself whether "the prospective juror is humane." He said he tried to find people "who can understand, can comprehend why, and that leaves no field for condemning." Those were the principles he used in the Scopes evolution trial, and the Leopold and Loeb murder trial, and he would now use them to select a jury in the trial of Ossian Sweet.

On Wednesday morning conditionally accepted jurors filled the temporary box. Any one of them could have easily come from Sweet's neighborhood. Among them were a painter, a Ford Motor Company employee, an axle assembler, an electrical experimenter, a foundry superintendent, a streetcar conductor, and supervisors of various factories. One was retired. Only three had been there since day one, nearly a week before. Of the four women who were initially approved, one asked to be excused and the others subsequently were. Any one of the twelve still could be.

Judge Murphy was growing mindful, perhaps a little apprehensive, about how a delay in seating the jury could compromise a trial. By the fourth day of selections, the list was again exhausted. Murphy showed frustration as he announced his intention to send police into the streets and subpoena prospective jurors. It was highly unorthodox.

Darrow seized the moment. He waived his remaining peremptory challenges and accepted all the men in the temporary box. By doing so he displayed his confidence in the twelve already present. Then he sat down.

His partner, Arthur Garfield Hays, however, was not as trusting. One juror was elusive and Hays was perplexed by his impassive appearance. Counsel asked to address the jury. A tall, thickset man with a full head of wavy brown hair, Hays walked toward the jury box and stood still while his eyes slowly swept the faces of all twelve men.

Forty-three, born in Rochester, New York, the son of Jewish-German immigrants, Hays carried the names of three American presidents. As he looked at the men before him, he wanted to see whose eyes brightened, whose lips turned down, who among them showed a pounding heart. He peered at one who had about as much expression as a tea towel. Arthur Garfield Hays had only one question: "Is any man in this box a member of the Ku Klux Klan?"

Hesitating hardly a moment, one juror, Charles Kinney, said he was. But this was not the juror whom Hays doubted, the one he called "hardboiled, stoney-faced," the one whom he would later nickname Mr. Pokerface. Rather, it was a different juror who confessed membership in the Klan and said that it would not stop him from rendering a fair verdict. "The principles of the Ku Klux Klan make fair and just decisions the real test of membership," he said.

Before the rolling laughter subsided in the courtroom, Judge Murphy had excused him for cause. From that moment on, however, Hays could not shake his suspicion about Mr. Pokerface, who seemed expressionless, unmoved by events that would normally elicit warmth, such as the time Gladys Sweet brought her daughter, Iva, to court. Hays wanted to read the jury's reactions. But Pokerface would not comply. As much as Hays tried, this juror remained enigmatic, refusing to reveal himself until the last days of the trial.

In the meantime Darrow put down a crossword puzzle and approached the bench. He told Judge Murphy he had confidence in the eleven jurors who remained after Mr. Kinney left, and fully displayed his reputation as a brilliant if risk-prone tactician, attuned to the psychology of the court, when he said he would accept the next candidate at face value as long as the prosecutor, Mr. Toms, would do the same.

Darrow's move was another calculated gamble to win the jury's trust, and he would have to wait until the end of the trial before he knew if it worked. On the afternoon of November 4, nearly two months after Ossian and Gladys Sweet were arrested, a jury was impaneled. *People of the State of Michigan v. Ossian Sweet* would call its first witness the next day.

The defense team had started collecting information immediately. But with only two weeks to work, they were still scrambling when the trial began. Walter White had already started tutoring Darrow about lynchings, about mob violence and the attack on Dr. Turner in June. The NAACP had forwarded copies of *Thirty Years of Lynching* to Arthur Garfield Hays. He absorbed it and asked for more. Even if details did not come out at the trial, Hays wanted to learn as much as he could about the history of America's racism "for our own information," he said, "in order to get the background." It would help him pursue his goal of portraying "how these things begin in a small way but develop." He told White he hoped to build a defense around how a black man knowing about the history of lynching might feel "his life was in danger under circumstances such as those that existed in Detroit." Johnson inundated Hays with documents including President Woodrow Wilson's statement on lynching and mob violence, descriptions of specific lynchings in Tennessee, Mississippi, and Georgia; reports of the massacres in East St. Louis and Tulsa, Oklahoma; and of the 1919 Washington race riots.

Hays also needed information about the Sweets. What magazines did they read? Did they know about other riots? "What sort of general stories of oppression of Negroes by white mobs" influenced their thinking? he asked.

Gladys wrote back that they read five black newspapers—*Chicago Defender* and *Pittsburgh Courier* among them—they received *The Crisis,* had read White's novel, *Fire in the Flint.* Her family was affected directly by the 1919 Chicago riots. Ossian was in medical school and was "impressed most by the riot at Washington, D.C., because he was attending Howard University at the time." They had read stories about East St. Louis and Tulsa. And Ossian had relatives who lived near Ocoee, Florida, and remained terrified by the massacre on election day five years before. In short, they were well-informed, involved bystanders.

Gladys outlined her suspicions that police were complicit in much of the violence. She and Ossian were friendly with some of the mob's other targets, and she mentioned Vollington Bristol and Dr. Alexander Turner, both of whom had troubles that summer. She said they did not believe the Waterworks Improvement Association would resort to violence but would rather do what the Tireman Association did in Dr. Turner's situation, which was use moving vans. That was why they delivered their own furniture, what little they had. And having seen the crowd die back on the first night, they had presumed the fracas was behind them when they shopped for furniture on the next day.

Gladys gave Hays leads to four witnesses who might challenge the state's portrait that all was quiet and peaceful until the "unprovoked" shooting attacked the crowd and killed Breiner. Locating witnesses to testify about the size and nature of the crowd was difficult. People like Mose Walker and Hayes McKinney were scouting. White had hired investigators.

The prosecution would surely try to discredit the Sweets' story. On the night of his arrest, Ossian Sweet deposited spent rifle cartridges into a cuspidor at police headquarters. When confronted with his deed, he initially denied having done so. All this was part of the record. So was the appearance of the house. It was alleged to be entirely dark, creating a sense of mystery and terror after sundown. When the police searched the premises, they discovered cigar butts mounding windowsills and mattresses placed under the windows. The physical evidence included nine guns. With this, and based on the testimony of reliable police and citizen witnesses, the prosecution intended to show the Sweets and their friends had gathered together with "malice aforethought" and "conspiracy to murder."

Absent the information they needed, the team of defense lawyers— Clarence Darrow, Arthur Garfield Hays, Herbert Friedman, Walter Nelson, Cecil Rowlette, Julian Perry, and Charles Mahoney—readied themselves as best they could for the next day, when prosecutors Robert Toms and Lester Moll would read the state's opening charge in *People v. Ossian Sweet.*

CHAPTER 11

"Nobody Is Molesting You"

Long before the sun rose at 7:14 A.M. on the fifth of November, hundreds of men and women started lining up for a seat at the Ossian Sweet murder trial. That Thursday morning they waited in forty-degree weather behind policemen who were having difficulty controlling the crowds surrounding the Municipal Court Building on the corner of Clinton and St. Antoine. At eleven o'clock spectators were still thronging the lobby and the stairwells, lawyers and newspapermen were still blocking the corridor and halls. Even associates of Judge Frank Murphy, people with access to his private elevator, could not penetrate the crowd trying to get into Recorder's Court that morning.

Inside the courtroom stood the chief prosecutor, Robert Toms. He was an affable, blue-eyed, blond-haired lawyer in his forties, ready to plead the people's case before Judge Murphy. By the time Toms met Darrow, he had already tried to calm himself by thinking, "just because I was up against a giant," there was no reason to be afraid. In truth, Toms was more than a bit nervous, and years later he recalled how hard he tried not to be foolish. He told himself he should not even attempt to match Darrow in wit, "invective and abuse." Instead, Toms said he became solicitous, adopting "a studied course of humility . . . almost obsequious at times, and I showed him the utmost deference." So careful was Toms that Darrow told him early in the trial that he was too "darned nice." That is, too nice for the conflict Clarence Darrow, attorney for the defense, usually engendered.

Behind Toms sat the other two prosecutors for the people: Lester Moll, chief assistant prosecutor, who was widely regarded as the best litigator and the most unfriendly person in the office; and Edward J. Kennedy, a younger man who had interrogated the defendants the night of their arrest. A few feet away were chairs for eight defense attorneys around a table; a short distance from them, another table accommodated reporters with their writing paraphernalia. In the spectators section behind the wooden railing sat Clarence Darrow's fashionable wife, Ruby. She had come to Detroit earlier in the week. The press trumpeted her arrival wearing a stylish, soft-fabric hat. Rosella Mitchell, Gladys's mother, had a ticket, as did the widow of Leon Breiner, who sat, undisturbed and unrecognized, in the first row of the spectator section. Another two hundred people who were unable to secure tickets stood behind the benches, shifting from foot to foot, for the entire trial.

Robert Toms started the trial by presenting a bill of particulars—the detailed summary of what the state intended to prove—which Arthur Garfield Hays had requested earlier. Toms initially tried to bypass this step, but Hays was insistent, forcing the prosecution to reveal its order of attack.

Toms claimed that on Wednesday night, September 9, the Sweet family and their friends acted with malice aforethought with an intent to "shoot to kill" anyone who trespassed on or threatened their property. It was premeditated. And, he said, "a bullet fired by one" killed Leon Breiner.

Toms was clear, direct, and brief. But he was too brief for Arthur Garfield Hays, who objected instantly. Could not the state disclose more than "a bullet fired by one"? A large part of the decision about whether to hold individual trials or a group of eleven turned on the question of the likelihood of the state's linking Breiner's death to a specific weapon. Nine of the ten guns had been fired. This made it more difficult, perhaps impossible, to point to a single person who shot the lethal bullet. A more definite bill of particulars would hold the state to a higher level of accountability. But Murphy denied Arthur Garfield Hays's request. The bill of particulars sufficed, said the judge, and he ordered the jurors into the courtroom. After the jury was seated, the trial would begin.

Prosecutor Toms opened by directing the jurors' attention to a map of the neighborhood, examining in detail the intersection where the Sweets' house stood. Using a chalkboard, he marked the two-family flats and the apartment building figuring in the story. Ossian Sweet's house, with its three-car garage, sat on the northwest corner of Garland and Charlevoix. An alley ran behind the house, parallel to Garland. Across from the Sweets' house, on the southwest side of the intersection, an apartment building fronted Charlevoix. Its walls came close to the curb. Continuing (counterclockwise) across the street from the apartment building, on the southeast side of Garland, was the Howe School, a brick elementary school set back from the street, surrounded by a grassy lawn. Across the street from the school, on the northeast side of the Charlevoix and Garland intersection, were commercial stores, the Morning Star grocery store and a tire shop. In front of the grocery store, on Charlevoix, the owner had parked his red Ford on the evening of September 9. Overhead street lamps brightened the intersection at night.

Later Toms would mark the spots where policemen had been positioned. Witnesses would use the diagram to show the court where they stood when startled by gunshots, the route they used to walk from their houses on the adjacent streets—Bewick, Goethe or St. Claire— to reach the intersection of Charlevoix and Garland Avenues. They would point to where they were standing when police urged them and others to move back from the curbs and onto the pavement.

The prosecutor pointed to the map to show where bullets lodged in trees and doors, where they shattered neighbors' windows. One bullet went through a glass door of an upstairs flat, and nearly "grazed or missed by a matter of inches a woman with a child in her arms." One bullet injured Eric Hogsburg in the leg. Another killed Leon Breiner.

After the Sweets were arrested, police found:

> a scant supply of furniture . . . and an ample supply of food. [T]here was a whole ham, a large dish of sweet potatoes, and another dish of spinach on the stove being cooked at the time the officers got there; at the time that the officers entered, the pantry was well stocked with dry groceries.

The empty rooms contrasted with the full supply of weapons. "[T]he police found one shotgun, two rifles and seven revolvers." Boxes of ammunition were stacked on the windowsills. More turned up on the floor of the patrol wagon that transported the prisoners to police headquarters. Toms maintained that in the Sweets' house no one that night had reason to believe his life or his safety was in jeopardy. "This killing was felonious," he said, "it was premeditated; premeditated because they went there with it in mind, and kept it in mind . . . armed until the time of the shooting." He concluded this summary by promising:

> Witnesses will testify that there was no disturbance, that everyone was going about his business; that there was no loud talk; that there were no groups of people together; that no violence was threatened and committed; that suddenly, without warning, from the front windows of Dr. Sweet's house, there was a volley of shots.

Tom's address to the jury contained far more graphic details about the crime scene and the Sweets' home than appeared in the bill of particulars. The state expected to prove, Toms said, that the defendants agreed to a preconceived conspiracy to murder. When the police entered the house, "There was no dining room furniture, no living room furniture, but upstairs there was one bedroom suite, some clothing, small amount, some bedding, and that is about all. In other words, the house was not ready to be lived in . . . The lights [were] all out, anticipating some possible disturbances.

Toms's opening and his focus on the jury were interrupted several times, sometimes by his own staff. Darrow broke his pace, too, by engaging in his trademark witty repartee to which the prosecutor responded. Toward the end, the defense ruined Toms's focused energy by objecting to his promise to take the jurors to the scene of the disturbance at 2905 Garland Avenue, where they could view the house. His momentum destroyed, Toms sat down.

Now the defense had an opportunity to tell its story. Darrow had a memorable courtroom style that was usually soft-spoken and chatty. Frequently he sat on the ledge of the jury box, leaning toward the jurors, speaking directly to them. Over the years he had cultivated a folksy persona, and his signature wardrobe, ill-fitting, out-of-date clothes, drove his wife mad but served to disguise his wealth and sophistication. It was exactly how he wanted to look in court, as a regular guy, perhaps a commoner, the jurors' friend, not an argumentative lawyer. In this stylized manner, he would personify the humility of a defendant's cause, he would appeal to the core values of the Golden Rule's "Do unto others," which would find its way into his sermonlike arguments.

Darrow's unadorned image contrasted with the debonair splendor of Arthur Garfield Hays, whose finely tailored suits draped his large, trim frame with elegance. Hays was the tactician, the strategist maneuvering through complex legal principles and traditions on behalf of civil liberties and universal rights. The two complemented each other's strengths. During the numerous court recesses, when the judge called lawyers into his chambers to discuss a legal text or the precision of a point of law, it was Hays who would attend the sessions. Darrow's strengths came from his personal appeal, his ability to get jurors to think about a dramatic event or calamity from the inside, not through statutes or precedent or legal texts. During sidebar conferences at the judge's bench, he frequently remained seated, scratching in words of a crossword puzzle. One time when the group adjourned to the judge's chambers, he told Toms he would let "Arthur take care of that."

For the trial of Ossian Sweet, the defense team would be joined by a Chicago colleague of Darrow's, Herbert Friedman, and a local white attorney from Detroit, Walter Nelson. The three local black lawyers contributed to a public relations blitz about black and white collaboration. Together they were a strong cadre, large for the era and the case, and they would have to work in harmony for as long as the trial took.

When Toms finished his preliminary remarks, instead of the defense delivering its own statement as was customary, Darrow asked to postpone his opening until after the prosecutor presented its side of the case and called its witnesses. The defense actually needed more time to search for usable facts. Judge Murphy had no reason to deny the request because, however unconventional, it was an option under Michigan law.

If the defense startled the prosecutors by postponing its opening statement, they didn't show it. The state called its first witness without delay.

The state started with technical witnesses. They identified the dead man as Leon Breiner and described how he died. However much hero worship the case had generated for Darrow and Hays, or however much it exemplified the essence of racial conflict, it was also a murder trial, and Toms made sure these details were introduced early to establish the necessary legal foundation for the state's charge. Dr. William Ryan, the medical examiner, explained how the lethal bullet entered through Breiner's back, ripped through the abdomen, and exited at hip level, near the umbilicus. Its trajectory was horizontal. The defense did not challenge, object, or waste time or sympathy by calling attention to the grisly particulars. Darrow and Hays had a larger picture in mind. They would return to the bullet's trajectory when they had reason.

The most important witnesses for the state would be policemen, the majority of the seventy people prosecutors intended to call to prove there were no crowds or reason for alarm on the night of September 9, 1925. Key for both sides would be the size of the crowd. Did people congregate on the streets or walk to the corner? It was important to pin down where bystanders stood, what they did, and whether they posed a threat sufficient for the Sweets to feel endangered. Michigan law was clear about what constituted a mob. Ordinance 15001 of "Offenses Against the Public Peace" defined a mob as "twelve or more people armed with clubs or other dangerous weapons . . . or thirty or more, whether armed or not."

Inspector Norton Schuknecht, from Detroit's Fifth Precinct, a twenty-four-year veteran, was the first to appear. His success as a police officer depended, in part, on his fluent German, which enabled him to converse with a large percentage of Detroit's foreign-born citizens. Schuknecht had worked his way up from his first post as a patrolman and had been promoted to the rank of inspector six years before. On the day Sweet moved into his house, and the day following, he was assigned to protect them and their property. For this, he detailed four extra policemen.

Schuknecht spent the better part of the trial's first day on the witness stand. He described how he had explored the neighborhood a few times on Tuesday, when the Sweets arrived in the vans carrying belongings to their new home. By early evening, when it was still light at seven o'clock, he said he saw only "ordinary people walking up and down."

On Wednesday, the day after the Sweets moved, Schuknecht reassigned the four policemen to the vicinity of the Sweets' house. Later he increased the number to eight, and he testified that at the three o'clock roll call he told his men they "were there to preserve peace and order, and that man, Dr. Sweet could live there if we had to take every man in the department to protect his home." In addition to the eight uniformed policemen, he added three plainclothes officers, one sergeant, and one lieutenant. Schuknecht testified that when he arrived on the scene about 6:30 P.M. all was calm.

Were there people on the streets? Toms asked.

People were walking up and down, but they were not congregating and definitely there were no crowds, Schuknecht said. It was like the night before, there was "nothing more than the ordinary person walking by the place. I don't believe there was more than two or three at a time that walked by," he said.

"At any time was there as many as ten people gathered in one group in that place?"

"No sir, there was not."

"Were there ever as many as five?" Toms asked.

"No sir."

"Were there any that stopped and stood there for more than half a minute?"

"No."

Schuknecht acknowledged, however, that it was a very warm night and women and children were relaxing on the Howe School's front lawn. Under cross-examination, he estimated that there might have been "a couple of hundred people within a block each way." His admission was difficult to reconcile with the prosecutor's description of a night absent reason for alarm.

While Toms was questioning Schuknecht, Darrow appeared to be more than a casual observer. He scooted his chair away from the defense table and closer to the jury box. As Toms talked, Darrow seemed to listen the way one might follow a chum whose story he was at liberty to interrupt, even to prompt for clarification from time to time. Toms and Darrow even engaged in a conversation that might have seemed like a private chat, appropriate between colleagues talking in confidence, except that it was taking place in front of a judge, twelve jurors, and three hundred spectators.

Toms took care not to inflame Darrow. But the banter, the irreverence in the court bothered Murphy, who was watching from a judge's bench, wearing the court's dignified black robe that exuded authority. One can imagine a grimace knitting his thick eyebrows, arched like protective awnings over saucer-round blue eyes. It mattered not that Darrow was twice his age and his hero, the judge sought to maintain his authority and asked Darrow to show more respect for protocol. Chagrined, Darrow promised not to talk across the table to Toms, saying he would address all future remarks to the court.

When it came to the cross-examination, Darrow comported himself respectfully, even when he believed the police were lying. In these early days he did not overtly challenge anyone with a caustic remark that might have cost him the jury's regard. Worse yet, sarcasm could show him to be an adversary. Instead he tried to chip away at the prosecution's image of a calm September evening, suggesting a different picture of the events that night. Darrow tried to pin Schuknecht down on the number of people he saw. Could it have been two hundred?

"Where?" Schuknecht asked.

"Around the neighborhood of Dr. Sweet's house?"

"Oh, within a block either way of the house, I would figure for everybody sitting on their porches and out in front of their lawns, there may have been a couple of hundred people within a block each way," Schuknecht admitted.

Darrow continued to prod. Could the inspector describe what action the police took and what Schuknecht personally did while standing in front of the store across the street from the Sweets' house?

Schuknecht said the police broke up groups, asked them to move on, sometimes repeatedly. But the police stopped no one or asked why he was walking back and forth either day or night.

None of the officers, even those who had been on duty since three o'clock, he said, mingled with the crowd long enough to overhear a bystander's utterance. Nobody bothered to tell them what Inspector Schuknecht had told the patrolmen, that it was the policemen's duty to protect the Sweets' home. With the exception of officers Williams and McPherson, no other policeman had even introduced himself to the Sweets. Despite assurances about guaranteeing safety and securing the streets, from the inspector's testimony, it did not appear that any of the policemen knew what was happening, or who was in control.

The crowd's appearance, how it swayed and bobbed or moved with ease, whether it had grown into a shapeless, faceless mass of blond Caucasians, whom Darrow would later call "noble Nordics," would become a central element to each side's argument about the mood on the night of the shooting. Were they more than thirty unarmed individuals visiting the neighborhood and leaving after glimpsing the house owned by Ossian and Gladys Sweet? Or were they fifteen neighbors initially, but growing in size and strength and armed? What role, if any, had the police played before the shooting? The law was clear about the number of people, the presence of weapons, and what was required of the police.

Schuknecht testified that he had been standing on the southeast corner of Garland and Charlevoix when he heard shots. He said he then knocked on Sweet's door to complain. That was when Sweet supposedly told him, "They're ruining my property."

"What has been done? I haven't seen a man throwing stones, and I haven't heard any commotion or anything else," the inspector said.

The officer's choice of words landed heavily on Darrow. He remembered reading testimony of the preliminary hearing and recalled that the inspector used the word "molest." More precisely, Darrow remembered Schuknecht testifying that he told Sweet, "Nobody is molesting you." Darrow asked him who was "the first one who mentioned the question of stoning." The inspector answered that it was Sweet. But Darrow suggested that the inspector contradicted his own testimony from the preliminary hearing.

Schuknecht then testified that after he left Sweet's house, he learned that Breiner had been shot. He returned and told Dr. Sweet, "We have got men around your house; we have got them in the alley;

we have got them on the side; we have got them on the front." This might have been his way of showing concern for the Sweets' welfare, but it is hard to imagine that it brought comfort to the Sweet brothers, who had grown up neighbors to a lynching tree.

Lieutenant Paul Schellenberger, Schuknecht's deputy, testified the next day. He said the pedestrians gathered in "knots" of six to seven people each. He estimated there might be as many as half a dozen of them, no more than thirty-five people. And they were not disorderly, he said. But, tellingly, he also estimated the total number of people on the streets was slightly more than the two hundred Schuknecht admitted.

One of Sweet's neighbors, Ray Dove, followed Schellenberger. Dove had moved to Detroit from southern Indiana three and a half years earlier. He lived in the two-family flat at 2914 Garland, across the street from Sweet and next door to the grocery store. The state used Dove to attempt to introduce pictures of the scene, focusing the jury's attention on bullet holes in trees, porches, and windows near where Dove was standing when Breiner and Hogsburg were shot. Taken the next day, the pictures had an artificial stillness. Emptiness was not the impression the defense wanted to the jury to absorb.

"If we had a photograph of the people there that night, and the traffic being stopped," Hays said, "there would be no objection." The defense maintained "there were mobs of people" at the time of the shooting, but the prosecutor's photos showed something quite different. "This is a very peaceful scene," said Hays. He doubted that words could alter the powerful impression these images conveyed.

The defense conceded that gunshots came from Sweet's windows—an admission Toms celebrated—but it did not want the jury to dwell on close-up pictures of bullets lodged in doorframes.

"I choose to prove that bullets struck there," Toms said, emphasizing why he wanted to include pictures of the porch and steps. Injecting a heavy dose of sarcasm, Darrow quipped, "Will they show who fired them?"

"We will get to that point too," Toms replied. It was a sloppy answer giving Hays the opportunity to create an expectation that the prosecution would prove who fired the shot, something Toms had tried to avoid. Now this strategic moment in the prosecution's case became part of the jury's expectation, exactly what Hays wanted specified in the bill of particulars, knowing it would be difficult, if not impossible, to prove.

Murphy next handed the defense a small victory when he ruled against admitting the pictures with bullets lodged in different parts of Dove's porch. It would distract the jury from the major issue, he said, "the murder of the deceased."

When Dove resumed testifying, he could not remember how many people were standing near his house or on the adjacent lot, how many he knew by name, how many he could recognize. Because many of Dove's answers were surprisingly vague or contradictory, those that were clear and well-crafted raised suspicions. He had not counted them, he told Darrow, but he was absolutely confident that women and children outnumbered men.

"Did you ever make an estimate of the number of men, women and children in a crowd before?" Darrow asked.

Dove said he had not.

By changing the pitch of his voice, or looking at the jury a certain way, Darrow conveyed skepticism without offending. He would gesture by throwing up his arms, open palms, followed by a shrug. Sometimes he made self-effacing remarks when witnesses stumbled badly. But Darrow reiterated that he was not trying to confuse him. He was just "trying to get it straight" in a tone half earnest, half mocking.

Darrow next implied that Dove had been coached by the state about how many people he had seen. Darrow and Toms traded barbs several times before Darrow accused the witness of saying what the state wanted him to say. "As long as the question was asked by the State, you thought you were safe in answering it the way you did," he said.

"Wait a minute," screamed Toms. Jumping to his feet, with blood turning his face red, he stammered a passionate objection.

Murphy allowed the question to stand because, he said, it probed "the credibility of the witness."

The press described Darrow radiating a "perfect calm" while he challenged Dove and accused him of being the prosecution's parrot. When had Dove first spoken to the prosecution? Darrow asked.

Dove said he met Toms only that day.

What about other policemen? Darrow insisted. Did he meet with an officer named William Johnson, the one who collected the evidence?

"Yes," Dove said.

"You talked with him how many times?"

"Well, just a few times. He was generally out there during the day when I am at work."

"Have you been down to their offices to talk to him?" Darrow asked.

"Have I been down to his office?" Dove repeated.

"Yes."

"I came down to his office before coming up here."

"[H]ow long were you there?"

"All, all the witnesses came to his office," said Dove.

"How long were you there?"

"Oh, ten or fifteen minutes, something like that."

Darrow was finished.

Toms could not allow the impression to stand. Before dismissing Dove he led him through a disavowal of having been coached by the police.

Until Officer Frank Lee Gill was sworn in as a witness, the prosecution had not introduced any evidence pointing to who had fired shots. Gill was the state's last witness late on Friday afternoon, the second day of testimony.

Patrolman Gill was one of eight sent to Garland and Charlevoix after the three o'clock briefing at the McClellan Street Station. He said his job that night was to maintain peace and protect property. Around eight o'clock, before light faded from the sky, he described having walked into the alley. He stayed there for about ten minutes before moving closer to the house, standing next to the garage, behind Sweet's house, to relieve another officer. Two or three minutes later, Gill saw two men walk outside, onto the upstairs back porch of Sweet's home. Gill could not see the men clearly enough to make out their features or to identify them in court. But he could see them go to opposite ends, about twelve feet from each other, on the back porch. Suddenly each fired, perhaps six or eight shots altogether. Gill said it looked like one of the bullets entered the property north of Sweet's, the Getke house. And the other shot was fired across Charlevoix. At no time did Gill believe he was a target, nor did he indicate he was possessed of fear standing between the garage and the house. Yet he aimed toward the men. He remembered shooting only one bullet, a .38 caliber lead bullet that was never found. Gill testified that he believed it hit the porch door and the overhang of the roof. Then the men ducked and disappeared into the house.

Like many of Detroit's new citizens, Gill was Southern, having migrated from Tennessee. In July, just two months before he fired at the Sweets, he joined the police force—a fact Judge Murphy drew out of him before allowing him to step down from the witness stand.

When Gill concluded testifying, the clock read four forty-five. The prosecution prepared to call its next witness, but, expecting to leave by five o'clock, Darrow asked the court to adjourn. He had scheduled an appointment to speak with someone who might become a witness for the defense. When Judge Murphy acceded to Darrow's request, he made it clear that he expected to work until five o'clock, later if warranted, most days. The only exception was Saturday, which convention dictated would be half day. This was going to be a long trial, the judge said, and leaving early would not hasten its momentum.

The prosecution's witnesses echoed police testimony concerning the peaceful conditions in Sweet's neighborhood on the night

Breiner was shot. On Saturday, Edward Wettlaufer testified. He had lived in the neighborhood for eleven years and worked downtown as the manager of a billiards hall. He was not an excitable person, or at least that is what he would have told anybody who asked. But going to the grocery store after dinner on the night of September 9 upset him.

After leaving his house on Bewick, one block away from the Sweets', he walked down Charlevoix, past several policemen and about fifteen people. Nobody looked familiar. On route, he heard glass breaking, and a minute later he heard shots, maybe twenty-five all together. Then he saw a policeman take out a flashlight and shine it at the man he later learned was Leon Breiner. By the time he reached the grocery store on the corner, he was so nervous that he didn't bother to purchase the bread, bananas, cream, and milk that he set out to buy for his morning's breakfast.

Wettlaufer first learned that Sweet had bought the house at 2905 Garland by attending a meeting of the Waterworks Improvement Association. But he had not known that the Sweets had moved into it. The next witness, Otto Eberhardt, attended the same gatherings. He similarly had trouble remembering the details and could not say when the first of two meetings took place, but it must have been the summer, he said, because "it was hot weather." Eberhardt's memory failed when it came to describing what had been discussed, whether Dr. Ossian Sweet was mentioned by name, or even who invited him to the meeting. He said "one of the men" notified him.

Eberhardt's testimony on Saturday morning was brief. The defense asked what took place at the Waterworks Improvement Association meeting. Had anybody discussed blacks moving into the neighborhood? Toms argued that the question was irrelevant. Michigan law permitted racial restrictions on the purchase of property, and the conversations took place several weeks before the shooting. Murphy permitted it, however, "to show interest."

Darrow was pleased. He then asked whether members of the association had discussed "arrangements whereby undesirable people could be kept out of the neighborhood?"

Toms objected again. Murphy overruled him again. Darrow repeated the question. He was trying to pin Eberhardt down. Toms objected that the question called for a conclusion. The court instructed Eberhardt to answer. He answered, "No."

Darrow then asked, "You didn't want colored people to come into the neighborhood, did you?" Toms objected one more time. Murphy overruled him for a third time.

By the end of his testimony, Eberhardt's memory had improved significantly, enough that he could recall that he was one of the men—there were five to a block—who formed the Waterworks Improvement Association.

The final witness that Saturday morning was Eben Draper, a salesman who, for seven years, had been living at 2625 Garland, in a house south of Charlevoix and across from the Howe School. On the night Breiner was shot, Draper was standing near his own house before going to the grocery store. While he was there, he saw nobody standing in front of the Sweet home and of those he saw walking elsewhere, none was armed. At the time of the shooting he did see fire, perhaps five or six spurts, flashes coming from a window on the Charlevoix side of the house.

Darrow continued to ask about the Waterworks Improvement Association. Draper had trouble remembering when he attended the first meeting, which took place in a garage a few doors away on Charlevoix. Nor did he recall the time elapsing between that small, private meeting and the second larger, public gathering in July at the Howe School. When Darrow tried to push Draper about the purpose of the Waterworks Improvement Association, Moll objected and the court sustained it. On his feet, Hays challenged the court. "Your honor, before you sustain that objection," he began, "I wonder if this ought not to be considered."

[I]f we bring out that there was an association formed for certain purposes, and that they agreed to do certain things, and they were present on that night, it throws very considerable light on the character of the testimony as to conditions being peaceful on that night.

Murphy sustained the objection and advised Hays to take it up during cross-examination.

Draper was a difficult witness to cross-examine. Like many others, his voice reflected the tension of the courtroom. It barely carried to the jury box. On several occasions the judge, prosecutors, and defense attorneys asked him to speak up and to take his hand away from his face. When he did speak, he was both vague and laconic. After Draper answered a question by asking, "What do you mean?" one more time, Darrow flung his arms in a gesture of helplessness.

Darrow abandoned his line of questions about the Waterworks Improvement Association and changed gears to ask, "What were the police doing to keep the crowds in check on Garland Avenue the night of the shooting?

Moll cried out, "I object to the use of the word 'crowd.' "

"Why? This is cross examination."

"There has not been any evidence up to date that there were crowds in any particular spot," Moll said.

It had been a tedious day and a long day and it was almost over. In a style that typified what *Free Press* reporter Philip O'Hara called "the latent force" of Darrow's personality, before sitting down the famous lawyer disparaged Moll and his question in a flippant tone by saying, "You must have been asleep."

CHAPTER 12

Your Fight / My Fight

The prosecution of Dr. Ossian Sweet did not excite the interest of investigative journalists. The press may have wanted to see Clarence Darrow conduct the trial, but newsmen did not search behind the scenes for evidence. The NAACP knew that if it could shape how people viewed the events, it could promote newspaper coverage, and it might be able to mold public opinion that would contribute to the success of this trial. In its own way, it might become as important as the team of defense attorneys. The association needed a talented person to work the press.

Walter White embraced the challenge enthusiastically. It was a way to fight for race equality that also affirmed his self-image as an intellectual, a man of belles lettres. White requested a press pass, based on the occasional story he had written for the *Nation* or the *New York World,* and Judge Murphy granted it. White then sat at the table of journalists, among the insiders, and he freely whispered into the ear of one reporter, traded notes with another, or let the man from the *Free Press* mooch his cigarettes.

Darrow realized White's greatest impact could come from influencing other reporters. Just two days into the trial, White took note of how he could induce small changes by dropping hints. Simple banter could lead to success. "I have been able to influence the stories in the local press considerably," he wrote to Johnson. "My flimsy connection with the *World* makes me a somewhat important figure in the eyes of the local newspaper men and they listen with respect thus far to my suggestions." Felix Holt's stories, from the *Detroit Times*, "are already getting better . . . He's eating out of my hand," White boasted. White's relationship with Holt was complicated. A Southerner, Holt bragged how an influential press could twist race relations. "Do you know we newspapermen can hang any innocent man no matter how guilty?" Holt asked White. "I'm from the South and I know what Negroes suffer from."

White could hear in Holt's voice the combination of diphthongs that cradled the rhythm of Paducah, Kentucky, reason enough for initial distrust. He grew especially uncomfortable when Holt repeatedly invited him for dinner. Finally White took Holt aside and whispered that despite his appearance, he was considered a man of color. Holt said he knew, leading White to accept the first of many invitations in a friendship that would last well beyond the trial.

Nothing quite compared to the glow that warmed White after he alerted the press corps to errors in police testimony. He never believed the police were telling the truth, and their inconsistencies provided an opportunity to push his view. Familiarity with testimony from the pretrial hearing helped White inform his press confidants how Inspector Schuknecht contradicted himself when he estimated the numbers of people around Sweet's house.

When not sitting in the crowded courtroom, White consulted with influential NAACP board members, on whom he had come to rely for strategic advice. These were men like Ira Jayne, now a judge but once a social worker who had come to the aid of the Urban League during the Southern Exodus. Judge Jayne had a keen understanding of Detroit's underbelly, its backroom deals, and how white liberals could be swayed. He counted lawyers, judges, and politicians as friends, and as a judge Jayne kept White abreast of intricacies of the bench, of strategies the association might adopt. He was the only person whom Darrow specifically mentioned wanting to see by name before he decided to take the case. Jayne informed many of the recommendations White urged upon the NAACP. White also met Judge Murphy, sometimes for lunch or dinner at the exclusive Detroit Athletic Club.

But White usually spent evenings with the defense attorneys, their wives and out-of-town guests, dignitaries such as the ambassador to Liberia, or celebrities who dropped in on the trial, such as the boxer Jack Dempsey. Some evenings they went to Berman's Restaurant, a favorite steak and chop house. Other nights they returned to the Book-Cadillac Hotel to have a private meal while talking strategy, comparing that day's impressions, sharing anecdotes about the judge, jury, witnesses, or prosecutors. And they planned for the next day. Usually White would return to his room at the Statler Hotel and type out a long letter to James Weldon Johnson with all the relevant information. In early November he reported how he and field organizer William Pickens "met with the Gomez crowd." Or he described how they "had a little trouble today when some colored people in the courtroom, over anxious and at high tension, made some remarks."

White kept Johnson well informed, sent him local newspaper stories to show the daily response, and itemized the receipts from his lectures. Johnson then turned White's letters and Detroit's news clippings into a formal press release and forwarded it to the Associated Negro Press, which reached more than 250 black weeklies. Many were one-man operations in hamlets and burgs anxious to carry news of Ossian and Gladys Sweet, their story of self-defense in the face of a mob.

The bigger papers, those with a national audience, sent their own reporters. The voices of Nettie George Speedy and Joe Coles brought detailed accounts to readers of the *Chicago Defender*. Speedy's stories were especially incisive, among the best of any press. Often contemplative, his accounts conveyed with biting description and telling detail the defendants' appearances, which attorneys jumped to their feet, and when the color drained from their faces. And Baxter S. Scruggs's byline appeared in two places, the *Chicago Defender* and the *Pittsburgh Courier*, which had a special interest in the case because Gladys Sweet came from Pittsburgh.

James Weldon Johnson remained in New York City, meanwhile, hunting feverishly for money to finance the NAACP's support of Sweet's defense. Even before the association knew of Sweet, Johnson guessed he would need about $50,000 for existing commitments. They needed money for other legal battles and an expensive trial in Detroit added to their existing obligations.

Shortly after hiring Clarence Darrow to head the defense team in October, Johnson threw himself into a vigorous pursuit of cash. He contacted friends, set strategies in motion, had lunch with Dr. W. G. Alexander, the president of the National Medical Association, the professional association of black doctors.

Johnson and White met Alexander, who lived in New Jersey, for lunch so they could explain to him how the NAACP's struggles affected all physicians. Of their current projects, doctors were among those most often victims of violence, if not with the full support of the law, often without substantial penalty for breaking it. Residential segregation posed the biggest threat for doctors, whose wealth set them apart from the mass of black migrants to the North. That is what made the appeal of Detroit universal.

White and Johnson explained that the association had overestimated *Buchanan v. Warley's* impact, the Louisville segregation case, for changing patterns of residential segregation. Other doctors had been denied access to a home of their choice, whether by private agreement, restrictive covenants, or by mob actions. At that moment, in Cleveland, Ohio, Dr. Charles Garvin was under attack for occupying a home he had built. In the state of Missouri, Dr. G. W. Holt spent his time and money in the courts, trying to overturn restrictive housing covenants. Dr. Holt's situation strongly resembled that of Dr. Arthur Curtis, in *Corrigan v. Buckley* pending before the Supreme Court in which homeowners agreed privately not to sell houses to black families in the District of Columbia. Nor was Dr. Ossian Sweet's the only family, or the only black physician's family, in Detroit to come to the attention of the NAACP that summer.

White and Johnson had no difficulty persuading Alexander of the peril doctors faced. By the end of lunch, Alexander promised his support; and within two weeks he had mobilized forty doctors into a committee to raise money from physicians attending the upcoming annual convention in Philadelphia. Having created a relief fund to aid victims after the Tulsa massacre in 1921, the National Medical Association presumed an activist tradition.

A "Dear Doctor" letter to the membership of six thousand explained why it was essential that they

> get favorable decisions from the court without delay. For with the tendency, especially of our own group to move in the more favored quarter of cities (and this is especially true where men are moving to the North from the South) these matters will become more frequent and more important.

Alexander asked each to donate $25, a steep amount, but failure would be more costly. "It is the other fellow's case today. It may be yours tomorrow" became the NMA's slogan. And all a doctor had to do was read the newspapers to see how close the threats came to one's own rights. The organization pledged to raise $5,000 toward the goal of halting the detestable climb toward segregation.

The community of Detroit's black doctors had actually been collecting money ad hoc since the weekend following Sweet's arrest, when Bradby's Second Baptist Church counted $355. The NAACP field organizer William Pickens arranged for a "Sweet Fund Baby Contest"—a beauty parade for babies—which he expected to net $2,000 by December. The wives of the defendants, including Gladys, attended a benefit hosted by the Arcadia supper club. The weekend the trial opened, Pickens went to Illinois, Ohio, Indiana, and Kentucky, eventually speaking at twenty-nine meetings in small towns or churches, doubling back and crossing once again to pick up $15 in one spot, $103 in another, $31.50 elsewhere, for a total of $909.67. And Walter White made his own whirlwind speaking tour in the Midwest. But eighteen appearances in four cities netted only $2,688.11.

It was a hard way to finance a major campaign, and the NAACP's efforts raised only a fraction of the need. The lawyers' fees amounted to $14,000. Darrow's high fees sometimes drew criticism. But he was careful to let the world know that he was not gouging the NAACP. Just as he wanted the public to know that his commitment to Leopold and Loeb was motivated by principled opposition to the death penalty, and that he had not been hired to buy justice for wealthy Chicago families, so he wanted it known that it would cost him more to conduct the trial than the $5,000 he was being paid.

Still, the legal costs seemed staggering to Sweet's supporters. Three sets of transcripts, which the defense requested daily, amounted to $150 a day. And there was the expense of sending prepared meals to the defendants in jail, and the costs of investigators looking for defense witnesses, who were not as plentiful as those for the prosecution. The Detroit NAACP branch paid the mortgage on Ossian Sweet's new house and rent for Otis Sweet's dental office. But national headquarters was responsible for telegrams; long-distance phone calls; ads in local newspapers; Gladys Sweet's living expenses; mortgage for Hewitt Watson, one of the insurance agents; a car payment for another insurance agent, Leonard Morris; carfare and wages for witnesses—they added up. The NAACP would come close to spending $22,000 by the end of the trial. (In 2003, that would approach $231,000.)

The NAACP experienced a chronic need for money, and there would be no easy way to raise it all from the grassroots. Johnson would have preferred to avoid leaning on his friends, tapping into deep wells of philanthropy among people who had already demonstrated largess by supporting the association for nearly all of its sixteen years. But he was growing desperate.

Johnson cleared his calendar to remain in New York City for the October 29 board meeting of the American Fund for Public Service, also known as the Garland Fund. Its benefactor was an eccentric socialist who wanted to spend down the principal of his multi-million-dollar inheritance. Johnson was on the board of directors, which was headed by ACLU's Roger Baldwin, to whom NAACP board president Moorfield Storey had already written. Storey asked for a contribution and outlined the dramatic elements of the Sweet case, emphasizing its example as a microcosm of the residential apartheid that greeted black Americans as they settled in urban centers. Nor was the segregation limited to owning homes. The antagonistic process that began with living in a house spread through the community to choke opportunities for education, as well as public recreation. Laws outlawing interracial marriage were being written in numerous states. And who knew where the hate mongerers would stop? Storey called upon the Garland Fund to arrest the "epidemic" of racism spreading through Northern cities. "[I]f colored men may be prevented from choosing their abodes as freely as whites," he wrote, "Catholics and Jews and any other body of citizens may be prevented as well."

The NAACP's was the kind of broad-based appeal that the fund admired. The Garland Fund had historically supported the NAACP's antilynching crusades. Now it donated $5,000 explicitly to the defense fund. While Johnson was too shrewd to appear ungrateful to such a generous benefactor, he knew $5,000 was hardly enough to carry all the cases the NAACP was managing. He appealed for an increase, perhaps as much as $20,000 toward a matching grant? That would put them well on the way to its target of $50,000. Holding firm, the Garland Fund offered $15,000, demanding a two-to-one match, which meant the NAACP had to raise $30,000. The problem, however, was not just the amount but the deadline. The Garland Fund gave the NAACP until January 1, 1926, just two months, to reach its goal.

Thirty thousand dollars seemed like a mountain of money in 1925, and the NAACP would have to race the clock to get there in eight weeks. New York officers personally tapped their wealthy and influential friends. The wealthiest realtor in Harlem happened to be James Weldon Johnson's father-in-law, business entrepreneur John Nail. But he was no more help than most other patrons donating $25. The association talked to race leaders, people such as Reverend Francis Grimke, to friendly politicians such as Congressman Leonidas Dyer from St. Louis. They contacted Alice Tapley of Boston, Julius Rosenwald of Chicago. Rosenwald declined at first, then agreed to donate $1,000 after the successful grassroots drive raised the majority. William White contacted Jacob Billikopf, the executive director of the Federation of Jewish Charities in Philadelphia and the son-in-law of attorney Louis B. Marshall, asking to be linked to wealthy Jews in Philadelphia. Billikopf donated $25, a generous sum, but regretted that he could only host a luncheon because the federation was in the midst of its own half-million-dollar campaign. Other friends took initiative without having to be asked. Mrs. G. N. Allen, from Detroit, was surely unaware that Henry Sweet was a student and that Ossian Sweet was an alumnus, when she wrote to Wilberforce to inform them of the crisis. "I know not one of you would refuse to help in this case since it is not a fight of the eleven prisoners, but it is your fight and my fight," she said. The campus did not disappoint. Each class of Wilberforce students and each academic department collected separately for the defense fund. President Gilbert H. Jones, the dean accompanying Ossian to Cleveland for a Kappa Alpha Psi event, gave $5. Most other faculty donated $1 and students less, with the collection netting $100.05, a proud sum in an era when a newspaper cost three cents and a year-long subscription to *The Crisis* was $1.50.

Support came from every part of the globe. From Nigeria $5 arrived. African students at University Union in Edinburgh, Scotland, collected 12 shillings—about $7. O. H. Tanner, the American artist living in France and son of an AME bishop, contributed $25, and William Hunt, the United States consul in Saint-Etienne, France, donated $50. When Reverend Charles Sumner Long, from the AME district office in Ocala, Florida, sent $25 to Johnson, he included a note telling him about the family connection and of meeting Ossian the night before he left for Ohio.

Johnson depended on enthusiastic local affiliates, numbering more than three hundred chapters, to garner attention to the NAACP's mission. New York handled the publicity. The contributions of all prominent people were celebrated. When Dr. A. A. Brill contributed $50, the NAACP announced that he was a "noted alienist and widely known as the leading exponent of Dr. Freud's psychoanalysis in America."

While working feverishly to raise money, White and Johnson also wanted to rein in Detroit's ministers. To bring Bradby into line, they arranged to feature him in a New York City speech where he could discuss the case. Then he could return to Detroit like a prince, not a bystander. Bradby's talk at Harlem's Mother Zion AME Church raised $470.75, and Johnson hoped the yield would help soothe the minister's self-image and promote more satisfactory cooperation. Not far from Johnson's purpose, however, was a hope that Bradby would contribute the $3,200 Detroit collected independently toward the Garland Fund's matching gift. The NAACP was still $19,657 short of its goal, and had seven weeks to go.

Reverend Joseph Gomez, from Detroit's Bethel AME Church, in-troduced his own set of problems. Gomez was Sweet's contemporary at Wilberforce, and later a fraternity brother in Detroit. Since Gomez's arrival four years before, eighteen hundred people had joined the church, giving him reason to view himself as an independent power broker. White doubted Gomez's alignment with the NAACP, consid-ered him serpentine, and told Johnson that Gomez had tricked him into a joint fund-raising meeting. Others thought Gomez fomented trouble by making invidious comparisons between the white and black attorneys, which, according to White, prompted Rowlette to go "all over town saying that if it hadn't been for the Gomez crowd all the money would have gone to white people."

Other fund-raising opportunities—rallies, sermons from church pulpits, and "better baby" beauty pageants—provided the forum for public education. Members of fraternal societies and professional or-ganizations, church leaders, and social activists were contacted. Robert Bagnall wrote a "Dear Home Owner" letter to names supplied by local affiliates, begging for help for the fight that "so dearly affects every Negro home owner who lives in a decent neighborhood." And James Weldon Johnson wrote to newspaper editors. "If it is possible, either for courts or mobs, to segregate colored citizens," he said, "they can segregate any minority group. The dangers to democracy are obvious." Memphis, he reminded them, had already tried "to segregate Jews . . . Similar attempts may be made against Catholics, Japanese and Chi-nese."

Donations started to roll in, often in amounts of fifty cents or less, from organized groups. Poorly educated and self-taught enthusiasts like R. W. Smith sent $5 from Los Angeles, California, with regrets

that I can't do what I would like to do for I only wish I COULD give then times as much as I can if we onily geat my peaple to SEE ther dutey and ack accordinly what a power we would be.

Mrs. Martha W. Contee enclosed a money order for $2 with simi-
lar regrets and hopes that "the little bit will help." If she were a laundry
worker living in Detroit, she would have had to work for an entire day
to earn that amount.

Most did not write a personal letter but instead sent back the form
in *The Crisis* with a few dollars addressed to J. E. Spingarn, treasurer of
the NAACP. Of the whites who wrote letters, many sounded like
Henry A. Todd, whose $10 accompanied a note saying: "I am an *Amer-
ican* as we used to consider them many years ago—a retired Presbyterian minister—white. I am becoming ashamed of our country—or a
large element in it for the barbarism that is displayed so often."

During a talk at the Citizen's Forum in Harlem, James Weldon
Johnson lamented, "When we won the fight against segregation
in the Supreme Court in 1916, we thought that we had wiped out segregation forever." He used every opportunity to remind listeners that
the Ossian Sweet crisis belonged to the larger army of the aggrieved.
This was not the first time the association had asked members to dig
deep. Several years before, after the massacre in Elaine, Arkansas, they
had launched a mass appeal. But it took more than five years to accu-
mulate $15,000, which dribbled into the office in contributions be-
tween $1 and $5. Now they had several weeks. Johnson had seen too
much in his years heading the NAACP to exude overconfidence about
success. In the meantime, as he always did in the past, he had to enlist
every available member, every friend of the NAACP, every foe of racial
injustice, doctors, white liberals, middle-class blacks, the Southern
chapters he helped organize on his tour of 1916, and many people he
had never met or heard of, to make a success of this crusade. And he
didn't have a lot of time to get it done.

CHAPTER 13

The Night of
September 9

When court convened at nine-thirty, on Monday, November 9, the press had already spent one week reporting the case closely. After the first day the *Detroit News* announced, CALL FIRST RIOT WITNESS TODAY. On day two the *Detroit Evening Times* shouted, TOMS BATTLES WITH DARROW. By Monday, day four, the public expected DARROW TO GRILL 7 OFFICERS.

Although Darrow had staged a few moments of laughter, and the prosecution had made a few blunders, testimony in the first week did not leave either side overly confident. Occasionally a witness flared, revealing a temper or even hostility to someone's questions, usually Darrow's. When he asked Inspector Schuknecht why he hadn't included broken glass and a rock in his findings of the search of an upstairs bedroom, the inspector snapped back, "Why didn't you ask me?" Darrow said that was exactly what he was doing.

These moments revealed Darrow's acerbic wit, exactly as his reputation implied. But the defense would need more than wit to damage the credibility of the police who provided eyewitness testimony about the events unfolding on the night of September 9. And the prosecution also needed to dismiss troublesome questions about cars parked on Garland Avenue, and where their owners might have been on the night in question.

The state led off that Monday with witnesses who testified that there were neither crowds nor aggression. Certainly there was no throwing of stones, no breaking of windows. The prosecution sought to draw a picture of a warm summer night, where neighbors were going to the corner grocery to stock up for the morning meal, perhaps for a snack for the kids, even for a pet.

Toms did not want any testimony that would credit the defendants' belief that a mob was forming. That would interfere with his ability to guide the jurors toward accepting a premise of the Sweets' *premeditated* conspiracy.

Each of the police witnesses stationed around Sweet's home stated the following: the time he arrived, where he stood on the night of September 9, whether he was stationed at the intersection of Garland and Charlevoix or on streets rimming the area. Several struggled over the details about where pedestrians were standing, what they were saying or doing. They were all certain, however, that nobody threatened peaceful assembly, and they all remembered the guns and rifles vividly. The press made it seem as if the weapons made up an arsenal.

It added up to a good day for the state. "The state's case developed considerably in the course of the day's proceedings," wrote the *Free Press*.

> A number of police officers testified to arresting the 11 defendants in the house, to finding a quantity of arms and ammunition, and to the fact that there was little disturbance in the district prior to the shooting.

The testimony most damaging to the Sweets came from Detective George Fairbairn, the arresting officer who identified the weapons. They found two .38 Colt revolvers hidden in a mattress in an upstairs bedroom, along with a black automatic Remington shotgun covered by a pillowcase. All were fully loaded. In an upstairs dresser were a German automatic revolver, two shotguns, and a bag of ammunition. More ammunition was discovered in a closet. Some had been stashed in a gutter spout over the kitchen roof. Spent cartridges littered the back porch and the hallway upstairs. The police discovered that William Davis, the narcotics agent who intended to live with Ossian and share a room with Otis Sweet, carried his own diamond-studded, blue-steel revolver, which he surrendered to police along with its cartridges. Under Darrow's cross-examination, Fairbairn described which guns had only unused cartridges, meaning they had not been fired.

Darrow conceded that gunfire had come from the Sweets' home, and he barely objected to the prosecution's entering the guns into evidence. Later he would take up Officer Gill's testimony that he had discharged his gun while standing at street level. He would also revisit the fact that the bullet that killed Breiner entered his body horizontally. But for now Darrow wanted to avoid squabbles that would alienate the jury or the judge or both. He would wait for an opportunity to have more control over the story. His main purpose in cross-examining the witnesses was to show which weapons were fully loaded, and he hesitated to remind the jurors about the piles of discharged cartridges.

Darrow, however, also strongly believed the police were lying about the events of that night, and he used his cross-examination to pin down falsehoods and tease out contradictions. He forced witnesses to expose inconsistencies and to create doubt that would make a juror stop and think. Why were the police so vague about the numbers of people congregating on Garland and Charlevoix? How could it be that the police department kept watch of the evidence yet had not supplied a written report of what had been confiscated? Inspector Schuknecht had testified there was no inventory of all the exhibits, including the boxes of bullets that Lieutenant William Johnson maintained for safekeeping. Darrow wanted the jury to realize how senseless some of it seemed.

Darrow asked Sergeant Joseph Neighbauer, a fifteen-year veteran, why traffic cops monitored the flow of automobiles at four different intersections on the night of the ninth. Was it normal to divert traffic from Waterloo, from Goethe, to have officers stationed at the intersection of Garland and Charlevoix?

Neighbauer said he did not know. But he also stumbled, as if he was confused and couldn't remember what he intended to say. Darrow practically taunted him.

"Now, don't you know why they were called in there?" Darrow queried.

"No, sir I don't," Neighbauer repeated.

Darrow aimed to pin him down. Where were people at eight o'clock? Had more assembled in the preceding hour? His tone was patronizing, the way a bully might speak to a child. "I want you to get it. I think I can make it simpler," Darrow urged with a controlled anger while the sergeant seemed shaken. Then Darrow stated his understanding of the officer's summary: "There was no more traffic and no more people and no more machines . . . going through there just before the traffic was blocked off than there was a half an hour before it was blocked off?"

"Well, there might have been," the sergeant said at first. Then he equivocated. "The traffic was very heavy and usually is in that vicinity."

"That is not what I asked you," Darrow said painstakingly. "I asked you if it increased in the last half hour before?"

"Not to my knowledge," Neighbauer answered, in a phrase that many of the state's witnesses would invoke. However aggressive Darrow's cross-examinations, however unpleasant and intense his questioning, the story the police told never varied.

To create reasonable doubt, Darrow would have to loosen the story the police held steady. But before he could do that, all hell broke loose in the courtroom.

Sergeant Joseph Grohm, the first uniformed man to reach Breiner after he fell, took the stand following the noon recess. Grohm recounted how he had just reached the corner of Garland and Charlevoix when he heard shouting about a man having been hit. Grohm rushed over to find Breiner unconscious. Blood covered his chest, his arms crossed his torso, and he was leaning against the porch steps. A smoking pipe rested across his lips. Grohm accompanied Breiner to the hospital, where he died soon after arriving.

Darrow had few questions for this witness and seemed impatient with the prosecutor. This time Lester Moll was questioning Grohm, and he intended to establish details about Breiner's death, such as what side of the two-step staircase his body rested against after a bullet brought him down. Darrow objected to none of it.

Just as Grohm was about to step down from what had been a fairly straightforward and noncontroversial recitation of facts, and without warning, a woman on the spectators' bench slipped to the floor.

"Step right out, gentleman," barked Judge Murphy, who, from his elevated chair, could see the fainting in slow motion from the time she began to slide off the bench until she was whisked away. The jury left while pandemonium roiled the courtroom, and two policemen hastily carried the woman away. It happened so quickly that for an instant nobody quite knew what the commotion was all about. It took Clarence Darrow several seconds to discover that the woman who had crumpled to the ground was Leon Breiner's widow.

After Mrs. Breiner was carried from the room, facts spilled forth. It was learned that she usually sat in the same place every day. She was either alone or with one of her daughters, and she spoke to no one. Judge Murphy had asked her to sit outside the railing, fearful that something might happen to upset the harmony of the trial. On this day, November 9, Mrs. Breiner was sitting in the second row of the public seats when her collapse brought calamity and suspense to the otherwise august court.

Immediately Darrow objected "to members of the family being in here." Chaos followed while the attorneys tried to sort out how often she had been attending the trial and what impact her fall would have.

Toms had not known that she was coming to court and seemed as surprised as Darrow. Family of the deceased attending a trial was uncommon, but so was an incident like this. For fifteen minutes defense attorneys huddled on one side of the room, prosecutors on the other. Murphy then met with both sides to discuss how to proceed. Darrow told the judge he had "no desire to enlarge on this," but he did want to query each juror about its impact for him. Darrow said he hoped only for a fair trial.

"In this incident," Murphy said, "I do not want either side to be hasty . . . It ought not be looked at by either side in a spirit of combat, but to do just what is the fair and correct thing to do. That is what I want to arrive at, and that is what I want done." Toms proved himself a respectful adversary in not exploiting the widow Breiner's faint to etch more deeply that a man had been murdered and his widow deeply affected. He called it a "hazy incident." All agreed that the defense had the most to lose. "[A]ny prejudice that could come up . . . would be to the accused," Murphy concluded.

Displeased, Darrow wanted each juror to disclose any impact the event might have had for him. Murphy thought this was excessive but agreed to ask who among them observed "a lady spectator in the courtroom [who] fainted, became ill?" Four raised a hand. None knew her. Murphy found this acceptable but Darrow did not. As expected, he moved for a mistrial; as could also have been predicted, Murphy denied his motion.

Mrs. Breiner's fainting did not interrupt the people's momentum. Now the state brought in the neighbors. Most testified that they saw flashes of fire from the second-story window on the Charlevoix side of the house. Almost all estimated there were between fifteen and twenty shots, and if there was a break in the shooting, it lasted only a few seconds.

The defense worked hard to introduce doubts about the rhythm of the shooting. Were the bullets fired consecutively in one continuous flow? Or were they fired in two distinct volleys, with several seconds in between? In addition to testifying about the rhythm of shots, almost everybody said he saw the grocer's car, the red Ford, and no others. Nor had anyone seen pedestrians congregating. The consistent, near uniform reply described people walking back and forth.

Darrow was anxious to establish the neighbors' frames of mind, what they knew about the Sweets and when they knew it. He tried to show the similarity between the Waterworks Improvement Association and the Tireman Avenue Improvement Association. Pundits thought these groups little more than fronts for the Klan, organizations to enlist voters for the mayoral election.

Delia Getke, Sweet's next-door neighbor at 2915 Garland, was a member of the Waterworks Improvement Association. She took the witness stand late on Monday afternoon when a gray sky dimmed whatever light was prying through the court's three large windows. Emblematic of the neighbors Toms subpoenaed, Getke and her husband were forgetful and tentative. She could not remember when she joined the Waterworks Improvement Association.

"Think hard," Darrow implored.

"I can't remember."

"What?"

"I can't remember just when it was."

Of nearly 150 questions Darrow asked Getke about what she did, where she was, or what she saw, she responded "I couldn't say," or "I cannot remember" thirty-two times.

Seeking to impeach her claims of forgetfulness, Darrow asked, "Have you ever tried to remember, or tried to forget, either one?"

"I cannot remember," she said predictably.

Darrow tried to establish the racial antagonism on which the Waterworks Improvement Association was based. Joseph Henley lived in an apartment upstairs from Ray Dove, at 2912 Garland Avenue. He testified that he had never met Ed Smith, the man who sold Sweet his house, but that after the sale, people learned that Ed Smith was racially mixed. They started talking about how the Smiths "sold out."

After the state's thirtieth witness, Walter Smith, repeated how policemen kept moving people along, allowing nobody to congregate on the streets, Darrow shot back only one question: "Do you know why nobody was congregated there?"

"Because the officers would not let anybody congregate," Smith replied. Under pressure, he guessed there were sixty to seventy-five noncongregating people.

Without Darrow's sarcasm, the witnesses seemed almost indistinguishable while the state built its case. At times the testimony melded like a familiar melody streaming through memory, and some of the witnesses appeared oddly dulled, anticipating questions even if they were somewhat nervous about what it meant to testify in a court. On several occasions a lawyer had to remind a witness to speak loudly enough for the last juror in the box to hear him. Occasionally it was a juror who yelled he could not hear. The state produced a stunning parade of people marked by inattention to their surroundings, and disavowing any knowledge of the events that conspired to deliver them to the corner of Garland and Charlevoix. Yet, on the night of September 9, nearly all of them had focused their attention on exactly the same spot—windows on the Charlevoix side of Sweet's house. All claimed to have seen momentary flashes of fire brighten the darkened sky when the elapsed time from beginning to end was a scant, indeterminable number of seconds.

On Tuesday, November 10, the fifth day of the trial, the State called local teenagers. Their testimony would turn out to be critical. The people claimed the lives of children were wantonly threatened by the defendants' malice and most likely called these boys to personify that threat. George Suppus, a student in the seventh grade, lived at 2996 Garland, and his friend Ulric Arthur, thirteen years old, lived four blocks away. After dinner every night, they went outside to play in the yard of the Howe School. Between them, they knew almost everybody their age in the neighborhood.

After having dinner at home on Wednesday night, each went separately to the corner of Garland and Charlevoix. For several weeks the boys had been hearing the neighbors talk over back alleys and gossip at the Charlevoix Avenue trolley stop about the imminent arrival of the Sweets. Now they saw the bustle, heard the din for themselves, but they wanted to be in the middle of the crowd and find out what everybody was doing at the corner on the day after the Sweets arrived.

When Suppus met Arthur at the intersection, the police asked them to move along. To get a better view of Sweet's house, they edged toward Ray Dove's front porch, where they sat down on the steps. Dove, his wife, the baby, and the upstairs neighbors were already lounging. On the vacant lot to the north stood several boys, perhaps as many as five, about the same age as they. Neither Suppus nor Arthur knew them, or where they lived, or where they went to school. But they told Toms that they could clearly see the boys hurling stones, throwing rocks. Then the shooting began. Under cross-examination, Arthur also told Darrow the sequence he remembered: Two black men got out of a taxi in front of Sweet's house; the strange boys started throwing rocks at the house. Glass shattered, and the sound of a thousand bursts of crystal carried more than fifty feet across the street, through corridors of many conversations, onto the steps of the front porch where he sat. Two minutes after the glass broke, there was a hail of bullets.

Up until now, all the evidence implied that broken windows and piles of rocks strewn about the front lawn came from the crowd's response to the shooting. Suppus and Arthur delivered the first break for the defense. It was the same thing the defendants claimed—the shooting followed an attack on the house. Their guilelessness, their authentic naiveté, suited them well for providing candid descriptions. None before had had the courage or perhaps the innocence to tell it this way.

The *Free Press* immediately grasped the importance of these boys' testimony. The next day's headline announced, SAW STONES HURLED AT SWEET HOME, CLAIM. The story said it was the "first direct testimony which indicated that any sort of disturbance preceded the slaying."

While Toms worked hard to move testimony along, Darrow slouched in a chair, working his crossword puzzle. His posture was as much of an affectation to camouflage his astuteness as were his clothes. After the teenagers revealed that the rock throwing preceded the shooting, skepticism eroded his patience, contempt replaced humility, and his posture straightened somewhat. But Darrow needed to do more than sit up straight if he was going to benefit from the testimony of Suppus and Arthur.

The boys sat down, and Darrow continued to chip away at the testimony of the state's next witness. Harry Monet was an eight-year resident of 2973 Garland Avenue, near Goethe, and Darrow hammered him for details about the Waterworks Improvement Association. He wanted Monet to testify about its purpose, goals, when and how it took shape.

Moll objected. "I suppose whether or not a meeting was held is more or less important," Moll said, "but what led up to it and how it was called, how it happened to be called, I think is immaterial."

Darrow disagreed. Knowing when the Waterworks Improvement Association met, how it canvassed the neighborhood for members, and when a specific witness joined would explain the ambition to keep the neighborhood racially homogeneous. "[I]t was gotten up for the purpose of driving these people out of the neighborhood, preventing their coming," Darrow told the court. Moll objected to Darrow's remark as prejudicial and Murphy agreed, striking the remark, but allowing Darrow to continue his line of inquiry.

Darrow's questioning led to descriptions of the July meeting at the Howe School. As with so many of the previous witnesses, hesitancy and tentativeness characterized Monet. He did not answer easily or fully.

Darrow then selected one of the Waterworks Improvement Association by-laws to read. He chose the one specifying how the organization aimed to maintain segregated neighborhoods, to control the transfer of property through "restrictions and ordinances; and originating and supporting other restrictions which may be deemed necessary to conserve this particular locality that it remain a desirable community and property owners may continue to dwell in peace, security and harmony."

Monet softened. He allowed that the Sweets' purchase had been discussed at the Howe School in July. He told Darrow how people wanted to "keep the neighborhood in the same high standard that it always has been." He was interested in maintaining his property, he told Darrow.

"Your purpose in joining was to keep colored people out of the neighborhood? . . . That is what you mean by keeping it the same high standard? . . . Just for white people? . . . And that was largely through your interest in your own property?"

Yes, yes, yes, Monet answered to all of the above. And yes, he cared deeply about the value of his property. So did most of the people on Garland Avenue or the streets south of Mack Avenue, between Cadillac and St. Claire, boundaries for the Waterworks Improvement Association. Many did not even own the homes they lived in. But that did nothing to dissolve the differences between them and Ossian Sweet. They were people for whom Vienna and Paris belonged to their parents' century. It mattered little that Sweet was a physician, had traveled extensively. So what if they pronounced Goethe as if it were two words, "go-the" and he spoke correctly with a German accent? That he continued his family's tradition of dining with a freshly starched white tablecloth at each meal? Culture and accomplishment mattered less than race in Detroit during the summer of 1925.

On day six of the trial, the defense got a boost when Dwight Hubbard took the stand. Wednesday, November 11, would be a short day because the court recessed after lunch to observe Armistice Day events. But it would be an important day. Hubbard was seventeen years old and lived two blocks away from the Sweets, on Goethe near Hurlbut. Toms was asking him what he saw while he was waiting to get picked up for work around eight o'clock on the evening of September 9. Hubbard fumbled his lines when he blurted there were "a great number of people and the officers—I won't say a great number—there were a large—there were a few people there and the officers."

Darrow brightened, then snapped, "Now, just a minute. Let's have that."

Toms, however, had the floor. He ignored Darrow and commanded Hubbard to continue. "There were a few people there," the boy said, "and the officers were keeping them moving; suddenly there was a volley of shots."

Darrow thought he could guess what just took place. He was willing to risk making an assumption that Lieutenant Johnson had met with Hubbard and that the teen erred by forgetting his instructions, telling the truth when he said "a great many" instead of "a few people." When Darrow asked if this is what happened, Hubbard responded, "Yes, sir." Darrow sat down abruptly, and the state made no attempt to rebut.

No matter how carefully Toms prepared his case, another admission of police coaching ran counter to his work and the state's credibility.

A loud crash, a rock falling to the floor, shattered the court's decorum during Alfred Andrew's testimony on Thursday, November 12. No doubt the assistant prosecutor, Edward Kennedy, was mortified and probably wished he had not accidentally dropped it, demonstrating for the jury the crash of sounds made by one of the rocks hitting the Sweets' home. The state introduced the stones into evidence to show how few the number police retrieved from the property, not to startle the jury with the terrifying sounds that reverberated through the home while the defendants ran for protective cover.

Darrow pointed to the tables holding the collection of rocks, stones, and pebbles. He asked Andrew to select the one he thought might have caused the sounds of marbles or gravel dropping onto the front porch that were heard right before the shooting.

A fter several days of testimony the court had heard from more than fifty witnesses. It was Friday morning, November 13, and Toms was nearly done, confident that the people had built a solid foundation, enough for a conviction of conspiracy—the simultaneous spray of bullets; Breiner's death; pedestrians who were walking, not gathering, on the streets; and ample police presence. Now Toms would use this day, his last, to harden the image, including malice aforethought for the jury.

Thirteen people would testify that Friday. The first two witnesses lived in Ray Dove's house. One of them witnessed Breiner's death. A third was going to the grocery store, which required him to pass through the eye of any gathering that might have been storming the street. The fourth was the highest-ranking officer that night, James Sprott, deputy superintendent of the Detroit Police Department, who said that he, not Inspector Schuknecht, assigned traffic cops. He testified that the scene was so ordinary that he left after no more than a twenty-minute visit.

The next two witnesses, Walter Doran and Ernest Stanke, were plainclothes policemen. They told the court how they sat in a car parked for four hours on Garland and Charlevoix, at the southeast corner, and saw nothing disturbing on the afternoon of September 9. While it was still light outside, around four o'clock, Stanke was reassigned to the roof of the apartment building abutting Charlevoix, facing the Sweets. From the roof he could observe the intersection and Ossian Sweet's home. Ray Schaldenbrand, another plainclothes officer, followed him. They stood sentry. Four hours later they heard shots explode in the air. They described for the jurors how they dropped to their bellies, lifted their heads up, and stretched to see, over a fourteen-inch protective ledge, while the instantaneous flashes of fire came from windows in the Sweet home.

Next came Inspector Bert McPherson, of the "Black Hand Squad"—a special detail assigned to monitor blacks and Italians. McPherson introduced himself to Gladys and Ossian Sweet about noon on the day they moved in, telling them he was there for "the purpose of giving protection if they needed it." If anything looked suspicious, he encouraged Sweet to contact him.

At this point Darrow asked for a clarification. He wanted to make sure the conversation between McPherson and Sweet did not apply to the other occupants of the house, relatives and employees who were helping the Sweets move. Prosecutor Kennedy, who was examining this witness, wanted to create a different impression. For the state's charge of conspiracy, it was important to establish that everybody in the home was aware of McPherson's offer. That would indicate a conspiracy.

Darrow objected.

Judge Murphy sustained his objection.

Moll didn't like the judge's ruling. Actually, he was incredulous. "[T]here is some question as to the correctness of that statement," he blurted.

> I disagree with it. I think we can produce some law to the contrary . . .
> That is where there is a conspiracy on foot, which we claim here, that testimony in the way of declarations during the course of that conspiracy are admissible against all the defendants.

Murphy did not agree. "At this time, I do not believe you have established the proof of that."

"Of the conspiracy?" Moll asked.

"Yes," replied the judge.

"Our whole proof has been directed to that," Moll said. The state reasoned that if all the defendants heard the same offer of help, no one of them could be exempted, could say he was ignorant and therefore not a party to the subsequent events, including murder. But at this time Murphy did not want to discuss the ramifications of Moll's re-marks, and he told the prosecution that he would allow the witness to testify only about the conversation with Dr. Sweet.

When Murphy declined Moll's request, saying, "I will hear you later on that," he stunned the prosecutor and silenced the courtroom. Moll's objection went to the heart of the case, what was at stake in the conspiracy charge, what was implicit in malice aforethought.

Toms tried not to betray his concern. He continued examining wit-nesses despite Judge Murphy's ruling. On this day, which was sup-posed to be the prosecution's last, Toms wanted to keep momentum moving. He called next Riley Burton, a policeman, who had been sta-tioned in the alley behind the house most of the day. Burton would de-scribe men who carried parcels—weapons—into the house.

Burton testified that at about six-thirty on the evening of the shooting, he saw three men arrive in a Buick coupe. They parked in the garage. A Ford sedan with two passengers followed. One passenger got out of the Ford. He carried a bundle, about three and a half feet long and six inches around, wrapped in newspaper. The other two packages were valises of some sort. The men went into the house, where they remained for the rest of the evening. About eight o'clock Patrolman Gill relieved Burton.

The last witness to be called that day was Lieutenant William John-son. His many roles made him a logical choice to conclude the people's case. He was a fifteen-year veteran and had been on the homicide squad for more than two years. Along with Edward Kennedy, he had interro-gated the defendants after they reached the police station. He visited the Sweet home on the day following their arrest. He told of finding rocks, spent cartridges, and bullet holes in Dove's porch. He said he found no broken windows in Sweet's home. He also identified seventy-five cartridges, two keys, and a pair of dice belonging to Ossian Sweet, which he found in a cuspidor at police headquarters. Johnson was in charge of the evidence for this case and was the officer who met with many if not all of the witnesses prior to their appearances in court. But most important of all, he had examined the guns and rifles in police custody and he knew how to tell "whether a gun had been fired or not."

Toms wanted Johnson to describe the weapons, to create the image of numerous guns and rifles, ten in all, in the jury's mind. He invited Johnson to step down from the witness chair and examine the exhibits, starting with a double-barreled shotgun. The right barrel had been fired, Johnson said. So far so good for the prosecution. Toms went on to identify each weapon, whether it was in the condition in which Johnson first saw it, and whether it had been fired. But Judge Murphy's impatience revealed itself when he asked if it was not possible to save some time and arrive at an agreement on this matter. Toms was in the middle of clicking off exhibit forty-one when Murphy renewed the request. "Can't you agree upon the fact that they have been fired or not?"

Darrow happily agreed to anything removing guns from the jury's view. Just then Johnson identified a gun that had been fired "lately." Darrow perked up and asked when, and Johnson replied, "Before it got into our possession, just shortly before it came into our possession."

"Can't you speak more definitely. You mean it has been fired at some time?" Darrow persisted.

"Yes, it has been fired, some time," Johnson said.

"That is all you mean by that, isn't it?" Darrow asked, but he was out-of-turn, for Toms had not yet released the witness for cross-examination.

"Well you cannot tell exactly the date it was fired, or give the number of days ago that it was fired," Johnson answered.

"Or the weeks or months ago?" asked Darrow.

"No, you cannot do that," Johnson told the court.

Judge Murphy then intervened to ask the prosecution: "There is no one who could tell, is there Mr. Toms?"

"Not that I know of," said the prosecutor. He had not yet realized where Murphy was heading. But in an instant, Darrow expedited the obvious when he moved to exclude all evidence related to when the guns were fired. Murphy concluded that Johnson's testimony was too speculative and ordered it struck from the record. "I will instruct the jury to gather no inference from it unfavorable to the accused," he said.

Stunned, the prosecutors leaped to their feet to object. A shouting match ensued, restrained only by the confines of courtroom protocol.

The *Detroit News* described the prosecution as completely "unprepared" for Judge Murphy's ruling. Moll jumped from his chair, saying that it was a question for the jury. Hays responded vigorously, arguing that Johnson's testimony was too speculative to be submitted to the jury.

Murphy then dismissed the jury while lawyers argued, for two hours, about what evidence could be introduced. Hays announced that "nothing can be further added to the inference from the fact that these guns were fired some time in the last six months." Murphy wound down the dispute and chastised Toms.

> There was a very strong inference that could be gathered by the jury, from the questions asked by Mr. Toms, and the answers taken, that the guns were recently fired. I do not think I ought to let it go in. That was my opinion before the objection was raised. The defendants here are charged with murder. It suggests an inference that may be very prejudicial to some of them, and on the most delicate and flimsy kind of proof.

Straining to maintain fairness in an emotionally charged court involving race and the future of segregated housing in Detroit, Murphy concluded that a murder trial required evidence exceeding vague and speculative considerations. He ruled that all the jury needed to know was that guns were usually tested before going to market. This particular set could have been fired in the last day, month, or year. Or any one of them could have been fired that night. There was no way to determine.

When the jury was brought back, Darrow finished his cross-examination of Lieutenant Johnson. After the lieutenant left the courtroom, it was reported, he changed into a dry shirt and collar.

CHAPTER 14

His Home Is His Castle

It was dark when court adjourned on Friday evening, and Hays and Darrow returned to their hotel, the Book-Cadillac, with Nelson and Friedman. Later Walter White would join them for a dinner meeting to work on strategy. The next day the defense would probably open its case.

Before White caught up with them, he wanted to return to his room at the Statler Hotel and write a long letter to James Weldon Johnson. News of the day, of the week, was good. Witnesses contradicted one another, teenagers introduced new facts about throwing stones, and the judge ruled there was no way to determine which guns were used on September 9. The "strong link in the prosecution's chain has popped," White told Johnson.

They have already admitted that they cannot prove which ones of the defendants fired and which ones did not fire; nor can they in any manner prove which finger pulled the trigger which caused Breiner's death.

Exhilarated and overly confident, White believed that the state's case had come apart over the last three days.

With this in mind, White told Johnson that Darrow and Hays would ask Judge Murphy to dismiss the case. White thought there was a good chance the judge might direct the jury to acquit the defendants. Even if Murphy denied the motion to dismiss, White believed there was considerable educational benefit to teaching the public about how tyranny, mobs, and violence, often in collusion with the police, had become extralegal mechanisms enforcing residential segregation. An optimist, White believed the publicity would give "the trial its greatest ultimate value."

After dinner, and with much work to do that night, White and Hays went to Hays's suite, where they discussed details about Ossian and Gladys Sweet. They reviewed the migration that resulted in expanding Detroit's black community, doubling it from forty thousand in 1920 to eighty thousand people just five years later, in 1925. White briefed Hays about lynching, filling him in on details he had acquired from his years in the field. They evaluated the state's testimony, which the defense would have to rebut to create reasonable doubt. Failing that, the defendants might spend the rest of their lives in jail.

When court resumed for its half-day Saturday schedule, as he had announced he would, Toms rested the state's case.

Arthur Garfield Hays, whom the press sometimes identified as "the lawyer from New York City," then summarized his understanding of the state's case: there were eleven people in the house; there were arms in the house; there was shooting and some of it came from the house. But, he emphasized, none of these facts proved the prosecution's charge that there was "a conspiracy on the part of the defendants to commit the murder of Breiner." Hays added:

> Every condition in the house was consistent with a lawful purpose. There were no lights because the people in the house feared they

would be killed from outside. There was no furniture because they had not moved into the house. There was food cooking on the kitchen stove because every man must eat, and because none of them could have gone outside the house to obtain food.

This whole case stands or falls with the proof or failure to prove a conspiracy to commit murder.

It was, he said, the "old principle of a man's right to protect his home as his castle."

When Darrow spoke, he minimized the question about whether "the Negroes had fired too quickly" because, he said, the prosecution failed to meet the burden of proving conspiracy or murder beyond a reasonable doubt.

If the prosecution desires to prove conspiracy against one man, it must submit evidence directly against that one man. So far in this trial, there has been no evidence against any one man of the 11 charged.

Only one bullet killed Breiner. Who fired that bullet? The man who fired the shot can only be guilty of manslaughter, but who was that one man? Let the prosecution pick him out.

For the next two hours the attorneys argued. Toms opposed the motion, saying there was a "unity of purpose" among the defendants. It was not possible, he said, to get a confession from them. "We will never have testimony as to the exact words of the conspirators except from the lips of the conspirators themselves." But that was not as important as the death of Leon Breiner. There was, he said, a "mutual meeting of minds, a coincidental thinking of the same things . . . We can hardly believe the words of any man when he is telling us what is in his mind, but we can fully trust his actions later will accurately interpret his mentally made plans."

Toms described what he considered damaging circumstances—the absence of furniture, plenty of food, and weapons with abundant ammunition.

Murphy responded with tough questions. "What evidence other than a deduction has been submitted in this case as to conspiracy?" he asked. Were the defendants entitled to protect their property, to possess arms?

"Certainly," replied the prosecutor.

"Excluding the shooting, what evidence is there that these defendants were there for any unlawful purpose?" the judge asked. Leaning toward Toms he said, "If there is no evidence of conspiracy there is no other theory upon which these defendants could be held?" Again he focused on Toms. "Do you believe Dr. Sweet had the right to have friends there to safeguard his property? That he had the right to keep arms for the same purpose?"

"People might have gathered for the purpose of protecting property and they might have fired arms for that purpose," Toms began, "but when they shot without sufficient provocation any agreement ceased to be lawful and instantly became unlawful." Toms was groping. "If Breiner had not been killed, there would have been no proof of a conspiracy."

Murphy tried to frame exactly what was meant by conspiracy, who could be included under the umbrella, what knowledge made one complicit. "Excluding the shooting, what evidence is there that these defendants were there for unlawful purpose," Murphy asked. "Was careless shooting the only unlawful act?"

"Not careless shooting," the prosecutor replied. It was "unjustifiable."

Noon approached, the time for quitting on a Saturday. Before the judge called to recess until Monday, Hays moved for a dismissal of all charges for all eleven defendants. The defense's motion requesting a directed verdict to acquit the eleven defendants was expected. But discussing at length what constituted a conspiracy had delayed everything. His Honor was already mindful about how long the case was taking, and wanted it to be finished before next week. This clarification jeopardized that likelihood.

Murphy was fastidious and methodical, and this case, as he had earlier predicted, would be important, too important to rush. When he adjourned court thirty minutes earlier than need be on that Saturday, he promised to have a decision on Monday about the defense motion to dismiss the case.

The *Detroit News* considered it newsworthy that the defendants were smiling when they left court that noon. But the *Free Press* reported the facts more precisely when it trumpeted SWEET MURDER CASE NOW UP TO JUDGE MURPHY.

Serious spectators hardly gave a three-inch snowfall a second thought as they waded through fresh mounds on their way to Recorder's Court Monday morning, November 16. Whether they expected justice to be done or undone, they stood shoulder to shoulder, breathing the smell of damp wool while dirty puddles spread from their rubber boots across the marble floor. They had come to hear what Judge Murphy would say about the defense request to instruct the jury to return a verdict of not guilty.

Before Murphy announced his decision, Toms wanted to argue why the judge ought to deny the defense's motion to dismiss. Otherwise, he said, "It means that the people of this city, both colored and white, are notified that it is entirely lawful for one or two hundred of them to gather in a house; to provide weapons in a sufficient number to arm them all; to fire volleys from the house and kill one or two dozen citizens on their own doorsteps under the pretext that they believe themselves endangered."

Toms usually comported himself seriously; some might say he was wooden. Cartoonists liked to exaggerate his long neck and shade his nose into a beak, giving him the appearance of a young bird. He thought this trial would be shorter, less frustrating. The many objections leading to conferences at the bench and to recesses lasting up to two hours seemed costly, denying Toms good publicity to eventually clothe him in a judge's robe. Now he suddenly attempted flamboyance and dropped the obsequious tone he had earlier adopted to avoid open conflict with Darrow. His sarcasm rivaled his opponent's when he outlined how to "kill another with impunity." Make sure, he said, that

- all the shooting is done from a place where the persons are lawfully entitled to be;
- that several of the weapons used are of the same caliber so that any bullets found in the bodies of citizens killed can not be traced to a particular weapon;
- Immediately after the shooting conceal or simply lay down all weapons so that no particular weapon can be traced to the hands of any particular occupant;
- Remain silent when arrested.

He sobered when he predicted that a dismissal would boomerang. "Mutual respect for the law and for the rights of others is the only solution of race hatred," he said. "[T]he decision asked by the defense especially in the form of a directed verdict

> must inevitably produce one result in the future, whether the person killed be black or white—that under the circumstances in this case, one racial group will know that it can literally get away with murder, and the other group will know *what* the law condones and permits. How can there possibly be any respect for law in either group under such an intolerable situation?

Murphy didn't need Toms to remind him of what he knew already. This case shone as bright a light on white man's justice as it did on the eleven defendants accused of murder. There was hardly a decision about introducing evidence or filing motions that did not have substantial repercussions and raise the stakes. How to handle Gladys was among them. At the time of the shooting she was in the kitchen. Could the defendants have carried on their activities without her help cooking dinner for them? Did this amount to aiding and abetting? Nobody claimed she was under duress, that her husband wielded extreme influence, that she was there for a reason other than her own choosing. And while there were ten weapons, everybody surmised that she did not use one. How, then, did she figure into the conspiracy? If she did not, did evidence point to holding anybody else?

Detroit did not even have a cell block for women prisoners when she was taken into custody. Prosecuting her carried a risk. She was a vibrant twenty-three-year-old mother who was viewed as a victim and could easily become a martyr. Hays knew this when he built his request to dismiss the case around Gladys. He tried to expand the logic to incorporate all the defendants, saying they were no more guilty than she. But when the state offered to selectively exempt defendants from the conspiracy charge, with Gladys the primary choice, she objected vigorously, saying, "If these men go to jail I want to go too." They were a group and unless they were all dismissed, they would all be tried. Toms agreed to drop the charges against her, but the defense believed her presence would be a softening "influence on the jury."

Murphy denied the motion to direct the jury toward a verdict of not guilty. Even if there were precedents to do so, he didn't want to fasten the panel. To restrain the jury, to bind them at this point in the proceedings would limit the broadest impact. Murphy told a friend that "the question of how to secure a fair trial for the eleven colored defendants is constantly on my mind. Above all things, I want them to know they are in a court where the true ideal of justice is constantly sought . . . I want the defendants to know that true justice does not recognize color."

As the judge said each time he declined a defense attorney's motion, they could renew it later. But the legal process must reveal itself naturally, maturely in the hands of the twelve jurors, all white men in this instance, who were chosen to personify a democratic nation's ideal of justice under law. Walter White told James Weldon Johnson that the jury's decision—he presumed it would acquit—"will influence public opinion infinitely more than a dismissal of the case by the judge."

The case was now at the halfway mark. The prosecution had put on its best witnesses, and the defense argued that it failed to meet its burden of proving conspiracy. After denying the defense's motion to dismiss the case, the judge was ready to proceed. Darrow and Hays were instructed to put the defendants' story before the jury. On this Monday morning, November 16, Arthur Garfield Hays delivered the opening statement that the defense had earlier postponed.

Hays's and Darrow's courtroom signature was to invoke passionate pleas drawn from humanitarian traditions and custom. Hays began the next hour by discussing Anglo-Saxon law based on a "sacred and ancient right." A "civilized society could not survive without the right of self-defense," he said. He appealed to history, to King George III, to the birth of America, and to the rights of the poorest subject to defend "his cottage."

He engaged the jury with humility and compliments, then he enchanted them with pithy examples from universal rights honored in Western civilization, then he tucked his remarks into this specific case. "We conceive the law to be this—that a man is not justified in shooting merely because he is fearful—but that a man is justified if he has reasonable ground for fear." Delaying the opening address allowed the defense time to research legal precedents, and they uncovered two Michigan decisions, and several from other states, that protected people under assault in their own homes. The defense had ammunition to now show previous favorable decisions, such as the nineteenth-century Michigan case *Pond v. People*, where the court ruled, "A man who is assaulted in his own house need not retreat in order to avoid slaying his assailant."

Hays wanted to establish credibility by assuring the jury that the defense team would not quibble over "facts which are sometimes subject to equivocation and avoidance." But neither would they accept excuses. "[I]t will be our duty and pleasure to show you the facts as they appeared from the inside of that little house on Garland and Charlevoix Avenues—the facts as they appeared to eleven people of the Black Race who had behind them a history . . . worried, distrustful, tortured and apparently trapped."

Having set the stage, Hays introduced the actors, beginning with Dr. Ossian H. Sweet. He asked Sweet to rise, to give the jury a chance to see him on his feet, standing tall, letting air fill his lungs instead of sitting crumpled, huddled on a bench where he had spent the last two weeks against the wall. Twenty-two times that hour Hays would refer to him as "the doctor," hoping to coax the jury into viewing him not as a criminal but a person of merit, achievement, and stature. Hays asked Otis Sweet to stand. Like his mother, Otis Sweet was small-boned, with fine features. He looked trim and stylish in a brown suit. Hays made sure the jury knew that Otis was a dentist. Next to him stood the third brother arrested that night, Henry Sweet, a pudgy-faced Wilberforce student, a college senior. Next Hays wanted the jury to meet Gladys. She stood alongside her husband, looking handsome and poised. She was worldly, a woman of apparent refinement, exactly the kind of person any juror ought to want for his next-door neighbor.

The scene took on the illusion of a series of personal introductions in the presence of hundreds of spectators standing behind the oak rail, or lining the corridors—any place they could catch a phrase or an impression from the trial. Hays then told the jury, "These are four of the defendants, and the first fact in our case of which we shall expect you, Gentlemen, to take notice is that they don't look like murderers."

Indeed, the defense widely believed that the Detroit police force consisted of Southern transplants whose hiring presumed they "would know how to handle a Negro." Hays promised to "prove that a Detroit policeman fired the bullet that killed Breiner." He cited the flat trajectory of the bullet, entering the body about hip level, moving on a horizontal plane. "It could not have come from the upper window in the home of Dr. Ossian H. Sweet, as indicated by the prosecution. The man who fired this shot is from Tennessee."

News of the long-awaited opening address spread well beyond Detroit. The *Detroit Free Press* called Arthur Garfield Hays's remarks a "masterly summing up." The black paper in Omaha, Nebraska, the *Monitor,* reported that he "stunned and electrified" a packed courtroom. And the *Chicago Defender,* which Sweet's relatives in Florida would read only after they closed the drapes, shut the windows, and packed around the dining room table, said, "It is in terms of humanity that Hays pleads."

The defense built a case by presenting witnesses who would tell a story very different from the prosecution's. The crowds were larger than the prosecution claimed, they said, ranging between three hundred and fifteen hundred people who crowded together stretching as far as St. Claire Street, one block east of the intersection. Garland Avenue was closed and incoming traffic diverted to Charlevoix. It was on Charlevoix where Philip Adler, a reporter for the *Detroit News,* saw a menacing group. It looked "more like people who were prepared for something," he later told the court.

Adler was on his way to dinner at a friend's when he happened upon the scene. A reporter's curiosity propelled him to investigate. After parking his car on Bewick near Mack, he elbowed his way between the men and women crowding Garland. He originally called the crowd a "mob" but the prosecution objected. Heading toward the corner, he heard spectators boasting, "We're going to get them out." When he reached the intersection, he spoke to a policeman who told him to mind his own business. In the meantime, pelting sounds carried. These Adler demonstrated by drumming a pencil on the arm of his chair in the rapid, rat-a-tat irregular pattern he had heard that night.

To challenge impressions that the Sweets were preparing for combat, the defense called two of Gladys's friends, interior decorators, who had come to advise them about furnishings. By the time the ladies arrived on Tuesday afternoon, crowds were already amassing. Soon, they estimated, between one hundred and two hundred people swarmed the street. Terrified, the women did not dare to leave the house that night. Wednesday morning, when they finally left, one of them overheard a woman telling the streetcar conductor what was planned for later that day. "A Negro family was here today but they won't be here tomorrow," she said. Later that afternoon, Serena Rochelle telephoned Gladys to tell her that they were all in danger.

Max Lieberman owned the furniture store where Gladys and Ossian shopped on the morning of September 9. He testified that they spent more than $1,100 to purchase a dining room set, a table with matching chairs, and a bedroom suite. His testimony cast doubt on the prosecution's assertion about why their home was empty. Delivery was scheduled for the next day.

Next Alonzo Smith described driving through the neighborhood with two of his nephews. They were heading home, he said, and it was nearly eight o'clock when they approached Garland and Charlevoix Avenues. Because they were black, someone mistakenly presumed they were going to visit the Sweets. Smith described how one of the men jumped onto the car's running board, but his nephew James pretended to have a gun and shouted that he would use it. He heard someone yell, "Here's some niggers, get a brick." When Smith applied the brakes suddenly, the intruder fell off the running board.

Charles Schauffner, his scar still visible from the cuts he endured from the mob, took the stand to talk about what he saw when he got to the intersection shortly after the defendants were arrested. An assailant attacked his moving car, broke the window glass, screamed, "There goes a Negro, catch him. Stop him!"

Prosecutors objected to Schauffner, who arrived on the scene later.

Darrow argued that his testimony would prove that racial hatred motivated the crowd. Murphy allowed Schauffner to testify, saying he helped establish an understanding of "the temper and character" of the crowd.

Dr. E. A. Carter, Ossian's colleague and fraternity brother, testified about bringing the Sweets a set of new dishes the night they moved. Months before, he had witnessed a conversation about Dr. Sweet's intentions to buy a house. Carter was a character witness able to speak about Sweet's fear after the call from Mrs. Smith, the former owner, informing him about the threats she received prior to the move.

When Hays asked Carter to describe a conversation he had had with Sweet about Dr. Turner, the doctor whom a mob moved out of his home in June, Toms renewed his objections. He said it was irrelevant to the conspiracy and murder charges. The defense argued that his testimony bore on Ossian Sweet's state of mind. The judge agreed and instructed the jury to consider not whether it was accurate but what it revealed about Sweet's point of view and how it shaped his expectations.

Sweet's defense could only benefit from mood-setting descriptions permitting Darrow to develop a defense based on psychology. Later it would be described as the psychology of fear. Darrow wanted the jury to hear testimony from witnesses who had survived violent crowds, who had been victimized by mobs, who had suffered because the police failed to protect them. The defense wanted the jury to hear about police who melded into the illegal activities they were hired to stop. After another lengthy conversation during which the jury was dismissed, Judge Murphy decided that Carter could describe his conversation with Ossian Sweet about how Dr. Turner's assailants falsely presented themselves as the mayor's representatives, then forced him to sign a deed at gunpoint before loading his furniture onto a moving van.

Carter described another factor influencing Sweet. It was the doctor's confidence in the neighborhood. While it now seemed misplaced, it had encouraged him to wait out the summer, to give the neighbors a chance to calm their fears before he and Gladys moved. It was, Carter said, Sweet's belief "that the white people in that neighborhood were of such a nature they would do no bodily harm." It was relevant that when Sweet asked Mrs. Smith about the Klan, she said no Klansmen lived on these streets. The neighbors were foreign. Or their parents were. Mrs. Smith never mentioned the Waterworks Improvement Association because it did not exist, didn't come into being until after the Sweets bought their house.

By the second day Darrow was elaborating his defense based on the psychology of fear. "[W]hat we learn as children, we remember—it gets fastened in the mind." Darrow argued. "The minds of the defendants were led to reasonably believe that great danger confronted them."

"Is everything this man saw as a child a justification for a crime twenty-five years later?" snarled Toms.

"Yes," replied Hays. "I might properly bring in the incidents his grandfather had told to him."

Ossian Sweet gained weight during his two months in prison. By the third week of the trial, he looked middle-aged. His thirty-year-old frame sagged. Shirt collars pinched at the neck, and a mustache looked like an afterthought more than a stylish touch to his appearance. What could he have thought about what he saw going on around him? While newspapermen pushed their way into the courtroom each day, his and Gladys's picture brightened the front page of the nation's major black weeklies, and the NAACP lavished praise. He remarked that he would never have moved into that house, he would not have accepted it as a gift, had he foreseen the disaster that lay ahead. However ambitious his earlier aspirations, performing on this public stage, moving from private obscurity to a national arena as a symbol of black oppression, was not among them.

Dr. Sweet took the stand on Wednesday, the day the defense had initially promised to finish. While Sweet was sworn in Darrow walked toward him slowly, assuming his trademark slouch. Darrow intuitively focused his attention on Sweet so intently that it almost seemed as if they were alone. The courtroom was still. Prosecutors who routinely interrupted Darrow's dramatic flourishes sat riveted. For the longest time Darrow just stood in front of Sweet, looking at him, before he spoke in a hushed tone.

"You are a Negro?" Darrow asked.

Whatever other witnesses had said, either to celebrate or to indict Sweet, his testimony brought the trial into a new phase. He spoke to the jury about himself and his ambition. He dwelt on images of Bartow, Florida, memories of local lynchings, his respect for the Wilberforce intelligentsia, his awe for the vanguard of Howard's medical school. The most dramatic exchanges would not unfold under the friendly interrogation of defense attorneys, but under the unrelenting staccato of Toms's swift cross-examination. When Sweet shot back answers, as a *Detroit Free Press* reporter said, he "dramatized the fear."

Thirty Years of Lynching, the NAACP's publication that kept alive the names of murder victims of the lawless, had an exclusive and a small distribution after it was released. Exhaustive research made it a jewel. By sending this pamphlet to Hays to read for background, the NAACP affirmed its belief that just knowing the prevalence of lynching could justify Sweet's fear of white mobs. What a surprise it must have been to see Robert Toms hold a copy of *Thirty Years of Lynching* when he began to cross-examine Ossian Sweet.

Was Sweet aware, Toms asked, that the last lynching in Michigan took place in 1891? Or that Michigan had had only four lynchings? "Did those facts tend to reduce your fear?" he asked.

"Not at all," Sweet answered briskly.

"Did you know lynchings in the United States were decreasing and decreasing fast?"

"That was true last year, but it is not this year."

"Do you know there has been a steady decrease over each four-year period, and that the last figures show a decrease of fifty-four percent?"

"Those things made me hopeful for the future," Sweet shot back, "but not confident for the present, for I know that many people from the south were moving to Detroit."

Sweet's testimony was bold and dramatic, and he refused to fawn or flinch. Toms persisted but Sweet held firm. Stillness settled in the court, while his baritone voice sounded across the room, giving pitch to his life, bouncing from the back wall as clearly as it carried to the judge sitting to his right.

Did Sweet know that of more than three thousand people lynched, almost all of them, more than ninety-nine percent, had been accused of criminal conduct?

Sweet said he did, but added confidently that he "knew what the South terms criminal conduct." Sweet reeled off the massacre of share-croppers in Elaine, Arkansas. He told about the murder of Dr. Jackson in the 1921 Tulsa riot; of the brothers Johnson, a doctor and a dentist who were shot in Phillips, Arkansas. He described the South Carolina sheriff who laughed while he condoned one hanging and explained, "The boys had a little lynching because they were blood thirsty."

Then he turned to his own plight. About eight o'clock on the night of September 9, while he was playing cards with friends in the dining room of his house, something hit the outside wall. He continued: "Someone went to the window and looked out. Then I remember this remark, 'The people, the people—we've got to get out of here; something's going to happen pretty soon.'"

Looking for Gladys, he went to the kitchen. He opened a side door. "I could see people but they couldn't see me. Then I heard someone say, 'Go to the front and raise hell; I'm going to the back.'" He locked the side door, turned off the bright lights in the kitchen, and immediately checked other doors.

Sweet said he wasn't armed. But before going upstairs, he took a gun from the closet. "Stones kept coming against the house," he recalled.

The intervals became shorter. After fifteen or twenty minutes, a stone crashed through the glass and some of it hit me. I got excited. It was pandemonium. Everybody ran from room to room. I made a dozen trips up and down the stairs. It was a general uproar.

Then I heard someone say, "Someone is coming. Don't open the door." I went to the door myself. It was my brother Otis, and William Davis. I heard people in the mob say, "They're niggers, get them."

As he opened the door to let them in, Sweet's eyes swept Garland Avenue. He saw a mob, and it surged ten, maybe fifteen feet forward. Davis saw a "human sea." Meanwhile the "stones were getting thicker and coming faster." Glass crackled. "By this time it seemed to me stones were hitting the house on all sides, mostly the roof," he said.

When I opened the door, I realized in a way that I was facing that same mob that had hounded my people through its entire history. I realized my back was against the wall and I was filled with a peculiar type of fear—the fear of one who knows the history of my race.

Schuknecht knocked on the door and asked, "What in the Hell are you shooting at?"

"They are destroying my home and my life is in imminent danger." Before Schuknecht left, Sweet took him upstairs to show him the window shattered by stones. The inspector looked and departed. Sweet closed the door behind him, but almost immediately the police returned to arrest the occupants. Ossian Sweet testified that he did not shoot. Toms conceded that the weapon Sweet was holding when they arrested him had never been fired, which the state later determined.

Toms, nonetheless, attacked Sweet's character, asking him to tell the jury, in his own words, why he lied about retiring to an upstairs bedroom to quiet his nerves and relieve his stress, why he denied having weapons in his house, why he later tossed bullets into the cuspidor at police headquarters.

"Fear made me say things that night . . . I thought if I told the truth it would be misinterpreted," Sweet explained. "It is generally known that Negroes are beaten up at police headquarters."

Toms asked about Breiner: "You admit of course, that Leon Breiner was killed by a bullet fired from your house."

"No, I don't."

"Why did you go upstairs and lie down on the bed?"

"To quiet my nerves and because from that point I had a clear view of the street. The bed is near the window."

"You did not take the revolver with you to quiet your nerves?"

"No, I did not."

"You were convinced that shots were not fired across Garland Avenue from your home?"

"I am."

"What is your theory of the bullet holes across the street."

Hays objected and Murphy sustained it.

Sweet then told the court how officials tried to intimidate the defendants. Lieutenant Johnson asked him "why did he move into a white neighborhood where he was not wanted?" Later there was a mock trial. Sweet described how Prosecutor Kennedy, Lieutenant Johnson, and a third officer

> [c]ame to the jail, handcuffed us, brought us out under the tunnel, declaring that we were going to our trial. He carried us to some strange room where there was a piano, and asked us if we wanted to verify whatever we had said the night of our arrest.
>
> I soon realized that we were being hoaxed and I refused to answer any questions, and advised the others not to answer any. When the three realized that we were not to be made fools, they carried us back to jail.

For the better part of two days, Sweet withstood Toms's pounding, and his testimony revealed how terror had spread through the house.

Just repeating the phrase "a human sea" from the witness stand was enough to send his friend, the narcotics agent Davis, shrinking back into his chair, covering his face with his hands. Observers thought it must have invoked memories for Ossian, too, because his body tightened and he looked to Gladys when describing how they were locked in the house, surrounded by strangers, with full knowledge of police complicity in racial conflict that summer.

The *Detroit Free Press* commended Toms for not trying to trip Sweet into "making absurd statements." But it also praised Sweet for maintaining his composure. Detroit's most widely read newspaper described him as "well educated and an astute student of the race problem." The general consensus was that he made "a good witness for himself."

Sweet's performance "swung public opinion," White told Johnson. In a detailed letter on the day Sweet testified, White described how Ossian "stood up under grilling examination . . . with restraint and simplicity." The local press, he said, has been turned around and their reports were "full and fair."

The information was welcome. Johnson had been uneasy because New York's papers were not covering the event, and he urged White to place something in the *New York World.* In the meantime Johnson advised him that fund-raising was behind schedule and they needed to distribute press releases. He would draft templates based on White's letter, which would make it easier for overworked editors to bang out copy. "No class of persons deserve more credit for the nation-wide response to the NAACP appeal for sinews of war than colored editors," he wrote, making sure to compliment all parties whose work mattered dearly.

White's description of Sweet's performance, his speaking with "restraint and simplicity," his holding "the courtroom breathless" appeared verbatim in the press release. Not a word was changed when the NAACP distributed it under the headline, PERSECUTION OF THE NEGRO RACE.

CHAPTER 15

A Reasonable Man?

J udge Murphy wanted the jury to have the case no later than the Wednesday before Thanksgiving. That would compact into the remaining week the rest of the defense testimony, plus any witnesses for recall, as well as the rebuttal for those who had been recalled, the closing statements, plus his own charge to the jurors. Despite the blustery predictions of a speedy decision with which the trial began, it had already been one week since Hays had promised to prove that a police officer killed Breiner. It now seemed to slow down again when the defense introduced more exhibits bearing on the trajectory of the lethal bullet. Murphy fidgeted and directed the lawyers to show all outstanding proof about the most important questions remaining.

The police could not locate the bullet that killed Breiner. Even had they found it, matching bullets to weapons in 1925 was crude at best, still more empirical than scientific, and based on eyeballing material evidence. But Toms believed he could affix blame for Breiner's death by showing how the bullet had come from an upper window of Sweet's house. Toward this end, Toms rigged up a primitive experiment and asked Lieutenant Johnson to witness the results, which he now described for the jury.

The experiment consisted of Toms placing an ordinary pencil in a bullet hole in the Getke house, on the north side of Sweet's. Toms believed the resulting slant of the pencil would show the direction from which the bullet came. In this instance, it pointed toward the "small upper window at the rear of the Sweet house." Proof enough, Toms thought, of the sight line of the lethal bullet.

The experiment was insufficient from the defense's point of view. No matter where the pencil pointed from the Getke house, Breiner was not felled there. He had been standing on a porch, fifty feet away, across the street. The medical examiner earlier testified that the trajectory of the bullet was horizontal, meaning a straight path through Breiner's body. Either the bullet was fired from street level or Breiner was leaning down to pick something off the floor or tie his shoes when he was struck. None of the witnesses had described the dead man leaning over.

"Does a bullet fired at an angle always take a diagonal course in the object it strikes," Hays asked Johnson, knowing where Patrolman Gill stood.

"Always," Johnson said emphatically.

With the answer that he wanted, Hays sat down with a smile.

Near the end of the trial prosecutors called Henry Sweet, Ossian's brother, to testify based on a statement he had given at police headquarters the night he was arrested. Objections immediately spewed from the defense attorneys.

The defense had made a strategic decision to try all eleven defendants in one trial. The strategy entailed grave risk if the testimony of one defendant could be used against the other defendants.

Judge Murphy recessed for thirty minutes to consider what to do about Henry Sweet's statement. When the judge returned, he told the jury to consider only those parts of the testimony pertaining to Henry Sweet's own actions and not to anything about anybody else.

In the statement that the prosecution asked to be read into testimony, Henry Sweet described sitting on the veranda at 2905 Garland Avenue early in the day, seeing police in front of the house. Prior to the shooting he had been in the kitchen. When he heard terrifying noises, he went upstairs for his rifle, a .38 caliber Winchester. Then he went to the front window, from which he could see stones sailing toward them.

> I looked out and saw the crowd across the street throwing stones. I tried to protect myself. I fired the rifle in the air the first time. The second time I fired at the crowd standing between the store and the first house.

Coming at the end of the trial when so much of the testimony ran together like the foamy backwash of waves returning to sea, Henry Sweet's confession stood out boldly. The prosecution aimed to keep it alive, to plant the details in the jury's mind, and the next day Moll linked Henry's shots to Breiner's death by saying perhaps the horizontal trajectory of the bullet occurred because the dead man was not standing "exactly perpendicular" to the ground.

To speed things up before Thanksgiving, Murphy extended court on Tuesday evening. It would be a long day, but Murphy insisted it would move along with dispatched precision, beginning with Moll's summation, followed by Hays's, then Darrow's. On Wednesday Robert Toms would finish. Murphy scheduled time slots, and after the lawyers concluded on Wednesday, he would take another hour to instruct the jury. The rest of the day would be theirs for deliberations. The judge presumed they could finish in a couple of hours and be home for the holiday. A nice plan.

The press termed Moll's two-and-one-half-hour summation "masterful." He rebuked the defendants, saying they should "repent in leisure for a crime of haste, preconceived, deliberate and uncalled for." The theory of fear was nothing more than a "smoke-screen advanced by the defense to obscure the facts," he said, "bunk," "poppycock." Rather than a menacing threat, Moll termed the crowd "neighborly." It was the defendants who were the cold-blooded murderers. They had not earned, did not deserve what he derided as the protection of the "fear complex."

It was apparent just how deeply Darrow had disturbed Moll when he scoffed, "Mr. Darrow is going to make his own witnesses liars when he tells of that crowd. I don't know how long he is going to talk—two hours, maybe; maybe two days. He is going to tell you about that howling, bloodthirsty crowd—"

With masterful timing, Darrow interjected, "Just neighborly." Laughter erupted in the packed courtroom; the judge's reprimand followed.

Moll did not pause to respond to Darrow's interruption. He moved ahead to describe the events of September 9 as unnecessary, unprovoked, and premeditated. Just look at the arsenal, he said. He denied that there was trespassing. Nobody attempted to invade the house, there was "nothing overt in the acts of the group outside." After Moll finished, the court recessed for lunch.

It was two o'clock when Hays stood up to speak. He moved toward the jury box. Hays looked once more at Mr. Pokerface but still glimpsed no response. In a relatively short talk, Hays criticized the police for failing to catalogue Patrolman Gill's weapon, the only gun the department admitted had been fired. By not doing so, the prosecution could not prove that the policeman from Tennessee fired only one shot. Hays reminded the jury of the Anglo-Saxon principle that "a man's home is his castle"; the famous assertion in the Declaration of Independence that "all men are created equal"; the Second Amendment's guarantee of the "right to bear arms"; the protection of using arms for "self-defense" in the Michigan constitution. He even unfurled the Emancipation Proclamation, which, he said, abhorred violence, "unless in necessary self-defense." He set his eyes on one of the jurors, Mr. Zann, who had served in France during World War I, and reminded him that when the government wanted soldiers to fight under the American flag, it was not "particular whether they were white or black." Elegant, erudite, and eloquent, he set the stage for Clarence Darrow, the man they really came to hear, the reason extra police were called that day to keep the crowds under control.

M y clients are here charged with murder," whispered Darrow, "but they are really here because they are black." With his hands thrust deep into his pockets, and his shoulders hunched, Darrow courted the jury one last time. He would speak for the rest of that day and part of the next. He wanted the jurors to accept that they all lived in an imperfect world where prejudice infused the soul. But could they also go further, take a giant step and imagine themselves in the dilemma of eleven black defendants?

It is so deep that if we stop to think of it we are ashamed of it, but it is there and we can't help it, and we have got it . . . I don't know how deep it is . . . but I have a right to ask you to overcome it for this case at least and treat these men as though they were white, and I ask no more than that.

Here are eleven people, which is about as many as there are on this jury, on trial for killing a white man . . . Reverse this: Supposing one of you were charged with murder and you had shot and killed somebody, while they were gathered around your home, and the mob had been a black mob and you lived in a black man's land and you had killed a black and you had to be tried by twelve blacks, what would you think about it?

All eyes—those of the press, the prosecutors, his own cocounsel, the spectators standing shoulder to shoulder crushed into the aisles, and Judge Murphy—followed Darrow's words, every gesture with rapt attention. Anticipation grew as he slowly glanced around the entire courtroom, his thumbs now anchored firmly in the armholes of his vest. The prosecutor broke the spell when he moved his chair quite suddenly, perhaps intentionally, making scraping sounds.

Then Darrow boomed. The state's witnesses lied, he said. "I think every one of them lied, perjured themselves over and over and over again to send eleven black people to prison for life." Was it possible one dozen policemen stood on the streets and never asked anyone what he was doing there? Could they really believe Sprott, the deputy superintendent of police, a man with a thirty-year career, when he did not know the elements of a riot? Did he seriously care about the Sweets' safety if he left the intersection after only twenty minutes? If all were so calm, so pacific and neighborly, why had the police deployed four officers during the day? Eight more after three o'clock? Two on the roof? And fill a station house with reserves? "Every policeman there knew that crowd was after Negroes," Darrow charged.

Darrow stopped just short of demonizing the police and the neighbors whose profiles were almost interchangeable with the jurors' in backgrounds, occupations, and, probably, aspirations. He needed to build bridges, not a battlefield, and he humbled himself for the task.

It does not mean that around Garland and Charlevoix, there are living people who are worse than other people picked from the community . . . I would not be afraid to go there to live, you would not need to be afraid to go there to live, but it means that almost instinctive hatred of the whites for anything that approaches social equality is so deep and so abiding in the hearts of most white people that they are willing to perjure themselves in behalf of what they think is their noble, Nordic race.

The picture he was portraying was one in which racial prejudice was a social problem, not an individual or personal failure, neither a sin nor a character flaw. He could influence what they thought but not change what they felt. "Prejudices do not rest on facts; they rest on the ideas that have been taught to us and that began coming to us almost with our mothers' milk, and they stick almost as the color of the skin sticks." Its hold on society meant that only the strongest could do battle, could meet the challenge. Were the jurors ready? "You twelve men are not only holding in your hands the future and the destiny of my eleven clients but to a certain extent [you] are determining the problems of two races."

Careful to avoid blame, absolving each juror of any guilt over his prejudice, Darrow affirmed his belief in the jury. "You are not responsible for prejudices," he said. He asked them to consider what a Christian community would do. It is not likely that Christians would "take a family who had as much right to buy that home as any other person in the community under the law . . . drive them out by force . . . send them to the penitentiary for life."

Before ending, he asked them to imagine themselves "in the position of these eleven defendants." As he had in countless other cases, Darrow asked them to stand in another's place. "Nobody can judge his fellow men in the world unless he does put himself in the other person's place." He cajoled the jurors as he challenged them: "Treat these men as though they were white, and I ask no more than that."

"Darrow's plea was marked by all the tense emotions," said the *Detroit News*, "of the deep pathos which won him his reputation."

The spectators kept a hushed silence, one or two dabbing at their eyes with handkerchiefs at his references to the plight of the black race. When Darrow finished he wiped an eye and sat down amid a hush shattered only as the judge found words and signaled the prosecutor to start his final plea.

Biographers consider Darrow a man with abundant contradictions, and his contemporaries, including Frank Murphy and Josephine Gomon, almost regarded their association with him as ennobling. But his inner passions were hardly invisible. The Evolution Society met at his ten-room apartment weekly in Chicago, crammed into a library spilling with books on every topic imaginable. Now Darrow's entreaties, rich with soaring visions of a world unfettered by the color of one's skin, came from a different view of paradise. His appeal cast the conflict not as eleven blacks versus a neighborhood, a city dominated by whites, but as the universal travail of millions who were fighting for the realization of America's ideals.

Despite the considerable disadvantage of following Darrow, Toms successfully held the jury's attention for three hours. He said he didn't care if Sweet spoke French in Paris, German in Vienna, saw a race riot in Washington, D.C. One man lay dead in Detroit and the rest was all a smokescreen, sophistry, he said. "The trouble with this case is that Darrow doesn't want to look at it as a criminal case, but as a cross section of human emotions. But that's not what we are here for. What an insignificant figure Leon Breiner has been, and yet, we started out to find out who killed him."

While Darrow enlisted the jurors to act as noble warriors battling with an unjustifiable prejudice in an impoverished world, Toms defended the status quo. "It is part of our instinct to herd into groups," he told the jury. "In Hamtramck, we have the Polish group; around this court house are the Italians; out Warren Avenue West the colored people have herded together. We gather with our little groups and we don't want anyone else to come in with us." This was a trial, Toms argued, not "a sociological clinic." "Maybe this is not right, but this court room is just a little spot in this world, and nothing we do here is going to change age-old things."

After lunch on Wednesday, Judge Murphy spoke to the jury. "Under the law, a man's house is his castle," he said. "It is his castle, whether he is white or black, and no man has the right to assail or invade it."

Murphy spoke succinctly for one hour, or at least he boiled down the legal issues as clearly as he could for a jury that might be growing weary after listening to arguments and summaries for nearly two days. Murphy wanted them to now understand that their duties began with a single question: Did the defendants kill Leon Breiner? "If you find that Leon Breiner was killed by the accused, your inquiry is only begun," he said. They must establish intent, circumstance, states of mind, and provocation. "By premeditation is meant a fixed design in the mind of the accused to commit the crime of murder." Without inducing to tedium, Judge Murphy explained what it meant to aid and abet a crime one did not commit; the necessity of presuming innocence until proven guilty; the definition of a mob; the relevance of character. He made it clear that their job as jurors was to determine facts and to accept the law as he described it. What would a reasonable man do if he believed what the defendants believed even if they, the jurors, did not share the beliefs? It was a difficult task, and Murphy explained the differences between first and second-degree murder and manslaughter.

"In your deliberations, try to be reasonable," he implored. "Be tolerant of the other man's viewpoint, try to understand, for in this way you will have the best chance of reaching a verdict." At three-thirty on Wednesday afternoon, he finished. He could have said more, but Murphy wanted to avoid annoyances, irritations, anything that might sabotage good judgment. He knew it was late to be handing a case over to a jury but he hoped they would reach a verdict quickly, perhaps in the hours before Thanksgiving.

After they had listened attentively, watching for the nuanced gestures in a witness, trying to remember what the judge said should be considered and forget what he said should not, it was time, and their turn, to put it all together. The jury left to deliberate.

Throughout the day and evening spectators wandered into and out of the courtroom. Along with the press, family, lawyers for defense, and prosecuting attorneys, the public would keep vigil until a verdict came down. Because Murphy expected people to bring children to court, he stocked his chambers with new toys for their amusement.

It would be nine hours before jurors sent a signal. It would come at 12:30 A.M., long past the bedtime of children who played with the judge's train sets, or even of the teams of attorneys and defendants who had to pinch themselves to stay awake. And then the jury only wanted to ask Murphy to clarify two questions: Did the jury have to return the same verdict for all of the defendants? Should they take into consideration a man's state of mind? To the first he answered no; to the second he advised them that they had to determine the defendants' states of mind, to consider all angles. At ten minutes past two in the morning, he sent them to bed in the dormitory for jurors on the sixth floor. The grayness that envelops Detroit from November to April had set in.

The mood was gloomy the next morning on Thanksgiving Day. More snow, more spectators, and indecision. Ruby Darrow had accepted an invitation to spend the day with friends in Grosse Pointe, but her husband wanted to stay behind, close to the court, downtown. He did not attempt to conceal his exhaustion and spent most of the time sprawled on a couch in the judge's chambers. He took at least one break to phone a local attorney, Thomas Chawke, to discuss a technical legal question. After seeing how long the jury was taking, Hays decided to postpone his departure for Washington, D.C., where his next trial was about to start. And Walter White, who already sent word to his wife that he would be returning home that day, had not budged. The prosecutors also stayed close to the courtroom. Nobody wanted to defer to another when it came time to hear the decision. At four-fifteen in the afternoon, a time that would have approached quitting for the day, the jury asked again to see the judge. Spectators lightened, presuming the moment was near. Not so. The jurors wanted another clarification.

After watching the twelve men climb aboard a bus to take them to a nearby hotel for turkey dinner, Darrow; White; Hays and his wife, Aline; other attorneys; friends with their children; and representatives of the local NAACP went over to the St. Antoine YMCA, where they ate a Thanksgiving dinner with the black community. To sidestep conversation about the impending decision that was now weighing on them, Darrow recited poetry. Arthur Garfield Hays regaled them with stories about his difficulty memorizing Countee Cullen's twelve-line poem "Baltimore." It was the story of a child who, after spending eight months in this border city, only remembered that someone once called him "nigger." Hays had used it masterfully in his closing remarks to the jury. Straining to appear relaxed, they could not conceal the tension that bound them.

Neither Thanksgiving nor bad weather kept Detroit's black citizens from the courthouse. Hundreds meandered in and out all day, some leaving only for rest or sustenance, or when they realized nothing had changed; others lingering for conversation, curiosity, or just to warm themselves before going on to spend time with family. Many came back more than once. The courtroom was still thick with spectators at quarter past eleven that night, when the jurors returned wearing somber expressions and stubbled beards, marking the third attempt to tell the judge that they had not reached an agreement.

Court officers already suspected that the jury was locked in battle. Frank Nolan, the judge's clerk, discovered a heating pipe carrying bits of sound and conversation with high-pitched exclamations. The pipe ran across the jury's room and through the judge's private bathroom before carrying its secrets into the halls. But members of the court could, and did, eavesdrop. They heard shrill protests and ill-tempered racial epithets, even crashing sounds of furniture hitting walls, shattering into piles on the floor. They would later discover that every piece of furniture had been smashed.

It was ill-omened for a consensus. After thirty-two hours of deliberations in a trial lasting nearly one month, the jury argued vigorously and now presented its indecision to the judge again. Time, money, and credibility were at stake, along with the destiny of ten men and one woman. His Honor sent them back to work and implored them to continue. At midnight they were allowed to retire.

Murphy thought he might give the jury additional instructions the next morning when court convened at nine-thirty. By the time he got to court they were far into their hot-tempered debates.

"What's the use of arguing with these fellows?" seeped through the closed doors from one juror.

"I would rot in hell before I would vote to convict a single one of them," came muffled from another.

Mr. Pokerface roared, "I'll sit here forever before I condemn those niggers," in a curious blend of principle and prejudice.

"I am a reasonable man," voiced another.

The impasse was too great, however, even for reasonable men. After forty-six hours, the judge brought them back to court, where, standing in a semicircle before him, they looked exhausted. The fore-

man, Charles Naas, told Murphy that since Thursday, when they alter-
nated between eating turkey in grim silence and arguing, they had
been stalemated.

Recognizing they could do no more, Murphy sent them home with
the court's appreciation. They brought back a divided opinion, which
meant nobody could be convicted. Some jurors wanted to acquit all the
defendants, some believed only eight of the eleven should be set free.
Five of the jurors would have convicted Ossian Sweet, Henry Sweet,
and Leonard Morris of manslaughter.

Manslaughter in the second degree, which the courts considered
willful and deliberate, but not a premeditated act, carried a maximum
jail sentence of up to fifteen years. It also carried a fine up to $1,000.
For the moment, they were all eligible for bail, and within one week,
they would each be sleeping at home.

In contrast to the eighty-four days the defendants spent in jail, nobody had been charged in the arson attempt on Ossian Sweet's home.
It had taken place ten days earlier, on the very day he testified in court.

Soon after the trial ended, the police department incomprehensibly
announced it intended to withdraw protection of Sweet's still empty
home. On behalf of the Sweets, Judge Murphy objected.

CHAPTER 16

More Than a Partial Victory

Perhaps because the outcome was ambiguous, so was the reaction to the jury's decision. Arthur Garfield Hays's immediate response was to lament its impact for people who fear "they cannot get justice in a white man's world." But he later changed his mind. Perhaps the hung jury might improve race relations, Hays mused. "From the public point of view, both as concerns negroes and whites, a disagreement was perhaps better than would have been a verdict either way," he told the NAACP.

Hays presumed that Toms, even Mayor John Smith, would react similarly, would see, as had he and Darrow, that a hung jury might appropriately reflect the complexity of the charges. A hung jury neither absolved nor incriminated anyone, reason enough for dismissing the charges, sparing the public expense, and patching tattered relations to avoid racial collision.

But "the attorney from New York" underestimated the pressures on Toms in a Klan-dominated city. The prosecutor expressed a willingness to call as many trials as necessary, a dozen if need be, to balance the scales of justice. Murphy was incredulous, while others believed Toms actually wanted to force Murphy into squashing a retrial, relieving the prosecutor of Klan pressure, perhaps criticism. It would shield Toms during his upcoming reelection campaign and might protect him later when he ran for judge. Darrow's "noble Nordics" made no secret of thirsting for a conviction, and no one had forgotten, including Toms, how well the Klan had done in the last election, handily winning seats on the city council.

The NAACP celebrated the fact that it had not lost the case, and was grateful that the name of Dr. Ossian H. Sweet became one of the sparks igniting its defense fund. Although the Detroit trial consumed a hefty amount of the association's resources, the NAACP immediately announced its commitment to the Sweets as part of its ongoing agenda. It would struggle mightily to "fight the case while there is any court in the land to appeal to until the eleven colored people were acquitted."

Walter White revealed his tendency to hyperbole when he claimed that the "case has largely changed public sentiment in Detroit. The better class opinion is now with the defendants, although the Klan is of course more bitter than ever." Actually, nobody had a clue about how any of this would play out in Detroit or in a second trial. All that could be predicted was it would be even more costly. By the end of the November the association had raised $14,364.7, nearly half of its goal.

December would be a make-it-or-break-it month for the association's drive to meet the Garland Fund's offer. And Ossian Sweet was clearly among those with celebrity appeal. After reports spread about his poise and confidence on the witness stand, it was apparent what a bonus he could be on the speakers' circuit. His first appearance came just two days after he was released from jail, when he delivered an address at Detroit's Ebenezer AME Church on Sunday afternoon, December 6. The NAACP recognized his value to the crusade, and Walter White had been negotiating with Judge Murphy to allow him to travel out of Michigan.

While the NAACP arranged a speaking trip for Sweet, donations streamed into the office. The Chicago branch raised $1,000 and the Banneker Relief Association contributed $300. Los Angeles asked its citizens to designate Sunday, December 13, "NAACP National Defense Day." Washington's women's groups scheduled a night at Howard Theater and a benefit dance at the Lincoln Colonnade on Christmas Eve. In New York City, book publisher Charles Boni wanted to host a musicale at a Park Avenue hotel, and Franklin Spier offered a ballroom large enough to hold three hundred people. Spier, however, was cautious about what people might think about his philanthropic or racial commitments. White told Johnson, "Mr. Spier felt it necessary to secure an imposing list of respectables to reassure the people of Park Avenue against becoming frightened at tendering an affair for legal defense of colored people."

By the second week of December the association counted $24,000 in contributions to the defense fund, which triggered a $1,000 gift from Julius Rosenwald. Coincidentally, smaller amounts arrived, including donations from the territory of Honolulu, Hawaii; Havre de Grace, France; Kansas City, Kansas; and Redlands, California. M. Thompson's note accompanied $135 from Florida, and remarked how Darrow's plea had impressed workers at the Florida East Coast Hotel Company. "I have never witnessed a willingness more pronounced than in this instance." New York City's Sleeping Car Porters donated $35, and the Hotel Traylor in Allentown, Pennsylvania, collected $8.50. Terre Haute's Deming Hotel sent in $15. Colored Cigar Makers raised $32. Passengers on the train going to Philadelphia for the Howard and Lincoln Thanksgiving Day football game collected $82. And $5 came from C. C. Johnson, a friend of the Sweet family in Bartow and former chairman of the board of directors at the Union Academy, from which Ossian had graduated before heading north to Ohio. Before the books closed on the drive in December, a total of $693 arrived from people donating sums less than $5.

Clarence Darrow contributed to the fund-raising campaign when he addressed four thousand people who were seated at the Salem Methodist Episcopal Church, the largest church in Harlem. When he finished speaking inside, he went outside to address the fifteen hundred people who hadn't gotten in but were still waiting on the steps. As usual, his remarks invited controversy because of his comments about how whites practiced Christianity, about the ambiguities of race, and about the excessive piety of religion. He spoke for more than ninety minutes, raised $1,601.94, and urged the audience to take to the ballot box. "Be independent, keep politicians guessing, never let them count your votes before election," he said.

As much as it depended on the press to promote its cause, the NAACP did not accept the offer of the *Negro News Weekly* to debut its newsreels with a story featuring Ossian Sweet. The Chicago-based company was starting out with a mission to "show worthy things and weekly happenings of the Colored race the world over." Producers wanted to hire "a motion picture man for half a day." They wanted a scene with "all the people talking, laughing, crying, walking—anything to keep them in action." The specifics of "action" were based on the impression, innocently construed, that it could obtain about "two hundred feet of film with Dr. Sweet in the jail yard," talking to representatives of the NAACP, other doctors, and "some of the people of the Detroit riot."

"We want Dr. Sweet and his wife there and the ruins of the home, about 50 feet of this. Then get the jury and Clarence Darrow. About 75 feet of Darrow and jury in front of court house if possible. Please get it when clear not cloudy. If you do this let us know at once and we will send 9 dollars for film and share the price of the motion picture man."

Too many distractions made the NAACP's time precious, and instead of staging a media event for a fledgling newsreel company's market debut the association relied on marquee names in known territory to gather $6,000. Oscar Baker, a prominent black attorney from northern Michigan and behind-the-scene advisor to Walter White, arranged to speak in Saginaw. Members of the National Medical Association renewed their pledges, and doctors rushed to submit $15 or $20, in some cases, $50 or $100. From others, gifts of $5 and $10 pushed the association toward the goal—from the Parisian Art Club of Detroit; Morris Ernst of New York City; Rabbi Max Heller of New Orleans; Pythagoras Lodge of Kansas City, Kansas. Nobody wanted to be left off the list, not the Girls Friend Club of the San Antonio Board of Education, not the Phyllis Wheatley Club of Frankfort, New York, or the Alphin Charity and Art Club of Fort Worth, Texas. Someone from a prison in New Jersey and a woman robbed twice in two weeks each wrote detailed accounts of their stories and their commitments and their intentions to contribute after their troubles cleared. And Mrs. W. C. Taylor from Manassas, Virginia, who read about the Sweets in the November issue of *The Crisis,* said she would have sent her donation of $5.50 sooner had she not "had the misfortune of being wrecked in a R.R. accident" and laid up in Freedmen's Hospital.

By December 31 the NAACP could announce a triumph in having raised $40,544.19—including the $200 that arrived while secretaries were typing out the final list with the names of hundreds of donors. It might have seemed a miracle to have met the Garland Fund's challenge had it not come from steady, determined, indefatigable work from secretaries and volunteers and passionate adherents clinging tenaciously to a promise of justice.

By the time the last penny was counted, the NAACP realized how much the defense fund had diverted money from the regular operating budget severely taxing the local chapters. Still, the drive was essential, desperately needed for expenses associated with ongoing legal work and for the second trial in the Ossian Sweet case in Detroit.

When the annual Kappa Alpha Psi convention hosted two hundred guests at its annual convention in New York City in December, 1925, Ossian Sweet was among the honored. The fraternity hoped that Sweet would speak from the podium, but the NAACP wanted his first public appearance to help them raise money. Ossian and Gladys were invited to attend the annual business meeting with members of the board in early January and to appear at Harlem's Mt. Olivet Baptist Church. On the same platform would be NAACP president Mary White Ovington and luminaries James Weldon Johnson, William Pickett, and Arthur Garfield Hays. And while Sweet was among the celebrities filling the church for that event, Hays did not want him to say too much while the second trial was pending.

People had come out of interest and respect, curiosity and favor, and Ossian and Gladys could enjoy the rapture their applause brought. The ordeal of this handsome, stoic couple had already worked its way into people's hearts, and everybody understood that their struggle continued. Still, just to have the public meet Gladys—self-possessed, brave, and stylish when she stood up in a blue silk dress—was a public relations accomplishment. Intermingled in the ovations filling the room were admiration for the NAACP, hope for the future, and a celebration of the success of the Sweets, who personified intelligence, passion, and grace.

As a way of making sure the doctor's voice was heard by the audience, Arthur Garfield Hays read from the transcripts of Ossian Sweet's trial testimony, which he introduced by saying, "In thinking of the Sweet case, it never occurs to me that it is the case of Dr. Sweet. I always feel it is a case of your people and a case of my people."

After their appearance in New York, Reverend Robert Bagnall, the director of NAACP branches, led the Sweets on a five-city tour to Philadelphia, Baltimore, Pittsburgh, Cleveland, and Chicago, where as many as six thousand people lined up to celebrate them and their mission. In Pittsburgh, Gladys's hometown, the audience fought its way through a blizzard. In Chicago spectators at the Eighth Regiment Armory heard Ossian Sweet modestly say he was not a hero. On the contrary, he declared, any red-blooded American man would have done the same to protect his home from hoodlums. "I have had the good fortune to have traveled in Europe and in many parts of Africa," he told them, referring to his stops in port cities on route to study abroad.

> Even in the jungles where the so-called barbarians and semi-civilized people live, a man's home is his castle. It was then that the thought came to me that the least we who claim to be civilized and more progressive can do is to uphold this principle at the cost of our very lives . . . I believe no man who thinks highly of himself and his own household can in any way disregard my stand by saying that there was another way out.

The NAACP considered the verdict of a mistrial in the Sweet case "more than a partial victory," and black citizens across the country celebrated what it termed "defiant unity." But Sweet alone was insufficient to overcome what Kelly Miller, dean of Howard University, called a "negative year." He thought Sweet was a "temporary standstill." Elsewhere members of the black intelligentsia pointed to eighteen people lynched that year. One of them was dragged from a guarded hospital bed in Orlando, Florida, the hamlet where Sweet was born in 1894, at the same time the jury was still deliberating in Detroit. The number of lynchings for the year was down from the all-time high of two a week, but higher than the previous year's total of sixteen.

The same time Ossian and Gladys Sweet toured cities on the East Coast and in the Midwest, Congress was getting ready to reconsider the Dyer antilynching bill, the same bill that Southern Democrats had filibustered to death three years before. And simultaneously an embarrassing story was making the rounds of the black weeklies. The celebrated black tenor Roland Hayes, whose accomplishments delivered him to the greatest concert halls in the world, had performed in a Jim Crow concert hall in America, forcing his large contigent of black fans to sit segregated in the balcony. Some questioned whether he ought to return the NAACP's highest award, the Spingarn Medal.

All agreed that the bright spot in 1925 was the NAACP's growth, with 380 active affiliates, and more than two hundred weeklies. Despite stagnation in some areas and setbacks in others, the NAACP believed the impact of the Sweet trial could be understood as having "stirred colored Americans as never before."

When the advisory board closed the books on 1925, it did so with hope that "the prospects for 1926 are most favorable."

CHAPTER 17

A Trial Fair

Though there were early hopes for a prompt retrial, the delay dragged into spring when longer, light-filled days edged out Michigan's gray skies. Optimists wondered if another trial would occur at all; others freely offered advice about how the NAACP should move ahead. Separate trials? A repeat event for all eleven? All sorts of rumors were printed about this issue, but whatever reports the press published, Darrow would wait until the opening day to settle the public's curiosity and announce his decision to defend Henry Sweet separately. Henry alone admitted to having fired a gun. Darrow knew the prosecution would have the strongest case against Henry, and if it couldn't convict him, it would never convict the others. If successful against Henry, the prosecution would almost certainly charge Ossian Sweet again. Darrow's strategy carried risk for them all.

In the meantime Darrow needed to decide which of the lawyers he wanted on his defense team. Criticism of Walter Nelson's contribution to the first trial, the local white attorney, removed him from consideration. Attorney Thomas Chawke, widely regarded as one of the best criminal lawyers in Michigan, could be enlisted as the substitute. Local black leaders discounted him at the first trial because his reputation had been made getting acquittals for bootleggers. But Darrow thought he would work well, and he was local. Arthur Garfield Hays had personal reasons for wanting to remain in New York, and was conflicted about disappointing his good friend Clarence Darrow, who accepted Hays's willingness to be available as "need be." And rather than include three black attorneys whom the defense did not really allow a large role in the first trial, it decided it needed—and could afford—only one, and retained Julian Perry, Ossian Sweet's best friend.

In late March White went to Detroit, and reserved a room at the Book-Cadillac, where he and Darrow would work out the remaining details for the second trial. Chawke was demanding a fee of $7,500, and the NAACP balked at paying him more than they were paying Darrow. Out of Chawke's salary would come the expenses for background searches on the 186 jurors listed on the April panel, which was some consolation. Darrow disposed of the NAACP's concern easily, telling them who got paid more was immaterial to him, and he reassured them of his commitment.

Many of the first trial's worries repeated with increased intensity. In some respects, selecting twelve jurors the second time was more demanding. Each side had accumulated more information emerging from the themes, personalities, and incidents stemming from the first trial. The defense hammered candidates with questions about whether concern over property values would make them fear living near blacks. Only one of three prospective jurors who admitted he lived next door to a black family made it into the final twelve. He lived on McClellan Avenue, five blocks west of Garland. People born south of the Mason-Dixon line, on the other hand, were unconditionally unacceptable.

Every time the defense asked whether a candidate's prejudice would interfere with his judgment, the prosecutors reminded the court that this was a murder case. "We are not trying the race question now. We are trying Henry Sweet for the murder of Leon Breiner," intoned Lester Moll on the third day. But the *Detroit Times* was unpersuaded, pointedly asking whether the trial was a case of "State vs. Sweet or State vs. the Negro." At the very least, the prosecutors wanted jurors who were not prejudiced against the police.

If Darrow's celebrity influenced the first trial, after banner headlines etched his personality across the front page of local papers for a month, it dominated the selection of a second jury. One routine question the prosecutors asked every potential juror was whether anybody's interest in serving as a juror was linked to Darrow's reputation. Candidates who said yes were summarily discounted, such as the potential juror who referred to Darrow and said in a disparaging tone that he heard that "Chicago was defending 'em." Those with closed minds were excused, such as one citizen who "wanted to know if the one he thought was guilty was the one on trial." Three repeated the exact same phrase, "I am convinced those people had no justification for firing," bringing Darrow to his feet, leading the *Detroit Free Press* to conclude DARROW MAY DEMAND SWEET VENUE CHANGE. One prospective juror had witnessed the police in front of Dr. Turner's house. Another boasted of ancestors who owned slaves.

Could it really be so much more difficult to replenish a panel than it had been the first time? "One after another," reported the *Free Press*, "the men were excused as they admitted being opinionated or prejudiced." Just as in the first trial, the court threatened to send policemen into the streets to compel citizens to fill a depleted jury pool moments before each side agreed upon the twelve white men sitting in the box.

A second trial had a different rhythm. It was remarkable enough that a dozen white men earlier judged eleven blacks fairly in a city that elected avowed members of the Ku Klux Klan to local office. Now Darrow and his colleagues had to bring forth new passions to convince new jurors. There were twelve different minds, each with his own concealed baggage, men who would observe the event as told by attorneys who had to behave as if it were opening night and not the second show with the identical witnesses. Many of the witnesses were now testifying for the third time, including the arraignment.

Error could not creep into the trial, and nobody was more vigilant than Judge Murphy in his goal to keep the proceedings untainted. Toward that end, he announced he would sequester the newly impaneled jurors. "Everybody wants to do everything humanly possible to procure a trial fair to the people of this state and fair to the defendants," he said just before telling the jurors they would reside in the sixth-floor dormitory. The court would take them to the theater that night and try to make them comfortable during the trial. Under the direction of a court officer, they could speak with their families or even visit their homes. They could read the newspapers but "all articles relating to the trial will be clipped out."

The burden of a second trial weighed as heavily on the NAACP as it did on the judge and Michigan courts. More was at stake in 1926 because *Corrigan v. Buckley* challenging the District of Columbia's protective covenants would be decided that spring. Since the case had been filed in 1922, it had been slowly wending its way toward the Supreme Court, and almost all the whites had moved away from the neighborhood where the aggrieved—another doctor's family—was prevented from moving into a home they bought. In January Moorfield Storey and Louis B. Marshall argued the NAACP's case, and asked the Supreme Court to rule that covenants restricting the sale of property to "Negroes, or persons of the Negro race or blood" would be declared unconstitutional. A decision was expected any day.

Henry Sweet would again be tried in Judge Murphy's black and white courtroom. The marble floors and marble wainscot covering the bottom half of the walls contrasted with the mahogany benches and oak railings. Again, spectators stood crammed behind the benches, resting against the walls, leaning onto the waist-high windowsills. This time spectators brought lunch boxes and ate in the courtroom so as not to lose a place during the two-hour recess. Attorneys dined at Berman's Steak House, and Clarence Darrow took Ossian and Gladys Sweet to lunch at the Wolverine Hotel, which had never before served blacks and whites at the same table or blacks at any table.

From the opening day of the trial on April 17 a steady parade of celebrities stepped into the court with the hushed reverence of tourists standing in the nave of a Gothic cathedral. Ambassador Joseph Johnson, minister to Liberia, attended often. So, too, Anita Loos, who excited interest when she came to Detroit for the premiere of *Gentlemen Prefer Blondes*. Tenor Roland Hayes visited the trial when he sang Haydn and Mozart for the season's only Detroit concert, which Ossian and Gladys attended in April. Actress Ann Harding, a friend of His Honor, came to court with Rollo Peters, her costar in *Tarnish;* and Jeanne Eagels, rehearsing for *Rain*, sometimes sat in the reserved section with Ruby Darrow or Marcet Haldeman-Julius, the socialist publisher of the *Blue Books* who wrote extensively about the trial. W. E. B. Du Bois made an appearance, and James Weldon Johnson, who stayed at the St. Antoine branch of the YMCA, traded places with Walter White. White held down the desk at the NAACP's headquarters in New York City. Now Johnson attended the trial daily.

Going into the second trial, Darrow had the benefit of knowing what to expect from Toms. He also knew Frank Murphy's earlier charge to the jury had recognized that a man's house is his castle, and as such he has a right to defend it. Based on this history, Darrow could also anticipate Robert Toms's objections. He knew that Toms would argue conspiracy; he knew the strategic weakness from the bill of particulars and that the state would attempt to prove that Henry Sweet fired the bullet that killed Breiner.

What Darrow had not expected was to enter the courtroom on the first day to find an arsenal displayed. Set on a table, in full view of the jury on the opening day of *People v. Henry Sweet,* were all the guns, rifles, and ammunition that had been confiscated after Breiner was shot. On the spot, Darrow and Chawke redesigned their defense strategy and opening remarks. They immediately acknowledged that the guns were taken into the house for the purpose of "defending the right of these individuals to remain secure within that home without being attacked by anybody."

Seizing the opportunity to diminish the impact of guns spread out before them, Darrow told the jurors "I don't know who killed Breiner. It might have been Henry Sweet."

> I can't tell and he can't tell. It is your task to determine if he was in a conspiracy to kill Breiner or anyone else, and under what circumstances.
>
> If Henry Sweet was there to kill someone on slight provocation, Mr. Toms is quite right in saying he would be guilty whether or not he fired a shot. But if he killed in defense of that home and that family, he is innocent. That is true if he shot when he believed it was necessary to shoot, even though it later became apparent that it was not necessary, but he at the time thought it was necessary.
>
> We will show that the white people in the neighborhood began to prepare for the reception of Dr. Sweet. They organized the Waterworks Park Improvement Association. It had nothing to do with waterworks or improvement. They organized to keep Dr. Sweet out of his home.

Witnesses entered the same labyrinth the attorneys had laid out in November. How many people on the streets? Did you see rock throwing? A taxicab? How many shots? Where were the police? Do you belong to the Waterworks Improvement Association?

Most of the answers sounded familiar. But new information crept into the previous testimony. Lieutenant Schellenberger admitted that rocks bounded off the front porch when he entered Sweet's house. Schuknecht acknowledged that he knew about the Waterworks Improvement Association, had actually assigned two men to find out what they could about its purpose. No single effort to reshape the story, to shade the details, or to reconstruct and revise the reality mattered as much as the testimony about how the Waterworks Improvement Association advocated violence.

Darrow was cross-examining a neighbor on Garland Avenue, Alfred Andrew, when he admitted that an official of the Tireman Avenue Improvement Association, the vigilante group that ousted Turner, advocated force to "keep Negroes out." Andrew provided the most comprehensive description yet about July's gathering at the Howe School. He even described one of the Howe speakers, someone from the Tireman Avenue group.

Darrow: Did he tell you about a race riot trouble they had had in his neighborhood?

Andrew: Yes, he told us about a negro named Dr. Turner who had bought a house on Spokane avenue.

Darrow: Did he say his organization made Turner leave?

Andrew: Yes.

Darrow: Did he say anything about the Turner incident?

Andrew: He said they didn't want colored people in their community and proposed to keep them out.

Darrow: Did he say that the association had made them leave their home?

Andrew: Yes he did.

Darrow: Did the speaker talk of legal means?

Andrew: No he was a radical. I myself do not believe in violence.

Darrow: Did anybody in that audience of 500 or more people protest against the speaker's advocacy of violence?

Andrew: I don't know.

Andrew made no attempt to hide his personal opinion that blacks should not be moving into the neighborhood. But he differed from some neighbors because he did not want protests to become illegal or violent.

Moll objected. Speeches made two months earlier could hardly provoke anger in September, he said. Darrow disagreed "There is a serious conflict of facts as seen by the defense and the State," he shot back. "I don't believe the State has put on one witness who was present at the shooting who told the truth." All of them, Darrow said, were "hedging, quibbling and lying."

Darrow wanted to make the Waterworks Improvement Association the central issue rather than Henry Sweet. "In the mind of spectators, and presumably the jurors, is the picture of a community organization, formed for mutual benefit, yet prowling abroad like a bloody jungle beast, showing its teeth to Negroes, interested in little else," wrote the *Free Press*. It was too soon to know whether the strategy, self-defense against a mob, would succeed.

Thomas Chawke proved a tenacious, dapper, and resolute replacement for Arthur Garfield Hays. A tall man with gray-blue eyes and dark hair slicked back, he stood while questioning witnesses as would a colonel, quasi-military, his feet planted firmly about shoulder-distance apart, his hands gripped behind his back, his head tipped slightly forward in readiness to hear the testimony. He rotated with Darrow, as had Hays, each one fully in charge of a witness while the other listened intently.

Observers said Chawke "rammed and battered" the state's witnesses with "merciless" cross-examinations and "searching questions." He and Darrow loaded their questions with information they assumed to be fact. Did not two officers go to the rooftop to watch the crowds? Chawke asked. Moll accused him of "bull-dozing a witness." Chawke accused Moll of trying to prejudice the jury against him. Judge Murphy stepped in to quell the running conflict between attorneys.

Julian Perry, meanwhile, turned pages of transcripts, cross-checking testimony from the first trial for consistency with the answers witnesses now gave about the size or actions of the crowd. When a state's witness amended or contradicted his earlier testimony, Perry alerted Chawke or Darrow, who displayed the conflict to the jury to undermine the witness and the testimony he was giving.

Henry Sweet did not take the witness stand. The state countered by introducing the statement he had given at police headquarters after his arrest. It confirmed he was an expert marksman, enrolled in ROTC at Wilberforce, and had fired a rifle over the heads of the people on the street. The police stenographer read his statement, including the details about his fear that he could have been killed if he had stayed in the kitchen, captive to a rock-throwing mob.

His brother Ossian Sweet did appear. Again he chronicled his life story and the background of persecution and lynching that so moved spectators during the first trial. Each incident he described was self-contained, like beads on a string, each locked into its own unique shape, separate yet cumulative and telling a story greater than the sum of its parts. The audience clung to his narrative. After two days, when he finished, the prosecution extracted the same admission that he had lied to the police when he was first arrested.

"Why didn't you tell them the truth about everything?" Toms asked, just as he had during the first trial.

"I made some untrue statements," Sweet told the second set of one dozen jurors. "I was scared and bewildered and denied the right of having an attorney. I thought they wanted to get me to make an incriminating statement so they could send me to prison. I was afraid I would be beaten if I didn't answer the way the police wanted me to."

Then Toms asked Sweet to clarify that nobody at police headquarters laid a hand on him. Chawke interrupted: "You aren't trying to suggest that such a thing never has happened, that the police never have beaten prisoners, are you?"

Toms flared. "If I had made the remark Mr. Chawke just made, this case would have been declared a mistrial," he said, implicitly accusing Judge Murphy of favoritism.

"Mr. Toms, that is not true," Judge Murphy responded.

Until John Dancy, head of the Urban League, took the stand, nobody challenged the assertion that black neighbors reduced property values. Dancy's testimony patterned a story of housing shortage, racial prejudice, and higher rents that resulted in increased housing prices when blacks moved into a neighborhood. Darrow heard Dancy deliver this talk one night when they shared a lectern at the Nacerima Club. He invited Dancy to appear as a witness and threatened him with a subpoena if he refused. Dancy needed no urging.

Toms, however, questioned the relevance of Dancy's testimony and objected to his brief time on the witness stand no fewer than twenty-six times. Dancy was not present at the Sweets' house, was not a witness at the first trial, and didn't live in the neighborhood, the prosecutor said. Moll, however, reassured Toms, whispering loudly that they could relax. Moll was convinced they could destroy Dancy's credibility by asking him about declining property values.

Unbeknownst to them, Dancy heard the remark and was ready when the prosecution began its cross-examination. Dancy had already spoken about his childhood and education, about Detroit's housing conditions, and about how the Southern Exodus had increased Detroit's population in a short time.

When Toms asked, "Isn't it a fact that when Negroes move into properties formerly occupied by whites that the property values go down?"

"No," Dancy said firmly.

"How can you say that?" asked a startled prosecutor.

Dancy outlined the practice of landlords doubling the rents charged to black tenants after whites moved out. Just next door to him on Chestnut Street, he said, one apartment that had rented for $35 to whites went up to $60 when a black family moved in. The same thing happened in the duplex houses on the other side of his own dwelling.

He shocked his listeners by saying exactly the opposite of what they expected. "Instead of the public values being depreciated," he said, "they were enhanced . . . The property values are intrinsic, and this is just a state of mind that people have that property values go down when Negroes come in."

After Dancy left the witness stand, and after two people from Wilberforce testified about Henry Sweet's character, and after Ossian Sweet finished his testimony, Chawke wanted to read a newspaper article appearing in the *Detroit Free Press* in July. It was the story about Mayor Smith's plea to end racial hostilities in Detroit. The court overruled the prosecutor's objection to reading the entire story, which described the "storm center" when Vollington Bristol moved into his home on American and Tireman Avenues, and the departure of John Fletcher, who, after forty-eight hours, moved out of his house, "in which not one window remained whole." It reported on "a big Ku Klux Klan meeting attended by more than 10,000 persons . . . with a member of the Tennessee branch of the organization standing on a platform illuminated with the red glare of fiery crosses." The *Free Press* sketched the perfect backdrop to Darrow's defense outlining psychological fears based on a history of racial tension. He read the entire story slowly and deliberately.

On Tuesday morning, May 11, James Weldon Johnson sat where he could hear every word of Darrow's closing remarks. For the occasion, the court allowed portable chairs set up between the judge's bench and the lawyers' tables, or in front of the jury box. Hundreds considered themselves lucky to stand cramped, chest to back, their arms tucked to their sides. An entire bench had been set aside for out-of-town judges who had come to hear Darrow's closing arguments. Johnson was lucky to have a seat from which he could see people stretching to hear while they gave Darrow their undivided attention.

Darrow spoke in low tones, Johnson said, "as though he were coaxing a reluctant child." He was angered by Moll's caustic remarks, and particularly by his reference to Sweet, describing him as "quasi-intelligent," fancying himself a second Lincoln. Darrow boiled at Moll's accusation that Sweet was a coward.

A coward, gentlemen. Here, he says, were a gang of gun men, and cowards—shot Breiner through the back. Nobody saw Breiner, of course. If he had his face turned toward the house, while he was smoking there, waiting for the shooting to begin, it wasn't our fault . . . Who are the cowards in this case? Cowards, gentlemen? Eleven people with black skin, eleven people, gentlemen, who didn't come to America because they wanted to, but were brought here in slave ships, to toil for nothing—for the white—whose lives have been taken in every state in the Union—who have been victims of riots in every state in the union.

Other times Johnson thought "his words came like flashes of lightning and crashes of thunder." "Did they shoot too quick?" Darrow shouted. "Why, you tell me just how long a man needs to wait for a mob? Why, the house was full of these guns . . . How long do you need to wait for a mob?"

"I am sorry for misfortune everywhere in the world," Darrow said, extending sympathy to Breiner's family. But Darrow made it clear that the dead man was not an innocent. "He was a conspirator in as foul a conspiracy that was hatched in a community; in a conspiracy to drive from their homes a little family of black people . . . and to destroy these blacks and their home." Darrow turned his outrage on those who urged violence that day at the Howe School meeting of the Water-works Improvement Association.

> So far as I can see, no officer has raised his hand to prosecute, and no citizen has raised his voice, while this man uttered those treasonable words in the presence of seven hundred people. Did anybody say a thing? Did anybody rise up in that audience and say, "We respect and shall obey this law; we shall not turn ourselves into a mob to destroy black men, to batter down their homes, in spite of what they have done on Tireman Avenue."

By the time Darrow finished, his passion stilled the court. He called the state's witnesses depraved: "They have lied and lied and lied." Why? To send the defendants "to the penitentiary for life . . . Which is the worst? They violate the constitutional law, they violate every human feeling and throw justice and mercy and humanity to the winds? . . . Which is the worst, to do that or lie about it?"

Darrow kept the court alert for more than seven hours. To some, to Frank Murphy in particular, no previous performance matched what he had just seen. None ever would, he expected. Murphy later said that Darrow was the most "Christ-like" figure he had ever seen. When Johnson walked over to thank Darrow on behalf of the NAACP, he could see the attorney's eyes "shining and wet." So were the judge's.

The next day Toms took his turn. He outraged Johnson by referring to the NAACP as an organization designed "for the purpose of foist-ing colored people into white neighborhoods, for the purpose of pro-moting social equality, and for the purpose of bringing about an amalgamation of the races." Defense attorneys objected. Too late. The jury had heard what Toms said and grasped his purpose. Toms asked jurors to consider what their white friends would say if they brought in a verdict of not guilty. The defense hollered, "Objection" once again. Toms skewered Henry Sweet for not speaking in court, despite his constitutional right not to take the stand. "Objection," screamed Chawke. The jury heard every one of Toms's allegations before it heard the judge sustain the defense attorney's objections, just as Toms had intended.

After Murphy delivered his charge to the jury on Thursday, Darrow, Josephine Gomon, Chawke, and ten others—including the visiting judges—took taxis over to lunch at Cohen's on Woodward Avenue, where "Scotch, Port and ginger ale mixed freely." Despite the official reign of prohibition, bootleggers were common in Detroit. With nobody in a particular hurry, they stayed until four-thirty before heading back to the courtroom.

Johnson was not hungry. He wanted to get a telegram off to Walter White in New York.

> Case went to jury twelve-thirty. Defense made and argued motion this morning to declare mistrial based on allusion by prosecutor in his argument to election of defendant not to testify. Motion denied. Defense however feels it sound foundation for reversible error. Charge of Judge very strong.

Then he stopped to speak with Judge Ira Jayne before going back to Murphy's courtroom to wait.

Johnson's belief that "public sentiment seemed favorable" left him guardedly optimistic. A conviction seemed unlikely. But it was difficult to imagine that an all-white jury would acquit Henry Sweet. The worst outcome, as well as the best he could hope for, he guessed, would be a mistrial. Preparing himself, he must have begun to calculate how to endure more court costs. Johnson returned to Murphy's third-floor courtroom to wait. Reporters began filing stories with their newspapers for the afternoon editions. Johnson saw mostly the faces of people who, although they sat through the trial, were strangers. Gladys, alone among the original defendants, also remained in the courtroom, where she mingled with friends.

"Suddenly, there was a pounding on the jury room door," Johnson later wrote. The jury, which had been out for three hours and twenty-five minutes, was seeking clarification of a legal point. Then, without waiting for the response, the jury announced, to everybody's astonishment, that it had reached a verdict. Caught off-guard, court officers were scattered and straggling back after a leisurely lunch. Murphy looked into the half-filled courtroom and commanded, "Don't bring that jury in until we are ready for them."

Terror spread through Johnson. He had seen enough verdicts to know that a fast decision usually signaled a compromise, often sacrificing a defendant to the importance of consensus. Haste implied jurors entered the deliberations with their minds made up, or jurors had not evaluated evidence carefully. What could Johnson presume when the jury, which heard the case for nearly four weeks, returned with a decision in under four hours, except that they had decided Henry Sweet "guilty as charged"?

Henry Sweet sat down. He glanced toward the wall, and Chawke whispered something, visibly trying to encourage him, reassure him. Johnson sat down next to Sweet. The man with somber gray eyes reached for Sweet's arm and whispered that the NAACP would continue its support if the verdict went against him. Sitting down, Darrow gripped the left arm of his chair, tightened his jaw. The courtroom was more crowded than it had been on any previous day. Judge Murphy cautioned spectators against demonstration.

When the room acquired the decorum Murphy demanded, the jury door was unlocked. Mr. George Small, the foreman, led them toward their seats. After they were settled, the judge asked the routine question, "Have you gentlemen in the course of your deliberations reached a verdict in the case of Henry Sweet? If so, who will answer for you?"

George Small stepped forward. As the foreman, he would deliver their decision, and he cleared his throat, hesitating a few seconds. Then, he said, "We find the defendant 'Not guilty.' "

It was better than anyone expected; it was stunning. Henry Sweet sank into his seat and covered his eyes with his hands. One person clapped, another said, "Ah," the judge rapped for order. Darrow slumped in his chair, and Robert Toms leaned toward Darrow, to pick him up, but Darrow—happy, weary, elated, weeping—waved him off. Toms asked to have the jury polled. As the last juror declared, "Not guilty," Ann Harding, the actress, leaped out of her chair and threw her arms around Darrow. And Johnson saw women "sobbing convulsively, and tears . . . running down the cheeks of men." Then things got confused, but he took note of

> Henry Sweet, Dr. Sweet and his wife shaking hands with the jury and thanking them, shaking hands with Mr. Darrow and Mr. Chawke and thanking them. They are followed by others. It seems that everybody is shaking hands and giving thanks.

He called it an "electrical moment."

CHAPTER 18

The Darker Brother

"I, too, sing America," wrote Langston Hughes in 1926, the year Henry Sweet was acquitted. In a sixty-two-word poem, Hughes caresses the hopes and dreams, and exposes the degradation and humiliation borne by a "darker brother"—the narrator—consigned to eat alone in America's kitchens. After he has grown strong and mannerly, will his oppressors be ashamed? he asks himself. Will they "see how beautiful I am"?

Back from Paris, living in New York City, Hughes was barely twenty-four years old when Alfred Knopf published his first book of poetry. Already he was emerging as one of the most promising talents of the Harlem Renaissance. There is no reason to think Langston Hughes intended to tell the story of Ossian Sweet; but he did.

Following the trial, racial tension abated in Detroit. Perhaps the exposure of police misconduct helped. One local NAACP official believed "the Sweet case has had a wonderful effect toward creating a better feeling."

The goodwill was local. In April, the U.S. Supreme Court announced it had no jurisdiction in *Corrigan v. Buckley*. In May, a member of the New York City Board of Education revoked an invitation for James Weldon Johnson and Arthur Garfield Hays to speak at Morris High School in the Bronx, saying they were "subversive to the highest American traditions." Dumbfounded, Johnson asked what values the NAACP represented that could disturb schools.

Thirty-five years after the acquittal of Henry Sweet, prosecuter Robert Toms said he knew he was fighting an uphill battle in the two trials. It was clear to him, he told historian Alex Baskin, that the "colored people involved were so far superior to the white people." Toms said the defense witnesses were "superior intellectually, in appearance, in culture and in sympathy."

Time may have softened Toms's attitude, shifted his memory. Nothing in his behavior during the trials indicated respect for defense witnesses, black or white, and following the acquittal of Henry Sweet, he took more than one year to drop the charges against the other ten defendants. It was believed that had he been able to, he would have brought them to trial yet again. By the time the state dropped the charges, the Klan's odious nostrums had subsided in Detroit—at least temporarily—imploding from its own scandals, corruption, malfeasance, a change in leadership, even prison. And in the next three decades, as public attitudes changed, perhaps Toms showed the influence of events subsequent to the 1920s.

As were the rest of America's cities, Detroit in the twenties was a cauldron with shape and language reconfigured by industry, made possible by prosperity, intensified by the strivings of immigrants black and white, threatened by xenophobes peddling counterfeit doctrines of racial worth. Upon hearing the jury's decision to acquit Henry Sweet,

Clarence Darrow told the press, "Both Negroes and whites have to learn the lesson of forbearance." Prejudice must be tamed, "reckoned with as much as fact," he said. "I believe the outcome of this case will benefit the white and black man alike."

For Ossian Sweet, the purchase of an ordinary house on an ordinary street inextricably altered his life. Sweet told a reporter that before the move, he could not have imagined "how bitter that neighborhood was going to be." But given the corner into which he had boxed himself, he said he had no choice. He could not permit a "gang of hoodlums" to keep him out.

During Henry's trial, he, Gladys, Iva, Henry, and Otis shared a second-floor walk-up apartment. After Henry's acquittal, Ossian and Gladys tried to stitch together a normal life. But within a few months their baby, Iva, came down with an active case of tuberculosis. It was a highly contagious disease that could lie dormant anywhere from months to years after exposure. It spread most rapidly in overcrowded and poor neighborhoods. It swept through prisons, ravaged prisoners. Most likely Gladys was infected awaiting the trial during her month-long confinement, and then transmitted it to her daughter. In the twenties, before the age of antibiotics, standard treatment was primarily quarantine and bed rest. After a brief illness Iva died in August 1926. She was buried in Roseland Cemetery in Detroit.

Gladys and Ossian moved back to their house at 2905 Garland Avenue following Iva's death. By now it had become a symbol as much as an abode, and in that house Gladys fought her own case of tuberculosis. But once the dormant infection became active, she had little chance. One month after turning twenty-seven she, too, was consumed.

In November 1928, two years after Iva's burial, Ossian Sweet had to return to the Roseland Cemetery to bury his wife next to his daughter. As had happened to him before, the guards stopped him at the front gate, which was reserved for whites. This time he was prepared, and when he was directed toward the back, Dr. Ossian Sweet pulled out a revolver, and threatened to use it until they allowed him to lead his wife's funeral cortege through the front gate.

Everything seemed to stall after Sweet lost Gladys. While she was ill, he played a minor role in the 1927 convention of the National Medical Association's meeting in Detroit. Later he founded Good Samaritan Hospital, a maternity center. He married twice more but each marriage failed; he ran for political office and lost the two elections. Otis, his brother, lived in the house with him at 2905 Garland Avenue. So did a sister who moved to Detroit, became a nurse, then was killed in an automobile accident. Nieces and nephews lodged with him when they visited Detroit for summer jobs. He helped Henry finish Wilberforce, then Howard University Law School, from which he graduated in 1933, a classmate of Thurgood Marshall.

Henry, too, moved into 2905 Garland Avenue, opened a law practice, busied himself with the Detroit branch of the NAACP. He developed an active case of tuberculosis, spent more than twelve months trying to stave off the illness, then lingered another twelve before dying at Herman Keifer Hospital in 1940.

If Detroit disappointed Ossian Sweet, sabotaged his dreams, broke his heart, Bartow did not. Although the glory days of this hardscrabble town were buried deep in the canyons of the phosphate mines, it was still home to his mother and many relatives. Here the Sweet family was legend, the envy of many. One person who grew up in Bartow under the Sweets' family shadow mused that they were "the image everybody wanted to set their standards by. That which we didn't see, we imagined. We may have made more of them," he said, "but that's imagination."

After the trials, public interest brought both visibility and danger. Vandals set fire to their orange groves, leading Bartow's east side residents to wonder if Klansmen were to blame. Similar questions percolated after an arsonist tried to burn a Sweet house. The Sweets never learned. But in the years that followed, Dora always left a light burning at night.

Even before his father, Henry Sr., died in 1941, Ossian had become a symbol of success in the urban North, which differed from the moral authority his father illumined in rural Florida. "Doc Sweet," as he was called, bought land in Bartow and rented it to farmers for grazing herds. He bought a house. Large by local standards, comfortable by any, it seemed like a castle to many. It was enormous—a white colonial, high ceilings inside, Greek columns outside, and green, leafy ornamental trees spreading across vast grounds dotted with seasonally blooming pastel petals. A long, winding driveway turned in from the road.

Every year Ossian Sweet drove home to Bartow from Michigan. After crossing the Mason-Dixon line, he donned a chauffeur's cap to trick the state police, patrolmen too willing to stop a black man for no other reason than that he was sitting behind the wheel of a big fancy Marmon. Along with his remaining brothers, Otis, William, and Sherman, Ossian returned each Thanksgiving. The sons hired a cook to free their mother of the kitchen's burden, stayed for Christmas, tucked celebrating her birthday into their relaxation of hunting, playing cards, enjoying music. He launched his boat in one of the local lakes where he cast a line to bring home sunfish. Anybody who wanted to go with him was welcome. Every January 1 he threw a large barbecue. On this anniversary of the date Lincoln set for freedom, the day for emancipation from slavery, Sweet walked tall in his white-brimmed hat. His lapel was scented with a fresh rose a nephew brought to him daily. And Sweet delivered a speech, an homage to the obligations of service, to the pride of accomplishment, to the gifts of freedom. He recreated the public stage he had lost in Detroit.

By the late fifties Ossian's visits home were longer, giving him the solace and warmth that eased his chronic pain from arthritis. Sometimes stiffness kept him from walking upstairs. Instead of sleeping in the second-floor bedroom, he spent the night on a chaise longue, downstairs in the library, where he could recline, rather than awaken to joints he could not bend.

One Saturday afternoon early in 1958, before he returned to Detroit, one of his nieces, Jackie, a student in the eleventh grade, paid him a visit. On this winter day when the Florida heat baked through his khaki pants and white shirt, he walked with her longer than his arthritis usually permitted.

As they walked, Jackie hoped Ossian would ask about her life—friends, classes, extracurricular activities. He usually did, and she valued his patience, his curiosity, his roving intellect. Now she wanted his help with a school project asking her to link the past to the present, not really a history, more of a debate.

For the first time since Reconstruction, political activism ripened in the late 1950s. The Supreme Court decision *Brown v. Board of Education* theoretically put Jim Crow in his grave in 1954 when it ruled that segregated schools were unconstitutional. Three years later, while the nation watched on television, nine youngsters put this to a test when they desegregated Central High School in Little Rock, Arkansas. It was September 1957, and President Dwight David Eisenhower reluctantly sent federal troops to guarantee the students' passage over the objection of the entrenched governor, Orville Faubus. Faubus would come to symbolize resistance to racial change, and the event became the first muscular test of that Supreme Court decision. New names were igniting passions, new leaders were personifying ambitions, new people were sacrificed in struggle.

The years between *Brown v. Board of Education* and the actual desegregation of a Southern public school would also see a teenager named Emmett Till lynched for sport in Mississippi. A few months after that, in December 1955, Rosa Parks inspired a generation and made Dora Sweet proud because she refused to move to the back of a bus in Alabama. The time gave voice to the twenty-six-year-old preacher Martin Luther King, Jr., gathering militancy in his call for a bus boycott that lasted thirteen months.

The year Ossian Sweet defied the angry mob surrounding his house, Rosa Parks was just twelve years old; Coleman Young, who would become Detroit's first black mayor, was seven years old; he had moved to Detroit two years earlier with his family, which came north from Alabama. None would claim a direct link between them, or their separate acts of conscience. But they were all schooled to believe that they were entitled to the best American society had to offer. Sweet's confidence and sense of entitlement to such reward could only attach to someone who had imbibed the expectation, whether false or true, that his destiny, the American destiny, was inextricably bound up with personal success diligently earned. Absent barriers of color, it should belong to him, to them, and to theirs, and they would fight for it the same way that Linda Brown's parents staked a claim for her that brought them to the Supreme Court from Topeka, Kansas, in 1954.

Helping his niece make sense of these events tapped Ossian Sweet's passions. For the rest of the day they discussed ideas she had barely considered, notions about equality, how everybody deserved the same choices, the same opportunities, a share in the same benefits of the rich land they loved.

Jackie returned the next day, and Doc Sweet helped her rehearse the speech. She read it aloud once. Then again. The second time he stopped her to show how to emphasize a phrase in one spot, pause at another. He taught her to speak confidently, to look at the audience, to let her voice rise, and when it might fall. He reminded Jackie of the traditional conversations around the dinner table, when family talked about how each of them could make a difference, what obligations they must pay to their country.

On this weekend in February before he returned to Detroit, Ossian Sweet continued that family tradition. Sitting at the desk in his library where the afternoon sun bowed through the windows, Sweet held a cigar in one hand, a pencil in the other, and helped his niece Jackie learn how to honor the past and prepare for the future in a talk entitled, "I Speak for Democracy."

After the Trials

- DR. OSSIAN SWEET lived the rest of his life in Detroit. He refused interviews and never talked publicly about the events of 1925. After the death of his family and the loss of four more siblings, marital and political failures, his reputation suffered as he was dragged into a paternity suit. Gnarled joints left him in chronic pain and depressed. He took his own life in March 1960. He was sixty-five years old.

- After the second defense trial, CLARENCE DARROW attended the NAACP's annual meeting in Chicago in June 1926 before he and Ruby took their long-awaited vacation abroad. In 1929 he accepted one more case before retiring to relative seclusion. One month shy of eighty, he died in 1938.

- JAMES WELDON JOHNSON left the NAACP in 1929 to spend time writing and speaking. The next year he accepted a teaching position at Fiske University and published five books including his autobiography, *Along This Way*, in 1933. In June 1938, Johnson died after a train collided with his car, on the way home from a weekend in the country. He was sixty-eight years old. His wife, Grace, recovered after a lengthy convalescence.

- WALTER WHITE succeeded Johnson as the executive secretary of the NAACP, where he remained for the rest of his life. He finished his novel *Flight* (1926) and wrote the entry for Ossian Sweet in the first edition of the *Biography of Colored America* (1927). In 1943 he returned to Detroit after racial conflict on Belle Isle led to a wartime riot. When he died in 1955, he counted world leaders as well as artists and writers among his friends.

- As he hoped it would, FRANK MURPHY's career soared. He was elected mayor of Detroit in 1930; President Franklin Delano Roosevelt appointed him governor of the Philippines in 1933. He returned to Michigan and became governor, serving in that capacity during the forty-four-day sit-down strike in Flint, Michigan, in 1937. His reputation as a progressive liberal was enhanced when he called up the National Guard but ordered them to protect the workers and not break up the strike. After he lost his reelection bid for governor, FDR named him as United States attorney general and then to the United States Supreme Court in 1940, where he remained until his death in 1949.

- ARTHUR GARFIELD HAYS continued his affiliation as general counsel to the American Civil Liberties Union and maintained an active law practice in New York City. Following the Sweet trial, he defended Sacco and Vanzetti, Italian radicals executed for murder in 1927, based on questionable evidence. He assisted in the Scottsboro defense of nine black Southern teenagers accused of rape on a train they were sharing with two women disguised as men. He died in New York City in 1954.

- CHARLES MAHONEY, one of the attorneys hired by the Liberty Life Insurance Company, maintained an active law practice in Detroit. In 1954 President Dwight David Eisenhower appointed him ambassador to the United Nations.

- ROBERT TOMS faced reelection as chief prosecutor and in 1929 was elected judge to the circuit court. Clarence Darrow wrote a letter endorsing his candidacy.

- JULIAN PERRY, Ossian Sweet's best friend and the only black attorney in both trials, ran for U.S. Senate in 1926. It was his second and last unsuccessful bid for elected office.

- In 1930 MRS. LEON BREINER dropped a civil lawsuit asking $150,000 for damages against Ossian Sweet.

- The American Social Hygiene Association declared Detroit the "wickedest city in the United States," and Police Commissioner Croul resigned under fire in 1926.

- The house at 2905 Garland Avenue has been placed on the National Register of Historic Places.

ENDNOTES

Abbreviations

AB = Alex Baskin Interviews, Bentley Historical Library, University of Michigan
AGH = Arthur Garfield Hays
ATW = James Weldon Johnson, *Along This Way*
GNJ = Grace Nail Johnson
JWJ = James Weldon Johnson
WW = Walter White

DT = *Detroit Times*
DN = *Detroit News*
FP = *Detroit Free Press*

Beinecke = Beinecke Rare Book and Manuscript Library at Yale University, New Haven, Connecticut
BHL = Bentley Historical Library, University of Michigan, Ann Arbor, Michigan
BHC = Burton Historical Collection, Detroit Public Library, Detroit, Michigan
LOC = Library of Congress, Washington, D.C.
MOMA = Museum of Modern Art, New York, New York
NAACP-micro = Papers of the National Association for the Advancement of Colored People on microfilm.
NAACP-LOC = Papers of the NAACP that were available only in the Manuscript Division of the Library of Congress.
NYPL = New York Public Library, New York, New York.
Schomburg = Schomburg Center for Research in Black Culture, a branch of the New York Public Library, New York, New York.
PUL = Papers of the Urban League—microfilm (originals in the Bentley Historical Library)
Trial Transcripts = *People v. Ossian Sweet, et al., State of Michigan in Recorder's Court for the City of Detroit,* November 1925. Original copy in the Burton Historical Collection. Microfilm at Bentley Historical Library.

Prologue

The incident involving Ossian Sweet is often mentioned in biographies of the principals as well as books about Detroit in the twenties. The fullest discussions appear in David Levine, *Internal Combustion: The Races in Detroit, 1915–1926* (Westport, Ct.: Greenwood Press, 1976); Kenneth G. Weinberg, *A Man's Home, A Man's Castle* (New York: McCall Publishing, 1971). Books with chapter-long accounts include Arthur Garfield Hays, *Let Freedom Ring* (New York: Liveright Publishing, 1937); Irving Stone, *Clarence Darrow for the Defense: A Biography* (New York: Doubleday, 1941), pp. 466–487; Arthur Weinberg, *Attorney for the Damned* (New York: Simon and Schuster, 1957), pp. 330–349; Kevin Tierney, *Darrow: A Biography* (New York: Thomas Y. Crowell, 1979), pp. 372–385; Sidney Fine, *Frank Murphy: The Detroit Years* (Ann Arbor: University of Michigan Press, 1975). Article-length accounts: Thomas J. Fleming, "The Right to Self-Defense," *Crisis* (January 1969), pp. 11–15; Fleming, "Take the Hatred Away," *American Heritage*, 20, no. 1 (December 1968), pp. 74–80, 104.

3 childhood hero: Clarence Darrow, "John Brown," *Crisis* (May 1926), pp. 12–16.

4 White told him: AGH, *Let Freedom Ring*, p. 196; Hays also repeated this incident at the annual NAACP convention in 1940. See Kenneth Robert Janken, *White: The Biography of Walter White, Mr. NAACP* (New York: New Press, 2003), p. 75. WW, *A Man Called White: The Autobiography of Walter White* (Athens: University of Georgia Press, 1995), pp. 75–76.

Chapter 1: Florida:"Incomparable and Indescribable"

7 On Florida's frontier and the Peace River Valley: Canter Brown, Jr., *Florida's Peace River Frontier* (Gainesville, Fla.: University of Central Florida Press, 1991); Larry E. Rivers, "Slavery in Microcosm: Leon County, Florida, 1824–1860," *Journal of Negro History* (February 1981), pp. 235–245; Leon County Farmers Club, *Leon County, Florida* (Tallahassee, Fl., 1883); "Life History of C. W. Wimster, Turpentine Man," Manuscripts from the Federal Writers' Project, 1936–1940, Library of Congress; Zora Neale Hurston, "Turpentine," reprinted in *Go Gator and Muddy the Water*, ed., Pamela Bordelon (New York: Norton, 1999), pp. 128–130; Charles Sumner Long, *The History of the AME Church in Florida* (Palatka, Fla., 1939). Long's antiquated work has been the standard source for the Florida AME. Robert L. Hall, " 'Yonder Come Day' Religious Dimensions of the Transition from Slavery to Freedom in Florida," *Florida Historical Quarterly* 65 (April 1987), pp. 411–437. On Polk County: M. F. Heatherington, *History of Polk County* (Lakeland, Fla., 1928). For Orlando, Orange County, see William Fremont Blackman, *History of Orange County* (Chuluota, Fla.: Mickler House Publishers, 1973); H. G. Cutler, *History of Florida* (Chicago: Lewis Publishing, 1923).

7   To reconstruct Bartow, the following were used at the Polk County Historical and Ge-
    nealogical Library: Florida Census (typescript), 1915 and 1935; Bartow City Directory,
    1911. I am indebted to Odell Robinson for sharing his work using Sanborn Insurance
    Maps for Bartow for the following years: 1889, 1895, 1901, 1906, 1911, 1917, 1924. Twelfth
    (1900) and Thirteenth (1910) Census of the United States (Bartow, Polk County, Fla.).

7   Historians and journalists are showing new interest in the history of lynching. For
    a landmark case involving the Supreme Court, see Mark Curriden and Leroy
    Phillips, Jr., *Contempt of Court: The Turn-of-the-Century Lynching That Launched a
    Hundred Years of Federalism* (New York: Anchor Books, 2001). Journalist James S.
    Hirsch has written an important book about the massacre in Tulsa in *Riot and Re-
    membrance: The Tulsa Race War and Its Legacy* (Boston: Houghton Mifflin, 2002).
    The obscene, American pandemic of lynching has received comprehensive atten-
    tion in three able works: Philip Dray, *At the Hands of Persons Unknown: The Lynch-
    ing of Black America* (New York: Random House, 2002); James H. Madison, *A
    Lynching in the Heartland: Race and Memory in America* (Palgrave/St. Martin's,
    2001); James Allen, Hilton Als, John Lewis, Leon I. Litwack, *Without Sanctuary:
    Lynching Photography in America* (Santa Fe, N.M.: Twin Palms, 2000). Also see a
    review essay by David Levering Lewis, "An American Pastime," *New York Review
    of Books*, November 21, 2002.

7   **Ossian Sweet witnessed:** AGH, "Opening Statement," November 16, 1925, Trial Tran-
    scripts. NAACP-micro, Part 5, Reel 3. Sweet also described the event to Marcet
    Haldeman-Julius, which she reports in *Clarence Darrow's Two Great Trials* (Girard,
    Kan.: Haldeman-Julius, Big Blue Books No. B-29, 1927).

7   **Rochelle's crime was murder:** The account of Rochelle's crime and the community ef-
    forts appeared in Bartow's local newspaper, *Courier Informant*, May 29 and June 5, 1901.

7   **settle a vendetta:** I am indebted to Lloyd Harris for this information.

8   **LYNCHING ALMOST CERTAIN:** *Courier-Informant*, May 29, 1901.

8   **as was the custom:** Personal communication, Lloyd Harris.

9   **black community tried to portray:** J. H. Lowe, C. H. Macon, Lee A. Smith, M. F.
    Boone, C. T. James, J. D. Brown, Phil Hall, M. Z. Rich, and C. T. Simons letter to
    the *Courier-Informant*, June 5, 1901.

9   **Newspapers from Sacramento . . . to New York:** *Sacramento*, May 30, 1901, vol. 101,
    no. 98; *New York Times*, May 30, 1901.

10 **"a hot-bed":** *Christian Recorder* (Philadelphia) April 3 and May 1, 1902. Professor
    Canter Brown, Jr., brought this to my attention.

10 **"no counterpart on the globe":** *Florida Times Union* [n.d.] 1890, Bartow, clipping
    file, Florida State Archives, Tallahassee.

11 **A STORY OF RUIN:** John Attaway, *A History of Florida Citrus Freezes* (Longboat Key, Fla.:
    Florida Science Source, 1997) provides exhaustive detail about weather conditions, ex-
    tent of damage, and migratory patterns following the decade of freezes. See pp. 30–31.

11 **Bartow was genteel:** Heatherington, *History of Polk County*, pp. 42, 43, 45. Bartow
    Board of Trade, *Bartow, Polk County, Florida* (1914), Florida State Library, Tallahassee.

12 **middle of a transformation:** Brown, *Florida's Peace River Frontier;* Joe Spann, "The South Florida Railroad," *Polk County Historical Quarterly* 12, no. 4 (March 1986).

12 This account of the phosphate industry comes from Arch Frederic Blakey, *The Florida Phosphate Industry* (Cambridge, Mass: Harvard University Press, 1973).

13 **the local press predicted:** (Tampa) *Weekly Tribune,* July 7, 1883, quoted in Blakey, *The Florida Phosphate Industry,* p. 19.

15 Professor Canter Brown provided generous help in confirming the prominence of the Argrett and Deaughn families. Also see Canter Brown, Jr., *Florida's Black Public Officials* (Tuscaloosa: University of Alabama Press, 1998), chapters 1, 2, and 5; Brown's biography of Ossian Hart informed my understanding of the politics of reconstruction and the AME Church. See *Ossian Bingley Hart* (Baton Rouge: Louisiana State University Press, 1997).

16 **He supported his family:** The Sweet family has been extremely generous in answering questions and providing information about their home in Bartow. These details have been culled from interviews with Hampton Green, Ruth Manning, Jacqueline Spotts, and Sherman Sweet.

16 **vagrancy laws:** Linda Kerber, *No Constitutional Right to Be Ladies* (New York: Hill and Wang, 1998), p. 64.

17 **a wood-framed house:** Louis and Sadie Milam sold Henry Sweet Lots 5, 7 and 8 of Block 4, Tier 3, land that had originally been granted to the South Florida railroad in exchange for its completion of track. Deeds Book 73, May 10, 1898, p. 445, Polk County Court House, Bartow, Fla.

18 **Wired street lamps lagged:** Marguerite B. Frisbie, "Historical Study," *Polk County Democrat,* October 6, 1939, in Clipping File: "Polk County, Bartow," Florida State Library, Tallahassee.

18 **It was the Sabbath:** Ruth Manning interview.

19 **"No town in Florida . . ."** *Courier-Informant,* September 12 and October 3, 1907.

20 **"good work for the colored people":** *Courier-Informant,* February 11, 1909.

20 **Long urged Henry:** Charles Sumner Long to JWJ, January 8, 1926, NAACP-micro, Part 5, Reel 23.

Chapter 2: The Education of Ossian Sweet

23 Descriptions of Jim Crow train travel may be found in C. Vann Woodward, *The Strange Career of Jim Crow* (New York: Oxford University Press, 1974); W. E. B. Du Bois, *The Autobiography: A Soliloquy on Viewing My Life* (New York: International Publisher's Company, 1968); David Levering Lewis, *W. E. B. Du Bois, Biography of a Race, 1868–1919* (New York: Henry Holt, 1993), chapter 10; T. Montgomery Gregory, "The Jim Crow Car," *The Crisis,* November 1915, December 1915, January 1916, March 1917.

23 Wilberforce Academy and University was the finest liberal arts education available to Ossian Sweet's generation. For descriptions of the campus, see Hallie Q. Brown, *Pen*

Pictures of Pioneers of Wilberforce (Wilberforce, Ohio: Aldine Publishing, 1937), pp. 67–68; C. Lowell, J. Silvius, and S. Darrow, "Tawawa Woods Natural Landmark: Geologic, Cultural, and Land Use History," *Ohio Journal of Science* 103, no. 2 (April, 2003), pp. 2–11; Du Bois, *Autobiography*, pp. 183–193; Frederick A. McGinnis, *A History and Interpretation of Wilberforce University* (Wilberforce, Ohio, Browne Publishing Co., 1941). Du Bois began his career at Wilberforce University, and David Levering Lewis includes a chapter on this fleeting year in his life. See *Du Bois, 1868–1919*, pp. 150–178.

23 **Long would describe it:** Long to JWJ, January 8, 1926, NAACP-micro, Part 5, Reel 23.

23 **not served food:** August Meier, *Negro Thought in America, 1880–1915* (Ann Arbor: University of Michigan, 1963), pp. 113–114. A discussion of the time Booker T. Washington was refused service at a train station is included in Louis R. Harlan, *Booker T. Washington, The Wizard of Tuskegee, 1901–1915* (New York: Oxford University Press, 1983), p. 422.

23 **Sweet's travel on the Atlantic Coast Line, Number 32** has been reconstructed from *Local Time Tables, Louisville and Nashville Railroad, Railroad (1909),* Railroad Museum, Sacramento, Calif.

24 **Charles Lokie:** NAACP, *Thirty Years of Lynching* (New York: 1918), p. 60.

24 **formal place setting:** Sherman Sweet interview.

24 Student origins are listed in *Wilberforce University Annual Catalogue,* 1912–1913.

25 **"deep impression":** *Xenia Gazette,* September 9, 1910.

25 **Carnegie Library:** *Forty-seventh Annual Report of the President, Secretary and Treasurer* (June 14, 1910), Wilberforce University Archives, Wilberforce University.

26 Scarborough has not received a full-scale biography, but many of his activities can be ascertained from his unpublished (typescript) autobiography, William Saunders Scarborough, "Autobiography" [micro], Ohio Historical Society, Columbus, Ohio.

26 **portrait painter from Boston, Darius Cobb:** See Scarborough, "Autobiography," p. 228.

26 **quest for knowledge:** *Xenia Gazette,* [September] 1926; McGinnis, *History and Interpretation of Wilberforce University,* p. 69; Lewis, *Du Bois, 1868–1919,* p. 153.

26 **"I forgot I was a colored boy":** Scarborough, "Autobiography," p. 24.

27 **Theophilus Steward:** William Seraile, *Voice of Dissent: Theophilus Gould Steward (1843–1924) and Black America* (Brooklyn: Carlson, 1991).

27 **local chapter on campus:** T. G. Steward to W. E. B. Du Bois, April 29, 1913, NAACP-LOC, Series I, Box G-170.

27 **course work:** W. A. Joiner, *A Half Century of Freedom of the Negro in Ohio* (Xenia, Ohio: Press of Smith Adv., 1915), pp. 78, 75, 101.

28 **buried Wilberforce in debt:** *Forty-Seventh Annual Report,* June 14, 1910, p. 4; Scarborough, "Autobiography," p. 200.

28 **forced to resign:** Alfred Moss, Jr., *The American Negro Academy, Voice of the Talented Tenth* (Louisiana University Press, 1981), pp. 102–104.

28 **"Many of the students need a helping hand":** *Forty-seventh Annual Report,* June 14, 1910.

28 **"repulsive sectarianism":** *Wilberforce Catalogue,* 1858.

29 **"the Mecca":** *Forty-seventh Annual Report,* June 14, 1910, p. 32.

29 **"I swept the recitation-room":** Details of Washington's life are included in his auto-

biography: Booker T. Washington, *Up from Slavery*, in *Three Negro Classics*, ed., John Hope Franklin, (New York: Avon Books, 1965), 23–207. He describes this incident on p. 56. Louis R. Harlan has written a two-part biography and edited Washington's papers. See *Booker T. Washington, 1856–1901* (New York: Oxford University Press, 1972) and *Booker T. Washington, 1901–1915*. Because of the antipathy between W. E. B. Du Bois and Washington before his death in 1911, he also figures prominently in Lewis, *W. E. B. Du Bois, 1868–1919*; Meier, *Negro Thought in America*.

30 **"slavery-bred imperfections and deficiencies"**: Grover Cleveland, quoted in Harlan, *Booker T. Washington, 1901–1915*, p. 134.

30 **"extremist folly"**: Washington's speech comprises chapter 14 in *Up from Slavery*. Washington included favorable reviews of the speech in *Up from Slavery*, p. 150; Harlan, *Booker T. Washington, 1856–1901*, p. 218; John Hope Franklin, Intro to *Three Negro Classics*, p. xi; Lewis, *W. E. B. Du Bois, 1868–1919*, p. 174; also see Meier, *Negro Thought in America*, pp. 100–118.

31 **American Negro Academy**: Scarborough, "Autobiography," pp. 131–132; Moss, *American Negro Academy*; Lewis, *W. E. B. Du Bois, 1868–1919*, pp. 168–174.

32 **single panacea**: Scarborough, "Autobiography," p. 86. Also see Meier, "The Rise of Industrial Education in Negro Schools," in *Negro Thought in America*.

32 **"disposing of the Negro's preparation"**: Scarborough, "Autobiography," p. 86.

32 **"Among his own people"**: W. E. B. Du Bois, *Souls of Black Folk*, pp. 242, 247; Du Bois, *Autobiography*, pp. 130–131, 245.

33 **"lynching really indicates progress"**: T. Thomas Fortune, ed., *Black-Belt Diamonds* (New York, 1898), p. 72. The entire book consists of a string of remarks Washington wrote or delivered. See Dray's comments on Washington's disregard of the victims of lynchings, *At the Hands of Persons Unknown*, p. 119.

33 **Working behind the scenes**: Harlan, *Booker T. Washington, 1856–1901*, p. 158, 238–265; W. H. Baldwin, Jr., to Booker T. Washington, Nov. 9, 1901, Vol. 6, pp. 311–312; W. H. Baldwin to Booker T. Washington, August 10, 1903, Vol. 7, pp. 303–304; Louis R. Harlan and Raymond W. Snow, eds., *Booker T. Washington Papers* (Urbana: University of Illinois Press).

33 **Southern Education Board**: On the Southern Education Board, see Raymond B. Fosdick with Henry F. Pringle and Katharine Douglas Pringle, *Adventure in Giving: The Story of the General Education Board* (New York: Harper and Row, 1962); Louis R. Harlan, *Separate and Unequal* (Chapel Hill: University of North Carolina Press, 1958), pp. 75–101; Lewis *W. E. B. Du Bois, 1868–1919*, pp. 266–272.

34 **In a letter**: Booker T. Washington to Jacob Henry Schiff, September 18, 1909, Harlan and Snow, eds., *Booker T. Washington Papers*, vol. 10, pp. 1909–1911.

34 **Deliberately and conspicuously**: Frederick Rudolph, *The American College and University, A History* (New York: Vintage Books, 1962), pp. 431–434.

34 **did not trust him**: Quoted in Meier, *Negro Thought in America*, p. 331.

34 **fund-raising trips**: *Forty-seventh Annual Report* (June 14, 1910).

34 **"So much wealth and influence"**: Scarborough, "Autobiography," pp. 166, 86, 131.

34 "a higher culture": Scarborough, "Autobiography," p. 135.

34 moment was tense: *Xenia Gazette,* June 13, 20, 1911.

35 without authority: When the school started awarding financial aid, according to the catalogue description, it was designed for seniors or other advanced students. Costs cited come from 1915–1916 fees. *Fifty-second Annual Report* (1915), p. 3.

35 Shorter Hall needed about $10,000 worth of repair when Scarborough became president. By 1915 Major L. F. Palmer, proctor of Shorter Hall and professor of military science and tactics, described in detail the deplorable conditions. In a letter to the General Faculty, dated December 2, 1915, he enumerated holes in the floor "large enough to get a foot caught," and rooms that were either damp or wet. *Faculty Minutes,* Wilberforce University Archives, Wilberforce University.

36 heart set on becoming a violinist: Author Interview with anonymous relative.

36 Entrance requirements are described in "School of Medicine, including the Medical Dental, and Pharmaceutic Colleges," (brochure, [1916] HUA.

36 "You better have your facts straight": Author interview with Ruth Manning.

36 nine acres of grazing land: Deed Book 109, April 10, 1912, pp. 308–309, Polk County Court House, Bartow, Florida.

37 vice president of the student athletic association: *Tawawa Remembrancer, 1914–1915,* Wilberforce University Archives.

37 letter of apology: Chester C. Horn, "Mr. President and General Faculty," June 2, 1914; O. H. Sweet, June 2, 1914, Faculty Minutes, Wilberforce University Archives.

37 "a marriage school": "Notes on Wilberforce," Reel 4, Theophilus Gould Steward Papers, Schomburg Library.

37 three young women: Faculty Minutes, January 13, 1914.

38 *Kappa Alpha Psi:* William Crump, *The Story of Kappa Alpha Psi* (Philadelphia: Kappa Alpha Psi, 1972), pp. 19–50. The importance of Kappa Alpha Psi to the Talented Tenth is discussed in Moss, *American Negro Academy,* p. 267. Sweet was elected Grand Lieutenant Strategus, a prominent leadership position, at the 1916 annual convention in Columbus, Ohio. Dr. Gilbert Jones spoke at the convention.

38 For a discussion of the cinematic significance of a *Birth of a Nation,* see David A. Cook, *A History of Narrative Film* (New York: W. W. Norton, 1996); Robert Sklar, *Movie Made America: A Cultural History of American Movies* (New York: Vintage, 1994). Griffith's cameraman, Karl Brown, describes the opening night in *Adventures of D. W. Griffith* (New York: Farrar, Straus, Giroux, 1973), pp. 86–88. John Hope Franklin, "The Birth of a Nation: Propaganda as History," in *Race and History—Selected Essays, 1938–1988* (Louisiana State University Press, 1989).

39 three publicists: This claim is part of the standard advertising on billboards and newspapers. Also see "Detail of Expanse Account as of May 20, 1915," and "Clipping File," Griffith Papers, Film Library, MOMA.

39 crescendos driving the audience: *The Moving Picture World* (March 13, 1915) reprinted in Robert Lang, ed. *The Birth of a Nation* (New Brunswick, Rutgers University Press, 1994).

39 National Press Club: *Washington Post,* February 20, 1915.

40 "It was all so terribly true": Wyn Craig Wade, *The Fiery Cross: The Ku Klux Klan in America* (New York: Simon and Schuster, 1987), p. 126.

40 NAACP student chapter at Howard University: Howard University College Chapter Annual Report, December 29, 1915, NAACP-LOC, Box 39.

40 Griffith's remarks were reported in the *New York Globe,* April 19, 1915.

40 $2,000 a day: Wade, *Fiery Cross,* p. 128.

40 trucked veterans: Seymour Stern, "Birth of a Nation," *Cinemages,* Special Issue #1 (1955), Griffith Papers, Film Library, MOMA. St. Louis: *New Republic,* June 5, 1915. *The Crisis* carried news of protests. See May, September, and October, 1915. *New Republic* also maintained vigilant watch over the controversy, with stories appearing in issues of March 20, May 8, and June 5, 1915.

41 Ohio's decision: *Cleveland Advocate,* July 1, 1916. The political fallout from *Birth of a Nation* in Ohio can be found in *Cleveland Advocate,* September 25, 1915; July 1, 1916; Feb. 10, 1917; and October 19, 1918.

41 *Atlanta Constitution* columnist: Ned McIntosh, " 'Birth of a Nation' Thrills Tremendous Audience in Atlanta," *Atlanta Constitution,* December 7, 1915.

41 On the Ku Klux Klan: David M. Chalmers, *Hooded Americanism: The History of the Ku Klux Klan* (New York: New Viewpoints, 1981) p. 28. Wade, *Fiery Cross;* Kenneth Jackson, *The Ku Klux Klan and the City, 1915–1930* (New York: Oxford University Press, 1967). Simmons has written his own account of the events. See William J. Simmons, *The Klan Unmasked* (Atlanta: 1923).

42 On the language and rituals, see Wade, *Fiery Cross,* pp. 142–147; Simmons, *Klan Unmasked,* pp. 87–97.

42 *Birth of a Nation* would premiere in Atlanta: *Atlanta Journal,* December 7, 1915.

43 Ralph McGill describes Simmons in *The South and the Southerner,* (Boston: Little Brown, 1963), p. 131. Also see Ward Greene, "Notes for a History of the Klan," *American Mercury* 5 (May–August 1925).

43 455 black Americans: *Crisis,* July 1921, p. 105.

44 On Howard University's reputation at the time, see D. O. W. Holmes, "Our Negro Colleges," *Opportunity* (March 1923), pp. 10–13; Kelly Miller, "Howard the National Negro University," in Alaine Locke, ed., *The New Negro: An Interpretation* (New York: Atheneum, 1992) pp. 312–321.

44 the Flexner Report: Abraham Flexner, "Medical Education, 1909–1924," *Journal of the American Medical Association* 82, no 11 (March 1924).

Chapter 3: Moving Up

46 General accounts of the Southern Exodus: Arna Bontemps, *They Seek a City* (Garden City: Doubleday, Doran, and Company, Inc. 1945); Florette Henri, *Black Migration* (Garden City, N.Y.: Anchor Press, 1975); Emmett Scott, "Letters of Negro Migrants

of 1916–1918, *Journal of Negro History* 4 (July and October 1919); Charles C. Johnson, "How Much Is the Migration a Flight from Persecution?" *Opportunity* (September 1923), pp. 272–274; W. E. B. Du Bois, "The Migration of Negroes," *Crisis* (June 1917), pp. 64–66; George Haynes, "Negroes Move North: I: Their Departure from the South," *Survey* 40 (May 4, 1918), pp. 115–122; Alfredteen Harrison, ed., *Black Exodus, The Great Migration from the American South* (University Press of Mississippi, 1991); George Edmund Haynes, *Negro New-Comers in Detroit, Michigan* (New York: Home Missions Council, 1918).

45   On black soldiers in World War I, see Athur E. Barbeau and Florette Henri, *The Unknown Soldiers: Black American Troops in World War I* (Philadelphia: Temple University Press, 1974); Lewis, *W. E. B. Du Bois, 1868–1919*, pp. 535–558.

46   On Robert Abbott, see Roi Ottley, *The Lonely Warrior* (Chicago: 1955);

47   **threaten to sue**: Ottley, *Lonely Warrior*, p. 140–141.

48   **"justice and fairness"**: *Chicago Defender*, May 23, 1918.

48   **"to become acclimated"**: *Chicago Defender*, May 12, 1917.

49   **"Not Belgium—America"**: *Chicago Defender*, September 8, 1917; Supplement to the *Crisis*, July 17 14, no. 3, (July 1917) JWJ, "Views and Reviews," *New York Age*, June 21, 1917; Dray, *At the Hands of Persons Unknown* pp. 231–234.

49   **"To die from the bite of frost"**: Ottley, *Lonely Warrior*, p. 169.

49   **Pullman factory**: Ottley, *Lonely Warrior*, p. 168.

49   **readers responded**: See the letters from 1916 and 1917, reprinted in Scott, "Letters of Negro Migrants of 1916–1918."

49   **"The colored people will leave if you will assist them"**: (April 21, 1917), in Scott, "Letters of Negro Migrants of 1916–1918," p. 331.

50   **observed how a teamster**: Ray Stannard Baker, quoted in "The Negro Migration of 1916–1918," *Journal of Negro History*, 5 (October 1921), p. 402.

50   **"Bound for the Promised Land"**: Bontemp and Conroy, *They Seek a City*, p. 136.

50   **could end up in Flint**: Many of the accounts appear in Elaine Latzman Moon, ed. *Untold Tales, Unsung Heroes: An Oral History of Detroit's African-American Community, 1918–1967* (Detroit: Wayne State University Press, 1993) pp. 27–103. Also see Coleman Young's description of his father's experience, *Hard Stuff: The Autobiography of Coleman Young* (New York: Penguin, 1994).

50   **the standard contract**: Henri, *Black Migration*, pp. 354–355; Gilbert Osofsky, *Harlem: the Making of a Ghetto* (New York: Harper and Row, 1963), p. 29. Harrison, ed., *Black Exodus*, p. 22.

51   **From Mississippi, 130,000 people fled, from South Carolina, 75,000**: E. Tolnay and E. M. Beck, "Rethinking the Role of Racial Violence," in *Black Exodus*, ed., Harrison, p. 22.

51   **they swelled cities**: Henri, *Black Migration*, p. 69; Du Bois, "Migration of Negroes," p. 64, provides figures for those leaving smaller towns.

51   **East St. Louis**: Elliot Rudwick, *Race Riot in East St. Louis, 1917* (New York: World Publishing, 1966). Also see the NAACP's coverage in *Crisis*, April 1917, September 1917, January 1918; Oscar Leonard, "The East St. Louis Pogrom," *Survey* (July 14, 1917),

pp. 331–333. Coverage in *Chicago Defender* runs from July 7 through August 18, 1917. Also see the account in *Crisis,* September 1917.

52 **property damages:** *New York Times,* July 3, 1917.

52 **public response was varied:** "East St. Louis Aftermath," *Chicago Defender,* July 28, 1917.

53 **German conspiracy:** *Chicago Defender,* July 28, 1917.

53 **Joseph P. Tumulty:** See Wilson's memo to Joseph Tumulty, July 28, 1917, Ray Stannard Baker, ed., *Woodrow Wilson, Life and Letters* Vol. 7 (New York: Doubleday, Doran, 1939), p. 207. *Chicago Defender,* August 11, 18, 1917.

53 **Congressional hearings convened:** Robert Zangrando, *NAACP Crusade Against Lynching, 1909–1950* (Philadelphia: Temple University Press, 1980), p. 37. The NAACP sent its own team to investigate East St. Louis. See *Crisis,* September 1917.

53 **Henry A. Cooper:** Quoted in *Crisis,* January 1918.

53 **"Make your own destiny":** *Chicago Defender,* August 2, 1917.

54 On the Silent Parade, *New York Times,* July 29, 1917; "The Negro Silent Parade," *Crisis,* September 1917, p. 241; ATW, p. 320.

54 **a sight as has never:** *New York Age,* August 2, 1917.

55 **fifty people:** NAACP, *Thirty Years of Lynching, 1889–1917* (New York, Arno Press, 1968), p. 29.

55 **"barbarism at its depth":** *Chicago Defender,* July 28, 1917.

55 Accounts of the Washington Riot: Arthur I. Waskow, *From Race Riot to Sit-Ins, 1919 and the 1960s* (New York: Doubleday, 1966), pp. 21–37; Constance McLaughlin Green, *The Secret City, A History of Race Relations in the Nation's Capital* (Princeton, Princeton University Press, 1967), pp. 184–214. The account of Professor Nelson is described in Rayford W. Logan, *Howard University* (New York: New York University Press, 1969), p. 189.

56 **Ossian Sweet himself saw:** Gladys Sweet to AGH, [1925] NAACP-micro, Part 5, Reel 3.

56 **"Negroes in Washington":** *New York Times,* July 21, 22, 23, 1919.

Chapter 4: Getting Settled

57 I used the following for a general history of Detroit: Allan Nevins and Frank Ernest Hill, *Ford: Expansion and Challenge 1915–1932* (New York: Charles Scribner's Sons, 1957), pp. 8, 10 for car prices. Joyce Shaw Peterson, "Black Automobile Workers in Detroit, 1910–1930," *Journal of Negro History* 64 (Summer 1979), pp. 177–190. Levine, *Internal Combustion;* Frank Barcus, *All Around Detroit* (Detroit: F. Barcus Art Studios, 1939). Oliver Zunz, *The Changing Face of Inequality: Urbanization, Industrial Development, and Immigrants in Detroit* (Chicago: University of Chicago Press, 1982); Thomas J. Sugrue, *The Origins of the Urban Crisis: Race, Inequality in Postwar Detroit* (Princeton, N.J.: Princeton University Press, 1996); Robert Conot, *American Odyssey* (New York: Morrow, 1974); David M. Katzman, *Before the Ghetto: Black Detroit in the Nineteenth Century* (Urbana: University of Illinois Press, 1973).

57 **Average wage of $2.74:** *Detroit City Directory* (1916), p. 9.
58 **"vast meadows":** Quoted in *Detroit Almanac,* eds. Peter Garilovick and Bill McGraw (Detroit: Detroit Free Press, 2000), p. 30.
58 **summer jobs:** AGH, "Opening Statement," November 16, 1925, NAACP-micro, Part 5, Reel 3. A description of BobLo Island: William Oxford, *The Ferry Steamers: The Story of the Detroit-Windsor Ferry Boats* (Ern, Ontario, Canada: Boston Mills Press, 1992).
58 **D. & C. Navigation Company:** Sunny Wilson with John Dohassey *Toast of the Town* (Detroit: Wayne State University Press, 1998), p. 30.
58 **"the colored population of Detroit":** Forrester B. Washington, "Part II: The Detroit Newcomers' Greeting," *Survey* (July 14, 1917), pp. 333–335. *Crisis* reprints this article, "The Lesson of Detroit" (September 1917), pp. 239–240.
58 On the history of the Urban League, see Nancy J. Weiss, *The National Urban League, 1910–1940* (New York: Oxford University Press, 1974).
59 **foot had frozen:** Minutes of the Urban League, February 1917; River Rouge post office, Report to the Board, January 8, 1920, Reel 1, PUL.
59 **"There seems to be no let up":** Report to the Board, September 18–19, 1917, Reel 1, PUL.
60 **"crime prevention":** Washington, "Part II: The Detroit Newcomers' Greeting," pp. 333–335.
60 **Roy Lubove:** *The Professional Altruist: The Emergence of Social Work as a Career, 1880–1930* (Cambridge, Mass.: Harvard University Press, 1965).
60 **"When the term 'Negro' is used":** Francis H. Warren, *Michigan Manual of Freedmen's Progress* (Detroit: The Commission, 1915), p. 21.
61 **"loud, noisy, type":** Directors Report, Minutes of the Urban League, October 1916, Reel 1, PUL.
61 **meeting trains:** Washington, "Part II: The Detroit Newcomers' Greeting"; Minutes of the Urban League, October 1916, Reel 1, PUL.
62 Descriptions of train travel may be found in Kelli B. Kavanaugh, *Images of America: Detroit's Michigan Central Station* (Detroit, Arcadia Publishing, 2001), pp. 41–52; *Rand McNally Guide to Detroit* (New York: Rand McNally, 1922); *Detroit City Directory* 1925 (microfilm), NYPL.
62 **"not make a nuisance of themselves":** Washington, "Part II: The Detroit Newcomers' Greeting."
62 **Bradby often went down to the station:** Ernestine E. Wright, in Moon, ed., *Untold Tales, Unsung Heroes,* p. 94.
63 **"blue book":** Quoted in Katzman, *Before the Ghetto, Black Detroit in the Nineteenth Century,* p. 138.
63 **"high yellow":** See Charles C. Diggs, in Moon, ed., *Untold Tales, Unsung Heroes,* pp. 51–57.
64 **already he was central:** Baskin Interview Osby. Most of the biographical material on the black middle class is featured in Warren, *Michigan Manual of Freedmen's Progress.* For Osby, see pp. 120–121.
64 The social life in Paradise Valley has been reconstructed from the autobiographical ac-

counts in Moon, ed., *Untold Tales, Unsung Heroes; Detroit City Directory* for the years 1916–1921; Wilson and Dohassey, *Toast of the Town.*

65 **"buffet flat":** Haynes, *Negro New-Comers in Detroit, Michigan,* p. 2. Also see Katzman, *Before the Ghetto;* John Dancy, "The Negro Population of Detroit," [1926]; John Dancy, Report to the Board, September 18 to October 9, 1919," Reel 1, PUL.

65 **nineteen renters:** Urban League Report to the Board, November 1922, Reel 1, PUL.

66 **the worst situations:** Forrester B. Washington, "The Negro in Detroit: A Survey of the Condition of a Negro Group in a Northern Industrial Center During the War Prosperity Period" (Detroit, 1920), pp. 6, 14.

66 **$45 a month:** According to the Consumer Price Index, $45 in 1920 was about the equivalent of $413 in 2003.

67 **two hundred of the eighteen thousand workers:** Joyce Shaw Peterson, "Black Automobile Workers in Detroit, 1910–1930," *Journal of Negro History* 64, no. 3 (Summer 1979), pp. 177–190. The figure two hundred comes from Haynes, *Negro New-Comers in Detroit, Michigan,* pp. 14–15.

68 **men began to leave Detroit:** Report of Director, September 18, 1919, PUL.

68 **"just what we are up against":** [John Dancy], Directors Report, Urban League Board Meeting, December 20, 1921, PUL.

68 **"colored people are being judged":** Urban League, Report of the Director, October 16, 1916, Reel 1, PUL.

69 **Detroit's Employers' Association:** Walter F. White, "Reviving the Ku Klux Klan," *Forum* (April 1921), pp. 426–434.

69 **Dancy wrote to college presidents:** Report of the Executive Director, May 12, 1921, PUL.

69 **People who were part of the Exodus:** For Oscar Lee, see pp 27–29; James E. Cummings, p. 34; Nathaniel Leech, p. 95; Helen Nuttall Brown, pp. 37–38; in Moon, ed., *Untold Tales, Unsung Heroes.*

70 **Later Dancy would write:** John Dancy, "The Negro Population of Detroit, ca. 1926" Reel 1, PUL.

Chapter 5: "Detroit the Dynamic"

71 On the evolution of medical practice, I relied on Paul Starr, *The Social Transformation of American Medicine* (New York: Basic Books, 1982); Charles E. Rosenberg, "The Therapeutic Revoloution," in *The Therapeutic Revolution: The Social History of American Medicine,* eds. Charles E. Rosenberg and Morris J. Vogel (Philadelphia: University of Pennsylvania Press, 1979), pp. 3–25; Morris Fishbein, *The History of the American Medical Association, 1847–1947* (Philadelphia: W. B. Saunders, 1947). On the lag between science and medicine, see Stanley Joel Reiser, *Medicine and the Reign of Technology* (Cambridge, Mass.: Cambridge University Press, 1978), pp. 143–165.

71 The Ku Klux Klan received a vast amount of attention in the twenties, and especially

informative was Robert L. Duffus's behind-the-scenes critique of the Ku Klux Klan for *Worlds Work* (now defunct) in 1923. See "The Salesmen of Hate: The Ku Klux Klan" (May), pp. 32–38; "How the Klan Sells Hate" (June), pp. 182–186; "Counter-Mining the Ku Klux Klan" (July), pp. 275–284; "The Ku Klux Klan in the Middle West" (August), pp. 363–372; "The March of Events" (September), pp. 573–575. On William Simmons, see: "An 'Imperial Wizard' and His 'Klan,' " *Literary Digest* (February 5, 1921), pp. 44–46. Ward Greene, "Notes for a History of the Klan," *American Mercury* 5 (May–August 1925), pp. 240–243. Scholarship has also delved into the Klan. See Michael Newton and Judy Ann Newton, *The Ku Klux Klan: An Encyclopedia* (New York: Garland Publishing, 1991); Jackson, *Ku Klux Klan in the City;* Chalmers, *Hooded Americanism;* Henry Fry, *The Modern Ku Klux Klan* (Boston: Small, Maynard, 1922); John Higham, *Strangers in the Land: Patterns of American Nativism, 1860–1925* (New York: Atheneum, 1975).

71 **"Imagine yourself in an aeroplane"**: William Kuenzel, Staff Photographer, "Aeroplane View of Detroit Today," *Detroit City Directory, 1920–1921,* p. 22.
71 **"Detroit the Dynamic"**: *Detroit City Directory, 1925,* p. 30.
72 Statistics come from *Detroit City Directory, 1925.*
72 **black professionals**: "Colored Detroit" provides biographical information about the community of black professionals in Detroit in 1925. BHC.
73 **Detroit's chapter of Kappa Alpha Psi**: Membership lists of Kappa Alpha Psi, 1920–1927, Archives, National Headquarters, Kappa Alpha Psi, Philadelphia.
73 **dinner dances for couples and smokers for men**: Twelfth Annual Convention (typescript), 1922, Archives Kappa Alpha Psi.
73 **A city doctor**: Starr, *Social Transformation of American Medicine,* p. 142.
73 **Dr. Alexander Turner operated two**: "Colored Detroit," BHC.
73 **loan Cyrus Drozier**: AGH, "Opening Statement," Trial Transcripts.
73 Requirements for Howard University Medical School and Freedmen's Hospital: Howard University, School of Medicine, 1916, Howardania, HU Archives.
74 **Harvey Cushing**: Cushing made this remark in 1914, by which time, he had left Johns Hopkins and moved to Harvard. Quoted in Reiser, *Medicine and the Reign of Technology,* p. 152.
74 **medical text on childbirth**: William George Lee, *Childbirth* (Chicago, Ill: University of Chicago Press, 1928), p. 286.
74 **NEGROES BUILD HOSPITAL HERE**: *FP,* May 31, 1919; Charles H. Wright, M.D., discusses the community of black doctors in Detroit in *The National Medical Association DEMANDS Equal Opportunity, Nothing More, Nothing Less* (Southfield, Mich.: Charro, 1955), pp. 52–55, 64–67.
75 Ethnic solidarity as a strategy for survival is discussed in David Rosner, *A Once Charitable Enterprise: Hospitals and Health Care in Brooklyn and New York* (Cambridge, Mass.: Cambridge University Press, 1982). Rosner's discussion of New York applies equally to neighborhood hospitals in Detroit; Fishbein, *History of the American Medical Association, 1847–1947,* pp. 898–901.

75 Detroit's health needs and medical services, are described in Section 6, "Health" in Forrester B. Washington, "The Negro in Detroit: Mayor's Inter-Racial Committee" (Detroit Bureau of Governmental Research, 1926); Wright, *National Medical Association DEMANDS Equal Opportunity.*

76 **Receiving Hospital:** *Detroit City Directory,* 1919, p. 55.

76 **deathly ill patients:** This comes from the report of Dr. James W. Ames, the inspector of the Board of Health of Detroit. His report noted the surge in tuberculosis is attributable to people "outside who come here and die . . ." Ames was a founding member of Dunbar Memorial Hospital. "Negro Mortality in Detroit," *Michigan Manual 1915,* p. 338. Also see G. Arthur Blakeslee, chief vital statistician, to John Dancy, March 11, 1926, Dancy Papers, Reel 1, PUL, BHL. Blakeslee also supplied the actual number of births, 2,237. Richard Wertz, and Dorothy Wertz, *Lying-In: A History of Childbirth in America* (New York: Free Press, 1977), p. 143.

76 **one-quarter of all babies:** "Detroit Today," *Detroit City Directory* (1921), p. 51. On the history of midwifery, see Susan E. Cayleff, "The Eradication of Female Midwifery," MA Thesis, Sarah Lawrence College, 1978. On contemporary obstetrical practices, see: Robert L. Dickinson, M.D., "A Program for American Gynecology: Presidential Address," read at the Forty-fifth Annual Meeting, May 24–26, 1920, *American Journal of Obstetrics and Gynecology* 1, no. 1 (October 1920), p. 9. Also see Edward Shorter, *Bedside Manners: The Troubled History of Doctors and Patients* (New York: Simon and Schuster, 1985), pp. 107–140; Judith Walzer Leavitt, *Brought to Bed: Child-Bearing in America, 1750–1950* (New York: Oxford University Press, 1986), pp. 36–86.

77 **five percent had hospital affiliations:** Starr, *Social Transformation of American Medicine,* p. 167.

77 **Crittendon Home:** Louise Hood to [Wayland D. Stearns] quoted in Wright, *National Medical Association DEMANDS Equal Opportunity,* pp. 64–67. Wright discusses Greenidge.

78 **Marie Curie's visit:** Susan Quinn, *Marie Curie: A Life* (New York: Simon and Schuster, 1995), pp. 388–399. Quinn's account, although clearly partisan, is more even handed than the biography written by Eve Curie, one of her daughters: *Madame Curie: A Biography* (New York, Doubleday, Doran, 1939).

78 Press coverage, including Marie Curie's arrival, is reported in the *New York Times,* May 12, 18, 19, 1921.

79 **"radium is still in the infancy period":** Thomas C. Jeffries, "The Story of Radium in America," *Current History of the New York Times* 14 (June 1921), pp. 448–454.

79 **Radium Institute:** For a discussion of the Radium Institute, see Dr. Claude Regaud, "Radium Institute of the University of Paris Departments of Radiophysiology and Medicine," *Methods and Problems of Medical Education,* 12th Series (New York Rockefeller Foundation, 1929).

80 **moved to Detroit:** Jackson, *Ku Klux Klan in the City,* p. 129.

80 **Couzens threatened:** "Police Trim Out Parts of Birth of a Nation," *DN,* September 6, 1921; "Mayor Orders Film Stopped," September, 1921.

80 **The exposé originally appeared:** *New York World,* September 5–19, 1921. In Detroit, the syndication appeared in the *Detroit Free Press.* Rowland Thomas, reporter for the *New York World,* describes his reporting in the hearings. See his testimony on October 11. U.S. Congress. House Committee on Rules. *Report on the Ku Klux Klan, 1921* (New York: Arno Press and New York Times, 1969), pp. 8–15. Fry, *Modern Ku Klux Klan,* chapter 4.

81 **fifty cents:** Jackson, *Ku Klux Klan in the City,* p. 129.

81 **most spectacular growth:** Simmons, *Klan Unmasked,* p. 11.

81 Photos of Clarke and Tyler appear in Robert L. Duffus, "The Salesmen of Hate: The Ku Klux Klan," *World's Work,* May 1923, pp. 31–38.

82 Details of Matty and the Klan's organizing activities after 1920, may be found in: Ward Greene, "Notes for a History of the Klan," *American Mercury* 5 (May–August 1925), pp. 241–245.

82 **They often spoke in code:** Wade, *Fiery Cross,* p. 142.

82 **"Klean Klansmens Klothes":** *Fiery Cross,* September 7, 21, 1923, BHC.

82 **Inches was a Klansman:** Inches denied this assertion. See *FP,* September 16, 1925; WW to JWJ, September 16, 1925, NAACP-micro, Part 5/Reel 2.

83 The hearings have been reprinted in *Report on the Ku Klux Klan, 1921.* Also see Fry, *Modern Ku Klux Klan,* chapter 17.

83 **C. Anderson Wright:** October 11, 1921. *Report on the Ku Klux Klan, 1921* pp. 15–27.

84 **"vigilante committees"** cleaned up **"fast and loose females":** Leonidas Dyer testimony, *Report on the Ku Klux Klan, 1921,* p. 6.

84 **Simmons had been waiting:** For descriptions, see *Atlantic Constitution,* October 10–14, 1921. Simmons's testimony appears in *Report on the Ku Klux Klan, 1921,* pp. 48–101.

85 **Simmons's testimony and collapse:** *Atlanta Constitution,* October 14, 1921; *Washington Post,* October 13, 1921.

85 The forms were printed as part of the syndicated series from the *New York World.*

85 **H. L. Mencken:** Quoted in Wade, *Fiery Cross,* p. 161.

86 Duffus estimates the memberships of different states in "The Ku Klux Klan in the Middle West," *World's Work* (August, 1923), p. 363.

86 **Warren G. Harding:** Wade, *Fiery Cross,* p. 165.

86 **Even a haberdasher from Independence:** David McCullough, *Truman* (New York: Simon and Schuster, 1992), pp. 163–164.

86 **on a farm in Royal Oak:** *FP,* June 14, 1923; Jackson, *Ku Klux Klan in the City,* p. 121.

87 **the scene repeated:** *Fiery Cross,* September 21, November 30, 1923, BHC. Jackson, *Ku Klux Klan in the City,* provides the most comprehensive account of Detroit. See chapter 9.

87 **towns such as Cairo:** *Fiery Cross,* November 30, 1923, BHC.

87 **The law was supposed to:** Burns Law outlawed masked men in Michigan: *FP,* August 30, 1923; Chalmers, *Hooded Americanism,* chapter 5; *Fiery Cross,* September 21, 1923, maligns Burns because he was Catholic.

88 **the annual luncheon at the Statler Hotel:** In his opening statement to the jury, AGH

refers to the event at the Intercollegiate Association. A story in *Detroit Saturday Night*, April 22, 1922 does not mention Cobb was planning to appear.

88 **black and white mixed:** Forrester B. Washington, "Recreation," in "The Negro in Detroit," p. 15, mentions the popularity of Mack Field, with an average daily attendance of 4,500, and Navin Field, home of the Tigers, as favorites for baseball fans.

88 **Ty Cobb:** Richard Bak, *Turkey Stearnes and the Detroit Stars* (Detroit: Wayne State University Press, 1994), pp. 110–112; also see Bak, *Ty Cobb: His Tulumtuous Life and Times* (Dallas: Taylor Publishing, 1994).

89 **Gladys Atkinson:** Gladys Atkinson is listed in the Student Directory, Detroit Teachers College, 1921–1922, Archives of Labor and Urban Affairs, Wayne Sate University. Details about her neighbors on Lamb Avenue come from the Fourteenth Census of the United States (1920).

90 When Gladys and Ossian departed, families traveled under the passport application of the head of household. Ossian's passport application specified the destinations and the anticipated duration of travel.

Chapter 6: Two Cities: Vienna and Paris

91 Study in Europe was the pinnacle of medical training in the twenties. This chapter benefited from Donald Fleming, *William Welch and the Rise of Modern Medicine* (Boston: Little Brown, 1954), pp. 33–34; Flexner, "Medical Education, 1909–1924," pp. 833–838; Ira M. Rutkow, "The Letters of William Halsted and Anton von Eiselsberg," *Archives of Surgery* 115 (August 1980), pp. 993–1001; William J. Mayo, M.D., "A Short Visit to Some of the Hospitals in Germany, Austria, Switzerland, and Holland," *Journal Lancet* 32, no. 16 (August 15, 1912), pp. 423–427; C. H. Mayo, M.D., *Staff Meetings of the Mayo Clinic,* September 11, 1929, p. 272.

91 The details about Vienna derive from the letters Dr. Carl Rosenbloom, Northampton, Mass., wrote home during his two trips to Vienna, the first during the summer of 1916, the second in 1925, two years after Sweet's.

91 **The Sweets planned to leave:** Departure from New York was scheduled for October 6. "Winter Tourists Sailing to Europe," and "The Weather," October 6, 1923, *New York Times.* Lloyd George's arrival occurred on the same day.

92 **Austria by train:** According to the "Meddezettal fur Unterpaarteien" which all travelers completed when they crossed the border. The Sweets arrived, in Austria on October 26, 1923. WienerStadt- und Landesarchiv, Vienna.

92 **Bartsch taught:** Paul Bartsch, *Who Was Who Among North American Authors, 1921–1939,* (Detroit: Gale Research Co., 1976), p. 109.

92 **She went to Vienna:** Anna Bartsch-Dunne, "Gynecology in Vienna," *Howard Medical News* 2 (February 20, 1926).

92 **Löwengasse 47:** Sweet lists his mailing address as Löwengasse 47 in December 1923 for

his fraternity membership. The Meldezettel gives his address as Löwengasse 49. This was probably a clerical error, which were common. The same document erroneously places Orlando, Florida, in Illinois. I am grateful to Professor Michael Hubenstorf, Institut ur Geschichte der Medizin, Austria, for calling to my attention the significance of Löwengasse 47. The building was controversial enough that it has become a part of the debate about Vienna's architectural legacy. See Janos Kamos and Andreas Lenne, *Jugenstil in Wien* (Vienna, Pichler Verlan GambH, 1998), p. 75.

94 **Pensions within walking distance:** Information about a pension could be obtained by writing to the Gremium der Pensionsinhaber. Tourists could also obtain a list of pensions based on classifications of comfort and amenities. *Grieben's Guide Books, Vienna and Enviorns, Vol. 199* (London: Geographia Ltd., 1930). Pensions also advertised on city maps.

94 **Over meals:** Carl Rosenbloom to Lena Rosenbloom, October 6, 1925, January 25, 1926, February 26, 1926. Also see a discussion of activities in *JAMA,* January 12, 1924.

95 **Vienna branch of the AMA:** The local activities of the AMA in Vienna are described by Jabez A. Mahan, *Vienna of Yesterday and Today* (Vienna: Halm and Goldmann, 1928), chapter 12. Official stationery listed Mahan as the treasurer of the AMA with a home in Ellensburgh, Washington.

95 **"Scientific investigators":** In a letter of November 28, 1925, Rosenbloom also describes the cancellation of classes. Carl Rosenbloom Letters, private collection.

96 **people of color were rare:** The permanent collection of the Leopold Museum displays two works of art by Hans Bohler. One painted in 1913 was *Black Girl with Blue Head Scarf (Jamaican Girl).* The other, *Black Boy with Blue Jacket,* is dated 1915. Professor Hubenstordf believes Ossian Sweet may have been the first black doctor from America to study in Vienna. The year after Sweet returned home, Dr. Alfred B. Xuma, a South African doctor who studied in the United States, arrived at the Allgemeines Krankenhaus. Xuma later returned to South Africa and became the first president-general of the African National Congress. Professor Richard Ralston, University of Wisconsin, kindly shared his research about Xuma. During one of his many trips to Europe at the end of the twenties, Dr. Charles Mayo wrote of meeting another "colored doctor" from New York. Black doctors were noteworthy because they were scarce. *Staff Meetings of the Mayo Clinic,* September 11, 1929, p. 272.

96 **"The French remind me":** Joel A. Rogers, *Amsterdam News,* September 23, 1925.

96 **"free to be merely a man":** ATW, p. 209.

97 **one guide book:** Ralph Neville, *Days and Nights in Montmartre and the Latin Quarter,* (London: H. Jenkins Limited, 1927), pp. 31, 275.

97 **On Paris in the 1920s see:** Petrine Archer-Straw, *Negrophilia: Avant-Garde Paris and Black Culture in the 1920's* (New York: Thames and Hudson, 2000); Michel Abre, *From Harlem to Paris: Black American Writers in France, 1840–1980* (Urbana and Chicago: University of Illinois Press, 1991), pp. 36–75; Neville, *Days and Nights in Montmartre,* p. 340 describes Café Florida.

97 **Paris of expatriates:** Langston Hughes, *The Big Sea: An Autobiography* (New York:

Hill and Wang 1940). For life on the Left Bank and the white writers' colony, see Ernest Hemingway, *A Moveable Feast* New York: Simon and Schuster, 1964); George Orwell, *Down and Out in Paris and London* (London and New York: Harvest Book, 1933);

97 **"Paris is Devine"**: Lorelei in Anita Loos, *Gentlemen Prefer Blondes* (New York: Boni and Liveright, 1925). Also see George H. Douglas, *Women of the 20s* (San Francisco: Saybrook Publishers, 1986), chapter 8. Gary Carey, *Anita Loos: A Biography* (New York: Alfred A. Knopf, 1988), chapter 8.

97 **"Slowly and deliberately"**: Neville, *Days and Nights in Montmartre*, p. 31.

97 *l'arte negre:* Abre, *From Harlem to Paris,* pp. 36–75.

97 **Joel Rogers:** *New York Age* September 14, 1927.

97 **references to a juvenile mind:** Georges Sadoul, "Sambo Without Tears," in Nancy Cunard, ed., *Negro: An Anthology* (New York: Frederick Ungar Publishing, 1979), p. 349.

97 **Folies Bergère:** Archer-Straw, *Negrophilia,* p. 32.

98 **Hughes wrote boldly about the rejection:** See Hughes, *The Big Sea,* p. 163.

98 **Opportunity to now learn:** A description of the research world in Paris at that time is found in Regaud, "Radium Institute of the University of Paris," p. 43. Also see Quinn, *Marie Curie,* chapter 18.

98 **Sweet donated 300 francs:** AGH "Opening Remarks." Transcripts.

98 **"facilities for taking care of Americans":** *Chicago Tribune,* June 20 [1924], Clipping Scrapbook, American Hospital of Paris. The fund-raising campaign for the American Hospital was covered extensively by the *Chicago Tribune* and the *New York Herald* throughout May and June 1924.

The exact date of Iva's birth is not known. A thorough search of the thirteen arrondissements in Paris failed to turn up her birth registration. May 29, 1924, is the date provided by the Roseland Park Cemetery where she is buried in Detroit.

100 **"quiet and free from visitors":** Dr. John S. Fairbairn, *Gynecology with Obstetrics* (London: Oxford University Press, 1924), p. 377.

101 **John W. Davis:** After defeat, Davis enjoyed a long career as a New York lawyer. In 1954 he argued against the plaintiffs in favor of segregation in the landmark *Brown v. Board of Education.* I am indebted to Paul Dodyk for calling this to my attention.

101 **debate over the Ku Klux Klan:** *New York Times,* June 29, 1924. Chalmers, *Hooded Americanism,* pp. 202–215.

Chapter 7: 2905 Garland Avenue

Descriptions of moving day have been pieced together from testimony presented at the trials, including newspaper accounts of the proceedings. In addition, journalist Marcet Haldeman-Julius visited extensively with the Sweets when she attended Henry Sweet's trial. One should read her cautiously because numerous unsubstantiated facts crept into her account. Where she is accurate, however, she provides effusive, often flamboyant descriptions. The originals were published in the now rare *Haldeman-Julius Monthly*. The first article, "The Defendants in the Sweet Murder Case," appeared in vol. 4, no. 1 (June 1926); the second, "Clarence Darrow Defends a Negro," in July 1926. More accessible is the condensed version, *Clarence Darrow's Two Great Trials*.

102 **making suburbia:** *Detroit Saturday Night,* March 29, 1925; *FP,* November 6, November 8, 1925; *DN,* May 9, 1925.

102 **reinforced housing segregation:** The Greater Detroit Realtors Committee announcement discouraging black ownership is reprinted in Washington, "The Negro in Detroit," section 5, "Housing," p. 26.

103 **description of Gladwin Park and waterworks tower:** Barcus, *All Around Detroit.*

103 **It was the kind of neighborhood:** Description of the neighborhood comes from testimony of *Trial Transcripts,* November 1925; *Detroit City Directory,* 1925; *Sanborn Insurance Maps,* Detroit, Michigan (1929), vol. 19, pp. 77–78; vol. 11, pp. 1–2, Geography and Map Reading Room, LOC.

105 **Wabash Railroad:** Marcet Haldeman-Julius; *Clarence Darrow's Two Great Trials,* p. 35.

107 **destroyed hope:** Detroit's street violence leading to the expulsion of black homeowners in the summer of 1925 has become the backdrop to the Sweets' story. The most succinct details are contained in Levine, *Internal Combustion,* pp. 154–157. Bristol Saw: Vollington Bristol provided details of the assault on his house in a statement to the defense attorneys. "Statement of Vollington Bristol, November 15, 1925," Clarence Darrow Papers, Box 5, Manuscript Division, LOC. John Fletcher primarily: *Pittsburgh Courier,* November 21, 1925.

107 **"mobbism against colored property owners":** WW to JWJ, September 16, 1925, NAACP-micro, Part 5, Reel 2.

108 **STOP RIOTING:** *FP,* July 12, 1925. The gunshot is described in *Pittsburgh Courier,* July 16, 1925.

109 **Smith disparaged:** This story also listed the agenda for the upcoming meeting of the Waterworks Improvement Association. See *FP,* July 12, 1925; Josephine Gomon, "The Sweet Trials," p. 12, in unpublished biography (typescript) of Frank Murphy. Box 9, Gomon Papers, BHL.

110 **nineteenth-century abolitionist:** The Sanborn Map (1919) lists the school at Garland and Charlevoix as the Julia Ward Howe School. All other sources refer to the Howe School.

110 **campaign in the summer:** Branch records, Detroit, March 2, 1925; press release, March 6, 1925, Branch records, NAACP-LOC, Box G-95.

111 **Bagnall responded to Bradby:** Bagnall to Bradby, July 30, 1925; Beulah Young to JWJ, July 30, 1925; JWJ to Robert Bradby, July 22, 1925; Robert Bradby to JWJ, July 27, 1925; JWJ to Bradby, July 30, 1925, Local branch records (Detroit), Box G-95, NAACP-LOC.

112 **suspicious of the police:** Gladys Sweet to WW, [nd], NAACP-micro Part 5, Reel 3; "Statement of Vollington Bristol", Darrow Papers, LOC.

112 **excessive force:** Accounts of police brutality are enumerated in Mayor's Intra-Racial

Committee of Detroit. *The Negro in Detroit* (Detroit Bureau of Governmental Research, 1926. Section IX (Crime) pp. 34, 35.

113 **Gladys reasoned:** Gladys Sweet to WW, [nd], NAACP-micro, Part 5, Reel 3.

113 **telephone call from Mrs. Marie Smith:** *DN,* November 18, 1925.

113 **Osby described the advice:** AB, William C. Osby.

114 **Clayton Williams:** Sergeant William's account, *Trial Transcripts,* November 9, 1925.

114 **food to stock a pantry:** Gladys Sweet to WW [nd], NAACP-micro, Part 5, Reel 3.

114 **friends visited:** Reports of threats to the Sweets are described in AGH, "Opening Statement, Address to the Jury, 16 November, 1925," *Trial Transcripts.*

115 **They scooped up:** Objects brought into the house are included in the eyewitness testimony of police officers Stanke and Doran, *Trial Transcripts,* November 13, 1925.

116 **entry of illegal liquor:** The narrow Detroit River made Detroit's proximity to Windsor, Canada, the distribution center for bootleg. From this advantage, organized crime radiated to Chicago. In 1920 Police Commissioner Inches estimated fifty bootlegers had earned more than $100,000 that year. See Larry Engelmann, *Intemperance: The Lost War Against Liquor* (New York: Free Press, 1979), pp. 72–89; Philip Mason, *Rum Running and the Roaring Twenties* (Detroit: Wayne State University Press, 1995). Detroit's future mayor Coleman Young wrote a biography with insight about these issues in *Hard Stuff.*

Chapter 8: James Weldon Johnson and the NAACP

Two major archival resources provide vivid documents of the activities of James Weldon Johnson. The James Weldon Johnson Papers comprise correspondence and papers spanning his entire life, as well as that of his wife, Grace Nail Johnson. They are deposited at the Beinecke Library, Yale University. The second resource is the substantial archive of the NAACP, and the Manuscript Division of the Library of Congress maintains the originals. A portion of them comprise 372 reels of microfilm, which are available in research libraries. For this project, both were consulted, and I used the microfilm at the Schomburg Center for Research in Black Culture, a branch of the New York Public Library. They are organized internally by reels within parts, and the initial selection for inclusion was made by general editors John Bracy, Jr., and August Meier. The project to copy more of the records continues. For this research, I relied heavily on the following records of the NAACP:

Part 1: Board of Directors Activities (Reel 2)
Part 2: Correspondence (Reels 2, 9, and 10)
Part 5: The Campaign Against Residential Segregation
(Reels 1, 2, 3, 4, 20, and 23)

Part 11: Special Subject Files (Reels 13 and 20)
Part 12: Local Branch Files (Reel 11)

In addition, the following books informed my discussion of the early years of the NAACP and James Weldon Johnson: Charles Kellogg, *The NAACP, Vol. I: 1909–1920* (Baltimore: Johns Hopkins Press, 1967); Mary White Ovington, *The Walls Came Tumbling Down* (New York: Schocken Books, 1970); Mark Schneider, *We Return Fighting: The Civil Rights Movement in the Jazz Age* (Boston: Northeastern Press, 2001); Zangrando, *NAACP Crusade Against Lynching, 1909–1950*, Eugene Levy, *James Weldon Johnson: Black Leader, Black Voice* (Chicago: University of Chicago Press, 1973); ATW.

120 **he wired for updated information:** JWJ to Bradby, September 11, 1925, NAACP-micro, Part 5, Reel 2.

121 **Kentucky's restrictive law:** On the Louisville case, *New York Age*, Nov. 9, 1916; ATW, p. 307.

121 **Moorfield Storey:** On Storey's influence in NAACP's legal strategies, see William B. Hixson, *Moorfield Storey and the Abolitionist Tradition* (New York: Oxford University Press, 1972).

121 **"If the NAACP never did anything else":** *New York Age*, December 22, 1917.

122 **William Stanley Braithwaite:** ATW, p. XV.

122 **Charles Evans Hughes:** Hughes campaign: *New York Times*, November 8–9, 1916, *New York Herald*, November 8, 1916. ATW, p. 307.

123 **Oklahoma law:** *Gunn and Beal v. United States*, No. 96, Supreme Court of the United States (June 21, 1915).

123 **William Jennings Bryan:** ATW, pp. 291–293. Also see Du Bois to Villard, March 31, 1915, Series I; Box 6, JWJ Papers, Beinecke.

123 **He loved the eight years:** ATW, p. 227–293.

123 **Bookerites:** ATW, p. 223.

123 **two hundred tunes:** Jervis Anderson, *Harlem: The Great Black Way* (London: Orbis Publishing, 1982), p. 33; Also see ATW, p. 157; Lewis, *W. E. B. Du Bois, 1868–1919*, p. 523.

123 **not relinquished:** Johnson tells his wife about his hopes for a restored career: JWJ to GNJ, June 12, 1916, Series III: Box 41, JWJ Papers, Beinecke.

123 **"We say 'Thank God' ":** *New York Age*, November 9, 1916.

124 **Johnson dropped:** ATW, p. 307.

124 **HUGHES WINS:** *New York Age*, November 9, 1916.

124 **On his Southern tour:** Both Johnson and White describe this in their respective autobiographies. See ATW, p. 125 for Johnson and *A Man Called White*, p. 35, for White.

124 **two violent incidents:** Kellogg, *NAACP*, p. 218.

125 **"work that must be done":** *Crisis*, April 1, 1917, p. 285.

125 **On branch growth,** see Kellogg, *NAACP*, p. 135; ATW, p. 315; [NAACP] *Annual Re-*

port 1919, p. 9, quoted in August Meier and Elliot Rudwick, *Along the Color Line* (Urbana: University of Illinois Press, 1976), p. 105.

125 **less than what was paid:** Meier and Rudwick, "Black Secretariat in the NAACP," in *Along the Color Line,* p. 125.

126 **Harlem's transition:** Several books document this period of Harlem's growth. See Osofsky, *Harlem;* Jervis Anderson, *Harlem, the Great Black Way;* JWJ, *Black Manhattan;* David Levering Lewis, *When Harlem Was in Vogue* (New York: Penguin Books, 1997).

126 **taboos of whites:** JWJ, *Black Manhattan* (New York: Da Capo Press, 1991), chapter 15.

126 **LeRoy's:** Willie "the Lion" Smith with George Hoeffer, *Music on My Mind: The Memoirs of An American Pianist* (New York: Doubleday, 1964), chapter 9; *The Memoirs of Willie the Lion Smith* (Liner Notes, Koch Jazz/BMG).

126 **In his soul:** Walter White's life has finally received a full-length biography. See Jenken, *White.*

126 **John Shalliday never completely recovered:** ATW, p. 343; Mary White Ovington to JWJ, April 9, 1920, JWJ Papers, Series I: Box 15, Beinecke. Johnson and Ovington subscribed to a different interpretation of this event than did Arthur Spingarn, which Jenken discusses in *White,* nb. 2, chapter 3, p. 382.

127 **"Shame of America":** ATW, p. 361; "Report of the Secretary," April 1921, NAACP-micro Part 1, Reel 4; Zangrado, *NAACP Crusade Against Lynching,* pp. 56–57.

128 **soon came to rely on him:** Report of the Secretary, February 1922, NAACP-micro, Part 1, Reel 4.

128 **booklet the NAACP had written:** *Thirty Years of Lynching, 1889–1918,* p. 7.

129 **Political maneuvering:** House debate on the Dyer bill is described on in several sources: ATW p. 366; Claudine L. Ferrell, *Nightmare and Dream: Anti-lynching in Congress, 1917–1922* (New York: Garland, 1986); Schneider, *We Return Fighting; New York Age,* October 21 and November 5, 1921.

129 **House of Representatives debate:** [JWJ] Secretary's Report, February 1922, NAACP-micro, Part 1, Reel 4.

129 **"Thanksgiving and jubiliation":** ATW

129 **Several were lawyers:** Ferrell, *Nightmare and Dream,* chapter 7.

130 **Johnson went to Washington:** [JWJ] Secretary's Report, February 1922, NAACP-micro, Part 1, Reel 4.

130 **appealing to a popular constituency:** *The Crisis,* October and November, 1922; Report of the Secretary, March 9, 1922, NAACP-micro, Part 1, Reel 4. Mary White Ovington to Louis B. Hertz, September 29, 1922; WW to Bessie Jacklin, October 26, 1922, NAACP-micro, Part 7, Reel 15.

130 **Walter White planned the press strategy:** WW to JWJ, November 23, 1922; WW to Editor of *New York Times,* December 27, 1922; JWJ to WW, November 30, 1927, NAACP-micro, Part 7, Reel 15.

131 **Marcus Garvey:** Zangrando, *NAACP Crusade Against Lynching,* pp. 90–91.

131 **Negro Press Association:** Zangrando, *NAACP Crusade Against Lynching* nb 49, p. 239. See *Afro-American,* December 20, 1922, pp. 5–6.

131 **"We should set up now"**: WW to JWJ, October 23, 1922, NAACP-micro, Part 7, Reel 15.

132 **"we still have a chance"**: JWJ to WW, November 30, 1922, NAACP-micro, Part 7, Reel 15.

132 **Senator Underwood**: *New York Age*, December 16, 1922; *New York Times*, November 29, 30, 1922.

132 **a national humiliation**: To the pastors of Greater New York, February 20, 1922, NAACP-micro, Part 7, Reel 28.

132 **full Senate would probably have passed the bill**: ATW, p. 371.

132 **He started to read diet books**: JWJ to GNJ, April 15, 1923, Series II: JWJ Papers, Beinecke.

132 **Congress as a forum**: JWJ, Annual Convention, Renaissance Casino, New York, January 6, 1924, NAACP-micro, Part 7, Reel 28.

132 **sounded listless**: Annual Convention, Renaissance Casino, New York City, January 6, 1924, NAACP-micro, Part 7, Reel 28.

133 **Income diminished**: Zangrando, *NAACP Anti-Lynching Crusade*, Report of the Secretary, November 8, 1923 and Board Minutes, November 12, 1923, nb 47, p. 239.

133 **Internal Revenue Service**: JWJ to A. B. Springarn, July 15, 1924; January 21, March 9, May 1, 1925, Series I: Box 19, JWJ Papers, Beinecke.

133 **Ira Jayne**: WW to James S. Cobb, May 24, 1924, NAACP-micro, Part 4, Reel 5.

133 **Louisiana imposed residential segregation**: Press Release, July 18, 1924, NAACP-micro, Part 5, Reel 2.

134 **Reviewing the galleys**: JWJ to GNJ, July 20, 1925, Series II: Box 34, JWJ Papers, Beinecke.

134 **barn in need of renovation**: The Great Barrington home is described by WW's daughter, Jane, in Anderson, *Harlem, the Great Black Way*, pp. 345–346; Ovington, *Walls Came Tumbling Down*, pp. 238–242.

134 **"The weather is perfect here"**: JWJ to Miss R. G. Randolph, [July]–August, 1925, Series II: Box 16, JWJ Papers, Beinecke.

134 **plethora of cases**: NAACP Press Release, July 18, 1924, NAACP-micro, Reel 5, Part 2. Minutes of NAACP Governing Board, July 13, September 14, 1925, NAACP-micro, Part 1, Reel 2.

134 **what worried him most**: JWJ to Moorefield Storey, September 12, 1925, NAACP-micro, Part 17, Reel 1.

134 *Corrigan v. Buckley:* No. 104, Supreme Court of the United States, 271 U.S. 323; 46 S. Ct. 521; 70 L. Ed. 969 (1926).

134 **need at least $50,000**: JWJ to Moorfield Storey, September 12, 1925, NAACP-micro, Part 17, Reel 1.

135 **roll onto the floor**: Ruth Manning interview.

135 **"voting rights were being murdered"**: Report of the Secretary, January 1921, NAACP-micro, Part I, Reel 4. Zora Neale Hurston has written a powerful description of the massacre. See *Go Gator and Muddy the Waters*, p. 146–150; WW, "Election Day in Florida," *Crisis* (January 1921) pp. 106–109.

Chapter 9: Send Walter White

Starting September 12, 1925, letters and telegrams went back and forth from Detroit to New York with great frequency. Sometimes multiple copies were delivered simultaneously to Mose Walker, Robert Bradby, Judge Ira Jayne, and W. Hayes McKinney from WW or JWJ. Because of the redundant nature of this correspondence, only consequential dispatches are cited. Of particular relevance to WW's first trip are: Mose Walker to JWJ, September 12; JWJ to W. Hayes McKinney, September 13; WW to JWJ, September 16, Mose Walker to WW, September 20; Mose Walker to WW, September 22; JWJ memo subsequent to conversation with Judge Ira Jayne, September 25, WW to Robert Bradby, September 25; WW to Mose Walker, September 25. All in 1925. NAACP-micro, Part 5, Reel 2.

136 **looked dismal:** Mose Walker to JWJ, September 12, 1925, NAACP-micro, Part 5, Reel 2.

138 **seventh green of a New Jersey golf course:** Ovington, *Walls Came Tumbling Down,* p. 198.

138 **Blanche Knopf:** September 15, 1925, NAACP-micro Part 5, Reel 2; October 8, 1925, NAACP-micro, Part 2, Reel 9.

138 **on the way out the door:** WW to Hussey, September 14, 1925, NAACP-micro, Part 5, Reel 2.

139 **"stay away from them":** WW, *Fire in the Flint* (New York: Alfred A. Knopf, 1924), p. 17.

139 **NAACP Twelfth Annual Convention:** Secretary's Report to the Board, July 7, 1921, NAACP-micro, Part 1, Reel 4; "The Twelfth Annual Conference," *Crisis* (August, 1921), pp. 161–164.

FP and *DN* each ran front-page stories on September 10, 1925.

140 **next best case was unraveling:** *New York World,* September 1924.

141 **successfully defended a woman:** The NAACP's celebration of the lawyers appeared in a press release, "Detroit NAACP Wins Three Cases for Colored People," June 5, 1925, One of the cases involved Mrs. Flita Mathis, who was also victimized by whites stoning her home after she refused to vacate. The attorneys of record were Cecil Rowlette and W. Hayes McKinney.

143 **prevent rumors:** The NAACP still felt shame about LeRoy Bundy, who bolted with money raised to defend him after he was accused of fomenting the riot in East St. Louis.

143 **book review:** WW to Sinclair Lewis, October 2, 1925, NAACP-micro, Part 2, Reel 9.

144 **White told Walker:** WW to Mose Walker, September 21, 1925, NAACP-micro, Part 5, Reel 2.

144 **family legend:** Sherman Sweet interview.

144 **"theory of Ku Klanism":** *Florida Sentinel,* September 26, 1926.

145 **defendants wrote a letter:** September 29, 1925; October 1, 1925, NAACP-micro, Part 5, Reel 2.

146 **"The question":** Oscar Baker to WW, October 4, 1925; WW to Oscar Baker, October 5, 1925, NAACP-micro, Part 5, Reel 2.

147 **"Did the defendants shoot":** WW repeats this scene in his autobiography, *A Man Called White*, p. 76.

148 **"boy-politician":** On Frank Murphy, see Fine, *Frank Murphy*, chapter 7.

149 **Walker gloated:** Mose Walker to WW, October 22, 1925, NAACP-micro, Part 2, Reel 5.

149 **personal reasons:** Josephine Gomon, "Sweet Trial," unpublished manuscript, "Biography of Frank Murphy," p. 15, Box 9, Gomon Papers, BHL

Chapter 10: Clarence Darrow Sets the Stage

I have relied on local newspapers as well as clips in the files of the NAACP to reconstruct courtroom scenes, especially for nuance, gesture, and emotions that would not be manifest in trial transcripts. For coverage in Detroit, I have culled the *Detroit Free Press, Detroit News,* and *Detroit Times.* I have benefited greatly from the exceptional descriptions in the *Chicago Defender* and the *Pittsburgh Courier* and heartily credit those journalists whose daily dedication indeed wrote "the first draft of history."

Scopes trial, see Edward J. Larson, *Summer for the Gods: The Scopes Trial and America's Continuing Debate over Science and Religion* (New York: Basic Books, 1997); Ray Ginger, *Six Days or Forever? Tennessee v. John Thomas Scopes* (Boston: Beacon Press, 1958).

151 **"RIOT TRIAL ON; DARROW HERE":** October 30, 1925 *DN.*

151 **DARROW AIDS NEGROES:** *Herald Tribune,* October 31, 1925.

151 **gestures and clothes:** description of Darrow: Gomon, "The Sweet Trial," box 9, Josephine Gomon Papers, BHC.

153 **Murphy told his close friend:** Gomon Diary, Josephine Gomon Papers, BHC.

153 **Darrow told a friend:** Josephine Gomon, "The Sweet Trial," p. 23, Box 9, Josephine Gomon Papers, BHC.

153 **Judge Murphy instructed:** Murphy's comments on the courtroom incident are reported in WW to JWJ "Saturday Night," [Oct. 31, 1925], NAACP-micro, Part 5, Reel 3.

154 **"stage is set":** *Chicago Defender,* November 7, 1925.

On 1924–1925 election, see Jackson, *Ku Klux Klan in the City; Detroit Saturday Night,* September 26, 1925; *DT,* September 23, 1925.

155 **"kleagles and loppers":** *Detroit Saturday Night,* September 12, 1925.

155 **"Detroiters of all races":** *Chicago Defender,* September 24, 1925.

156 **His criteria:** Clarence Darrow, "Attorney for the Defense," *Esquire,* May 1936, quoted in "FBI, Memo for Mr. Tolson from R. E. Joseph, 6/24/36," Darrow Papers, Box 5, Manuscript Division, LOC; Clarence Darrow, *Story of My Life,* (New York: Da Capo Press, 1996) p. 308.

157 **Mr. Pokerface:** AGH, "What's Wrong with Our Juries," *Pageant Magazine* (May 1955), pp. 88–93.

157 **"principles of the Ku Klux Klan":** *DN*, November 5, 1925.

158 **Hays wanted to learn:** AGH to NAACP, October 19, 1925, NAACP-micro, Part 5, Reel 3.

158 **information about the Sweets:** [WW to Gladys, October 21, 1925; Gladys Sweet to WW, [October 1925], NAACP-micro, Part 5, Reel 3.

159 **Locating witnesses:** WW to Darrow, October 20, 1925, NAACP-micro, Part 5, Reel 3.

Chapter 11: "Nobody Is Molesting You"

The references for this chapter are contained within Trial Transcripts, BHL, on the following pages. Day 1, Thursday, November 5: Norton Schuknecht, pp. 31–125; Paul Schellenberger, pp. 132–151; Day 2, Friday, November 6: Paul Schellenberger, pp. 185; Ray Dove, pp. 185–290; Frank Lee Gill, pp. 290–322; Day 3, Saturday, November 7: Edward Wettlaufer, pp. 320–364; Otto Eberhardt, pp. 364–396; Eben Draper, pp. 424–472.

161 **associates of Judge:** Josephine Gomon, "The Sweet Trial," typescript, p. 13, Box 9, Gomon Papers, BHC.

161 **Toms's recollection of his dealings with Darrow:** AB, Robert Toms, pp. 2–4.

162 **Toms started the trial:** Toms, State's Opening Statement, pp. 11, 17, 5, Thursday, November 5, 1925, Trial Transcripts.

165 **Signature wardrobe:** AB asked each of the people he interviewed about Darrow's attire and personal style. See AB. Josephine Gomon also commented that Ruby Darrow nagged her husband to the chagrin of those around her. See Diary, "Clarence Darrow," Gomon Papers, BHL; AB, Toms, p. 2.

166 **"Arthur take care of that":** AB, Toms, p. 3.

167 **the first to appear:** Lieutenant Norton Schuknecht, Thursday, November 5, 1925, pp. 40–42, 75–76, 97, 111–112, Trial Transcripts.

171 **Schellenberger, Schuknecht's deputy:** Lieutenant Paul Schellenberger, Thursday, November 5, 1925, pp. 132–151; Friday, November 6, pp. 152–184, Trial Transcripts.

171 **One of Sweet's neighbors:** Ray Dove, Friday, November 6, 1925, pp. 270, 274, 204–207, Trial Transcripts.

172 **face red:** Description of Toms's appearance in court comes from the *Detroit Evening Times*, November 6, 1925.

175 **first learned:** Wettlaufer, Saturday, November 7, 1925, pp. 320–364, Trial Transcripts.

176 **Murphy permitted it:** Eberhardt, Saturday, November 7, 1925, pp. 364–495, Trial Transcripts.

176 **Draper had trouble:** Eben Draper, November 7, 1925, pp. 434–473.

Chapter 12: Your Fight / My Fight

179 **two days into the trial:** WW to JWJ, Second Day, October 31, 1925, NAACP-micro, Part 5, Reel 3.

179 **Holt bragged:** WW to JWJ (October 31, 1925; Gomon typescript and Josephine Gomon. WW to JWJ [October 31, 1925]; Josephine Gomon mentions the Holt incident in "Sweet Trial," Box 9., BHL.

179 **Inspector Schuknecht contradicted himself:** WW to JWJ, November 13, NAACP-micro, Part 5, Reel 2.

180 **Some evenings:** Ruby Darrow discusses how they spent their leisure in a letter to one of Darrow's biographers, Irving Stone, January 24, [nd], Darrow Papers, Box 34, LOC.

180 **White's letters to Johnson:** WW to JWJ, "Second day," NAACP-micro, Part 5, Reel 2.

181 White and Johnson after their meeting wrote to Alexander, providing him with written documentation he could then turn into his own words for appeal. See WW to Alexander, October 19, 1925, NAACP-micro, Part 5, Reel 23.

182 **Dr. Charles Garvin:** February 1926, after Garvin moved in, his house was bombed. Report of the Secretary, Minutes, 1926, NAACP-micro, Part 1, Reel 4.

182 A notice raising money for victims of Tulsa appears in the *Journal of National Medical Association,* July–September 1921, p. 207.

182 W. Alexander to JWJ, November 2, November 4, 1925; JWJ to Dr. Alexander, November 4, 1925 contains the template for the "Dear Doctor" letter. All in NAACP-micro, Part 5, Reel 23.

182 **$5,000 toward the goal:** Alexander to Dr. Belsaw, October 28, 1925, NAACP-micro, Part 5, Reel 23.

183 **fundraising trips:** "Sweet Defense Fund, State of Cash Receipts and Disbursements," Part 2 Reel 11, NAACP-micro; Pickens to Jim and Walter, October 25, 1925, part 5/Reel 3; WW to JWJ, November 9, 1925, NAACP-micro Part 5, Reel 4.

183 **Darrow's fee:** *Detroit Evening Times,* October 16, 1925; WW to JWJ, Second Day, [October 31, 1925] NAACP-micro Part 5, Reel 3.

183 Expenses are enumerated in "Statement of Cash Receipts and Disbursements," September 30-December 1, 1925, NAACP-micro Part 5/Reel 2.

184 **Storey asked for:** Moorfield Storey to Directors of the American fund for Public Service, October 22, 1925, Papers of the American Fund for Public Service, Roll 10/Box 15, microfilm, Manuscript Division, NYPL; JWJ to Moorfield Storey, October 21, 1925, NAACP-micro Part 1, Reel 17.

Fundraising, including receipts for donations is included in: WW to Billikopf, 27 October; Billikopf to White, 29 October 1925. NAACP-micro, Part 12, Reel 12. Mrs. Allen to Wilberforce Faculty . . . The list of Wilberforce donors, "Faculty Minutes," November 30–December 1, 1925, Wilberforce University Archives.

184 **it donated $5,000:** "Contributions to the Defense Fund of the National Association for the Advancement of Colored People from October 19 to December 4, 1925," Box 15, Reel 10, American Fund for Public Service, Manuscript Division, NYPL.

185 **The family connection:** Reverend Charles Sumner Long to JWJ, January 8, 1926.

186 **Dr. A. A. Brill:** Press Release, November 20, 1925, NAACP-micro, Part 5, Reel 23.

186 **bring Bradby into line:** "Detroit City Wide Committee Makes Peace with NAACP, November 13, 1925," NAACP-micro, Part 5, Reel 3.

187 **White doubted Gomez:** WW to JWJ, November 13, 1925; W. Hayes McKinney to William Pickens, October 13, 1925. NAACP-micro, Part 5, Reel 2.

187 **Robert Bagnall wrote:** November 4, 1925, NAACP-micro, Part 5, Reel 5.

187 **"dangers to democracy are obvious":** NAACP Press Release, October 31, 1924, NAACP-micro, Part 5, Reel 4.

187 **Donations started to roll in:** All letters accompanying contributions are in NAACP-micro, Part 5, Reel 23.

Chapter 13: The Night of September 9

The references for this chapter are contained within Trial Transcripts, BHL, on the following pages: Day 4, Monday, November 9: George Fairbairn, pp. 423–483; John E. Hayes, pp. 487–495; Joseph Neighbauer, pp. 502–510; Joseph Grohm, pp. 579–602; John Getke, pp. 610–615; Mrs. Delia Getke, pp. 616–632; Joseph Henley, pp. 632–645; Day 5, Tuesday, November 10: George Suppus, pp. 698–726; Ulric Arthur, pp. 726–750; Harry Monet, pp. 756–796; Edward J. Belcher, pp. 817–833; Day 6, Wednesday, November 11: Dwight Hubbard, pp. 856–862; Day 7, Thursday, November 12, trial transcripts are missing. Testimony of Alfred Andrew reconstructed from *DI, FP,* November 13, 1925. Day 8, Friday, November 13: Walter Doran, pp. 1210–1223; Ernest Stanke, pp. 1223–1247; Bert McPherson, pp. 1247–1255; Roy Schaldenbrand, pp. 1255–1260; Riley Burton, pp. 1266–1281; William Johnson, pp. 1329–1375.

189 **Inspector snapped back:** Testimony of Norton Schuknecht, November 5, 1925, pp. 104–105, Trial Transcripts.

190 **"The state's case":** *FP,* Phillip O'Hara, "Darrow Hints a Demand for Another Jury."

193 On Mrs. Breiner's fainting, Trial Transcripts, November 9, 1925, pp. 588–602; *DT,* November 9, 1925; *DN,* November 10, 1925.

196 **local teenagers:** *FP,* November 11, 1925.

199 **Dwight Hubbard:** Trial Transcripts: November 11, 1925, Hubbard fumbled his lines, pp. 856–865.

200 **Alfred Andrew's testimony:** Andrew's testimony on the seventh day of the trial is missing from Trial Transcripts. This account comes from *DT,* November 13, 1925.

202 **Murphy did not agree:** *Detroit News* (November 14, 1925) and *FP* (November 15,

1925) have vivid accounts of Murphy's instructions and the conversation with the attorneys on the point of conspiracy.

204 **Judge Murphy's impatience:** Trial Transcripts, Day 8, November 13, 1925, pp. 1239–1376.

205 **changed into a dry shirt and collar:** *Chicago Defender,* November 28, 1925.

Chapter 14: His Home Is His Castle

206 **strong link:** WW to JWJ, November 13, 1925; November 16, 1925, NAACP-micro, Part 5, Reel 3.

207 **half-day Saturday:** Transcripts are missing after Friday, November 13. All subsequent courtroom accounts have been pieced together from eyewitness, diaries, or press coverage. Saturday's half-day session is described in *DN,* November 14, *FP,* November 15, *Detroit Sunday Times,* November 15, 1925.

209 **Leaning toward Toms:** O'Hara, "Sweet Trial Develops into Battle of Wits," *FP* [nd], NAACP-micro, Part 5, Reel 3.

209 **Toms was groping:** Toms's remarks to the court are reported in *DN,* November 16, 1925.

212 **"influence on the jury":** AB, Rowlette, p. 8.

212 **"justice does not recognize color":** Quoted in Fine, *Frank Murphy,* p. 156.

213 **he presumed it would acquit:** WW to JWJ, November 15, 1925, NAACP-micro, Part 5, Reel 3.

213 **Hays began:** AGH, "Opening Address," November 16, 1925, NAACP-micro, Part 5, Reel 3.

213 **two Michigan decisions:** *Augustus Pond v. People,* 8 Mich. 150 (1860); *People v. Lilly,* 38 Mich 270 (1878); "When Is a Homicide Justifiable Because Committed in Defense of Home," Typescript [8 pps], [nd], Darrow Papers, Box 5, Manuscript Division, LOC.

214 **"would know how to handle a Negro":** AB, Mahoney, p. 23.

215 **"the man who fired this shot":** AGH, "Opening Address."

215 **Packed around the table:** Ruth Manning interview.

215 **Adler was on his way to dinner:** Gomon, "The Sweet Trial," p. 8, BHL.

215 **"Hays pleads":** November 21, 1925, *Chicago Defender.*

216 **the defense called:** All testimony for that day, including Adler's, has been reconstructed from newspaper accounts, especially *FP,* November 18, 1925, and *DN* November 17, 1925; Darrow's remarks, *Pittsburgh Courier,* November 12, 19, 1925.

218 **"incidents his grandfather":** *FP,* November 20, 1925.

219 **Darrow's dramatic flourishes:** Gomon describes the tension in the courtroom when Darrow began his examination of Sweet. See "Sweet Trial," p. 28.

219 **spoke to the jury:** Sweet's testimony is repeated in *DN,* November 19, 20, 1925, *Detroit Evening Times,* November 20, 1925, *Chicago Defender,* November 21, 28, 1925; *FP,* November 19, 20, 21, 1925. The incident Sweet described occurred in the era before

Miranda v. Arizona gave some protection to prisoners and informed them that their words could be used against them.

223 **swung public opinion:** WW to JWJ, November 20, 1925, NAACP-micro, Part 5, Reel 3.

223 **PERSECUTION OF THE NEGRO RACE:** "NAACP Press Release," November 20, 1925, NAACP-micro, Part 5, Reel 3.

Chapter 15: A Reasonable Man?

225 **resulting slant:** *DN,* November 21, 1925 carries the testimony about the experiment with the pencil and the bullet hole and the smiles on Darrow and Hays.

226 **Henry Sweet's statement:** *DN,* November 21, 1925.

227 **press termed Moll's:** *FP,* November 25, 1925.

227 **Hays criticized:** AGH, Trial Transcripts, November 24, 1925.

228 **My clients are here charged:** Clarence Darrow, Closing Remarks in the Trial of Ossian Sweet," Trial Transcripts; *DN,* November 25, *FP,* November 26, 1925.

Local newspaper accounts describe the jury's interaction with the judge and the court. See *FP,* November 27, 1925; *DT,* November 27, 1925; *DN,* November 28, 1925; *Chicago Defender,* December 5, 1925.

233 **mood was gloomy:** The courtroom and spectators, the jury, the brawl and smashing of furniture, as well as the socializing of the defense attorneys is discussed in Goman, "The Sweet Trial."

234 **Thomas Chawke:** AB, Thomas Chawke, p. 1.

235 **"What's the use of arguing with these fellows?"** Quoted in Thomas Fleming, "Take the Hatred Away," pp. 74–80, 104–105.

235 **Mr. Pokerface:** AGH, *Pageant* (May 1955), p. 91.

236 **intended to withdraw protection:** Mose Walker to WW, December 9, 1925, NAACP-micro, Part 5, Reel 3.

Chapter 16: More Than a Partial Victory

Contributions and correspondence from donors large and small, as well as copies of thank-you notes from JWJ, are included in NAACP-micro, Part 5, Reel 23. "Contributions to the Defense Fund of the National Association for the Advancement of Colored People, from October 19 to December 4, 1925," are located in Box 15, Reel 10, American Fund for Public Service, Manuscript Division, NYPL.

237 **Arthur Garfield Hays's immediate response:** *DN,* November 18, 1925. AGH to NAACP, January 2, 1926, NAACP-micro, Part 5, Reel 3.

238 **ongoing commitment to the case:** "Press Release, NAACP, Special Extra" November 28, 1925, NAACP-micro, Part 5, Reel 3.

238 **White had been negotiating:** White reports a conversation with Murphy to Darrow in WW to Clarence Darrow, December 26, 1925, NAACP-micro, Part 5, Reel 3.

239 **$693 from people donating sums less than $5:** "Contributions to Defense Fund," NAACP-micro, Part 12, Reel 12.

239 **Clarence Darrow contributed:** Darrow's remarks are reported in *New York Age,* December 14, 1925.

240 *Negro News Weekly:* Mrs. Pankey to WW, November 27, 1925, NAACP-micro, Part 5, Reel 3.

241 **From others:** Eleanor Terrell, March 18; W. L. Brown to JWJ, March 22, 1926, NAACP-micro, Part 5, Reel 3.

242 **On the same platform:** AGH, NAACP Address, January 3, 1926, New York City, NAACP-micro, Part 5, Reel 3.

243 **traveled in Europe:** *Chicago Defender,* January 16, 1926.

243 **Kelly Miller:** *Afro-American,* January 9, 1926.

243 **eighteen people lynched:** NAACP Sixteenth Annual Report, 1925, American Fund for Public Service Records, Box 15, Reel 10, NYPL.

244 **"prospects for 1926":** January 1926, NAACP Report to the Board of Directors, p. 760, NAACP-micro, Part I, Reel 4.

Chapter 17: A Trial Fair

Transcripts do not exist for the trial of *People v. Henry Sweet.* All dialogue comes from reports in newspapers or eyewitness observations, including Josephine Gomon and Marcet Haldeman-Julius.

246 **reassured them of his commitment:** Darrow to JWJ, April 5, 1926; NAACP-micro, Part 5, Reel 3. Darrow's commitment was manifest again when, in 1930, he offered to help dispose of the civil case Mrs. Breiner brought against Sweet. Correspondence between Darrow, WW, Ossian Sweet, and William Pickens is contained in the NAACP—LOC, File G-96, December 12–20, 1930.

247 **"We are not trying the race question":** *DT* and *FP,* April 21, 1926.

247 **candidates who said:** Nettie George Speedy, *Chicago Defender,* April 24; May 1, 1926, *FP,* April 24, 1926.

248 **sequestered the newly impaneled jurors:** *DT,* April 25, 1926.

248 *Corrigan v. Buckley:* "The Battle of Washington and Detroit," *The Crisis* (December 1925), pp. 69–71.

249 **Wolverine Hotel:** In the six years he worked there, M. Kelly Fritz never saw a black sit down in the dining room of the Wolverine Hotel until Clarence Darrow brought

Ossian and Gladys Sweet with Charles Mahoney for lunch one day. Moon, ed., *Untold Tales, Unsung Heroes,* p. 83.

250 **what Darrow had not expected:** Thomas Chawke describes the scene when he and Darrow arrived in court the first day and found guns on the table. See AB, Chawke, p. 4.

250 **Darrow told the jurors:** *FP,* April 26, 27, May 2, 1926.

251 **Andrew provided:** *FP,* May 2, 4, 1926. Darrow accused the State's witness of "hedging, quibbling and lying," *Afro-American,* May 8, 1926. *FP,* May 2; *DN,* May 2; Speedy, in *Chicago Defender,* remembered him saying "no," May 8, 1926.

253 **police stenographer:** *DT,* May 5, 1926.

253 **did appear:** Ossian Sweet's testimony and the Toms-Murphy exchange, *FP,* May 9, 1926.

254 **Dancy's testimony:** AB, John Dancy, pp. 2–3; *DT,* May 7, 1926.

256 **Darrow spoke in low tones:** The courtroom during closing arguments, and the wait for a verdict, have been pieced together from JWJ to Arthur [Spingarn], Saturday [May 8, 1926], JWJ Papers, Beinecke; JWJ to WW, May 13, 1925, (telegram), NAACP-micro, Part 3, Reel 5; JWJ, "Detroit," *The Crisis* (July 1926) pp. 117–120; Marcet Haldeman-Julius, "Clarence Darrow's Defense of a Negro," *Haldeman-Julius Monthly* 4, no. 2 (June 1926), pp. 3–5 (July 1926). *DN,* May 11, 14, 1926; Darrow's "Closing Argument, *People v. Henry Sweet,* pp. 9, 79, 26, 14; Gomon, "The Sweet Trial."

257 **So were the judge's:** Charles Mahoney told Alex Baskin that he had heard "about lawyers making a judge cry but Darrow was the first man I actually saw do it." AB, Mahoney, p. 10.

258 **lunch at Cohen's:** Gomon describes the scene this way in her diary and another way in the "Sweet trial" a chapter in the unpublished biography of Frank Murphy. I have relied on the diary account because it was contemporary. Both located in Gomon Papers, BHC.

Chapter 18: The Darker Brother

261 **"the Sweet case":** Mose Walker to WW, September 27, 1926, NAACP-micro, Part 12, Reel 11.

262 *Corrigan v. Buckley:* James A. Cobb to James Weldon Johnson, November 13, 1924, Part 5, Reel 4; ADD NAACP minutes re this case from board meetings NAACP-microfilm.

262 **"subversive to the highest American traditions":** ATW, pp. 327–328.

262 **Toms said:** AB, Robert Toms, p. 11.

263 **"lesson of forebearance":** *FP,* May 14, 1926.

263 **"gang of hoodlums":** Haldeman-Julius, *Clarence Darrow's Two Great Trials,* p. 32.

263 **Roseland Cemetery:** M. Kelley Fritz worked at the cemetery when Ossian Sweet buried his daughter, then his wife. He describes this in Moon, ed., *Untold Tales, Unsung Heroes,* p. 83.

264 **"image everybody wanted to set their standards by":** Author interview.

266 **political activism:** Excellent accounts of the emerging civil rights movement in the 1950s may be found in Robert A. Caro, *Lyndon Johnson, Master of the Senate* (New York: Alfred A. Knopf, 2002), pp. 701–709; Taylor Branch, *Parting the Waters America in the King Years, 1954–63* (New York: Simon and Schuster, 1988). On Emmett Till, see Paul Hendrickson, *Sons of Mississippi* (New York: Alfred A. Knopf, 2003).

266 **made Dora Sweet proud:** Jackie Spotts Interview.

Epilogue: After the Trials

271 **American Social Hygiene Association:** WW to Clarence Darrow, July 26, 1926, NAACP-micro, Part 5, Reel 3.

BIBLIOGRAPHY

Abre, Michael. *From Harlem to Paris: Black American Writers in France, 1840–1980.* Urbana and Chicago: University of Illinois Press, 1991.

Allen, James, Hilton Als, John Lewis, and Leon F. Litwack. *Without Sanctuary: Lynching Photography in America.* Santa Fe: Twin Palms, 2000.

Anderson, Jervis. *Harlem, the Great Black Way.* London: Orbis Publishing, 1982.

Archer-Straw, Petrine. *Negrophilia: Avant-Garde Paris and Black Culture in the 1920s.* New York: Thames and Hudson, 2000.

Attaway, John. *A History of Florida Citrus Freezes.* Longboat Key, Fla.: Florida Science Source, 1997.

Bak, Richard. *Turkey Stearnes and the Detroit Stars.* Detroit: Wayne State University Press, 1994.

———. *Ty Cobb: His Tumultuous Life and Times.* Dallas: Taylor Publishing, 1994.

Baker, Ray Stannard. "The Negro Migration of 1916–1918." *Journal of Negro History* 6 (October 1921), pp. 383–498.

———, ed. *Woodrow Wilson, Life and Letters,* Vol. 7. New York: Doubleday, Doran, 1939.

Barbeau, Arthur E. and Florette Henri. *The Unknown Soldiers: Black American Troops in World War I.* Philadelphia: Temple University Press, 1974.

Barcus, Frank. *All Around Detroit.* Detroit: F. Barcus Art Studios, 1939.

Bartsch-Dunne, Dr. Anna, "Gynecology in Vienna," *Harvard Medical News* (Vol. II), Feb. 20, 1936, pp. 1–2.

Blackman, William Fremont. *History of Orange County.* Chuluota, Fla.: Mickler House Publishers, 1973.

Blakey, Arch Frederic. *The Florida Phosphate Industry.* Cambridge, Mass.: Harvard University Press, 1973.

Bontemps, Arna. *They Seek a City.* Garden City: Doubleday, Doran and Company, Inc., 1945.

Bracey, D. R. "University of Vienna Medical School." *Mayo Clinic Proceedings* 56 (October 1981), pp. 634–638.

Branch, Taylor. *Parting the Waters: America in the King Years, 1954–63.* New York: Simon and Schuster, 1988.

Brown, Canter, Jr. *Florida's Black Public Officials.* Tuscaloosa: University of Alabama Press, 1998.

———. *Florida's Peace River Frontier.* Gainesville: University of Central Florida Press, 1991.

———. *Ossian Bingley Hart.* Baton Rouge: Louisiana State University Press, 1997.

Brown, Hallie Q. *Pen Pictures of Pioneers of Wilberforce.* Wilberforce, Ohio: Aldine Publishing, 1937.

Brown, Karl. *Adventures of D. W. Griffith.* New York: Farrar, Straus and Giroux, 1973.

Carey, Gary. *Anita Loos: A Biography.* New York: Alfred A. Knopf, 1988.

Caro, Robert A. *Lyndon Johnson, Master of the Senate.* New York: Alfred A. Knopf, 2002.

Chalmers, David M. *Hooded Americanism: The History of the Ku Klux Klan.* New York: Franklin Watts, 1981.

Conot, Robert. *American Odyssey.* New York: Morrow, 1974.

Cook, David A. *A History of Narrative Film.* New York: W. W. Norton, 1996.

Crump, William. *The Story of Kappa Alpha Psi.* Philadelphia: Kappa Alpha Psi, 1972.

Cunard, Nancy, ed. *Negro: An Anthology.* New York: Frederick Ungar Publishing, 1979.

Curie, Eve. *Madame Curie: A Biography.* New York: Doubleday, Doran, 1939.

Curriden, Mark and Leroy Phillips, Jr. *Contempt of Court: The Turn-of-the-Century Lynching That Launched a Hundred Years of Federalism.* New York: Anchor Books, 2001.

Cutler, H. G. *History of Florida.* Chicago: Lewis Publishing, 1923.

Darrow, Clarence. *Story of My Life.* New York: Da Capo Press, 1996.

Dickinson, Robert L., M.D. "A Program for American Gynecology: Presidential Address." *American Journal of Obstetrics and Gynecology* 1, no. 1 (October 1920).

Douglas, George H. *Women of the 20s.* San Francisco: Saybrook, 1986.

Dray, Philip. *At the Hands of Persons Unknown: The Lynching of Black America.* New York: Random House, 2002.

Du Bois, W. E. B. *The Autobiography: A Soliloquy on Viewing My Life.* New York: International Publisher's Company, 1968.

———. "The Souls of Black Folk," in *Three Negro Classics,* ed., John Hope Franklin. New York: Avon Books, 1965.

Duffus, Robert. "The Salesmen of Hate: The Ku Klux Klan," *World's Work* 1923 (May), pages 32–38; "How the Klan Sells Hate" (June), pp. 182–86; "Counter-Mining the Ku Klux Klan" (July), pp. 275–284; "The Ku Klux Klan in the Middle West" (August), pages 363–372; "The March of Events" (Sept.), pp. 573–575.

Engelmann, Larry. *Intemperance: The Lost War Against Liquor.* New York: Free Press, 1979.

Fabre, Michel. *From Harlem to Paris, 1840–1980.* Urbana: University of Illinois Press, 1991.

Fairbairn, Dr. John S. *Gynecology with Obsterics.* London: Oxford University Press, 1924.

Ferrell, Claudine L. *Nightmare and Dream: Anti-lynching in Congress, 1917–1922.* New York: Garland, 1986.

Fine, Sidney, *Frank Murphy: The Detroit Years.* Ann Arbor: University of Michigan Press, 1975.

Fishbein, Morris. *The History of the American Medical Association, 1847–1947.* Philadelphia: W. B. Saunders, 1947.

Fleming, Donald. *William Welch and the Rise of Modern Medicine.* Boston: Little Brown, 1954.

Fleming, Thomas J. "Take the Hatred Away," *American Heritage,* 20 no. 1 (December 1968), pp. 74–80, 104–105.

———. "The Right of Self-Defense," *The Crisis* (January, 1969), pp. 9–14.

Flexner, Abraham. "Medical Education, 1909–1924." *Journal of the American Medical Association* 82, no. 11 (March 15, 1924), pp. 833–838.

Fosdick, Raymond B. with Henry F. Pringle and Katharine Douglas Pringle. *Adventure in Giving: The Story of the General Education Board.* New York: Harper and Row, 1962.

Franklin, John Hope, ed. *Three Negro Classics.* New York: Avon Books, 1965.

———. "The Birth of a Nation: Propaganda as History," in *Race and History—Selected Essays, 1938–1988.* Baton Rouge: Louisiana State University Press, 1989.

Fry, Henry, *The Modern Ku Klux Klan.* Boston: Small, Maynard, 1922.

Garilovick, Peter and Bill McGraw, eds. *Detroit Almanac.* Detroit: Detroit Free Press, 2000.

Ginger, Ray. *Six Days or Forever? Tennessee v. John Thomas Scopes.* Boston: Beacon Press, 1958.

Green, Constance McLaughlin. *The Secret City: A History of Race Relations in the Nation's Capital.* Princeton: Princeton University Press, 1967.

Greene, Ward. "Notes for a History of the Klan," *American Mercury 5* (May–August, 1925), pp. 240–243.

Gregory, T. Montgomery. "The Jim Crow Car," *The Crisis,* November 1915, December 1915, January 1916, March 1917.

Grieben's Guide Books. *Vienna and Environs, Vol. 199.* London: Geographia Ltd. London, 1930.

Haldeman-Julius, Marcet. *Clarence Darrow's Two Great Trials: Reports of the Scopes Anti-Evolution Case and the Dr. Sweet Negro Trial.* Girard, Kans.: Haldeman-Julius, Big Blue Books No. B-29 1927.

———. "The Defendants in the Secret Murder Case," Vol. IV (No. 1), June 1926, pp. 3–21 ; "Clarence Darrow's Defense of a Negro," Vol. IV (No. 2), July 1926, pp. 3–32.

Harlan, Louis R. *Booker T. Washington, the Wizard of Tuskegee, 1901–1915.* New York: Oxford University Press, 1983.

———. *Booker T. Washington, 1856–1901.* New York: Oxford University Press, 1972.

———. *Separate and Unequal.* Chapel Hill, University of North Carolina Press 1958).

Harlan, Louis R., and Raymond W. Snow, eds., *The Booker T. Washington Papers.* Urbana: University of Illinois Press, 1981.

Harrison, Alfredteen, ed. *Black Exodus, The Great Migration from the American South.* Jackson: University Press of Mississippi, 1991.

Haynes, George Edmund. *Negro New-Comers in Detroit, Michigan.* New York: Home Missions Council, 1918.

Hays, Arthur Garfield. *Let Freedom Ring.* New York: Liveright Publishing, 1941.

Hemingway, Ernest. *A Moveable Feast.* New York: Simon and Schuster, 1964.

Hendrickson, Paul. *Sons of Mississippi.* New York: Alfred A. Knopf, 2003.

Henri, Florette. *Black Migration.* Garden City, N.Y.: Anchor Press, 1975.

Hetherington, M. F. *History of Polk County.* Lakeland, Fla. Record Company Printers: 1928.

Higham, John, *Strangers in the Land: Patterns of American Nativism, 1860–1925.* New York: Atheneum, 1975.

Hirsch, James S. *Riot and Remembrance: The Tulsa Race War and Its Legacy.* Boston: Houghton Mifflin Company, 2002.

Hixson, William B. *Moorfield Storey and the Abolitionist Tradition.* New York: Oxford University Press, 1972.

Hughes, Langston. *The Big Sea: An Autobiography.* New York: Hill and Wang, 1940.

Hurston, Zora Neale. *Go Gator and Muddy the Waters,* ed. Pamela Bordelon. New York: W. W. Norton, 1999.

Jackson, Kenneth. *The Ku Klux Klan in the City, 1915–1930.* New York: Oxford University Press, 1967.

Jenken, Kenneth Robert. *White: The Biography of Walter White, Mr. NAACP.* New York: New Press, 2003.

Johnson, James Weldon. *Along This Way: The Autobiography of James Weldon Johnson.* New York: The Viking Press, 1968.

——. *Black Manhattan.* New York: Da Capo Press, 1991.

——. "Detroit," *The Crisis* (July, 1926), pp. 117–120.

Joiner, W. A. *A Half Century of Freedom of the Negro in Ohio.* Xenia, Ohio: Press of Smith Adv., 1915.

Katzman, David M. *Before the Ghetto: Black Detroit in the Nineteenth Century.* Urbana: University of Illinois Press, 1973.

Kavanaugh, Kelli B. *Images of America: Detroit's Michigan Central Station.* Detroit: Arcadia Publishing, 2001.

Kellogg, Charles. *The NAACP, Vol. I: 1909–1920.* Baltimore: Johns Hopkins Press, 1967.

Kerber, Linda. *No Constitutional Right to Be Ladies.* New York: Hill and Wang, 1998.

Lang, Robert, ed. *The Birth of a Nation.* New Brunswick, N.J.: Rutgers University Press, 1994.

Larson, Edward J. *Summer for the Gods: The Scopes Trial and America's Continuing Debate over Science and Religion.* New York: Basic Books, 1997.

Leavitt, Judith Walzer. *Brought to Bed: Child-Bearing in America, 1750–1950.* New York: Oxford University Press, 1986.

Leon County Farmers Club. *Leon County, Florida.* Tallahassee: 1883.

Levine, David Allan. *Internal Combustion: The Races in Detroit, 1915–1926.* Westport, Ct.: Greenwood Press, 1976.

Levy, Eugene. *James Weldon Johnson. Black Leader, Black Voice.* Chicago: University of Chicago Press, 1973.

Lewis, David Levering. *W. E. B. Du Bois. Biography of a Race, 1868–1919.* New York: Henry Holt, 1993.

——. *W. E. B. Du Bois: The Fight for Equality and the American Century, 1919–1963.* New York: Henry Holt, 2000.

——. *When Harlem Was in Vogue.* New York: Penguin Books, 1997.

——. "An American Pastime." *New York Review of Books,* November 21, 2002.

Local Time Tables, Louisville and Nashville Railroad, Railroad (1909), Railroad Museum, Sacramento, Cal.

Locke, Alaine, ed. *The New Negro: An Interpretation.* New York: Atheneum, 1992.

Logan, Rayford W. *Howard University.* New York: New York University Press, 1969.

Long, Charles Summer. *The History of the AME Church in Florida.* Philadelphia: A.M.E. Book Concern, 1939.

Loos, Anita. *Gentlemen Prefer Blondes.* New York: Boni and Liveright, 1925.

Lowell, C., J. Silvius, and S. Darrow, "Tawawa Woods Natural Landmark: Geologic, Cultural, and Land Use History." *Ohio Journal of Science* 103, no. 2 (April, 2003), pp. 2–11.

Lubove, Roy. *The Professional Altruist: The Emergence of Social Work as a Career, 1880–1930.* Cambridge, Mass.: Harvard University Press, 1965.

McCullough, David. *Truman.* New York: Simon and Schuster, 1992.

McGill, Ralph. *The South and the Southerner.* Boston: Little Brown, 1963.

McGinnis, Frederick A. *A History and Interpretation of Wilberforce University.* Wilberforce, Ohio: Brown Publishing Co., 1941.

McLean, Nancy. *Behind the Mask of Chivalry: Making of the Second Ku Klux Klan.* New York: Oxford University Press, 1994.

Madison, James H. *A Lynching in the Heartland: Race and Memory in America.* New York: Palgrave/St. Martin's, 2001.

Mahon, Alexander Jabez. *Vienna of Yesterday and Today.* Vienna: Halm and Goldmann, 1928.

Mayo, C. H. *"Staff Meetings of the Mayo Clinic,"* September 11, 1929, pp. 272–273.

Mayo, William J. "A Short Visit to Some Hospitals in Germany, Austria, Switzerland." *Journal Lancet* 32 (1912), pp. 423–427.

———. "Observations During a Recent European Trip." *Proceedings Staff Meeting of the Mayo Clinic* 4 (1929), pp. 272–273.

Mason, Phillip. *Rum Running and the Roaring Twenties.* Detroit: Wayne State University Press, 1995.

Mayor's Intra-Racial Committee of Detroit. *The Negro in Detroit.* Detroit Bureau of Governmental Research, 1926.

Meier, August. *Negro Thought in America, 1880–1915.* Ann Arbor: University of Michigan, 1963.

———, and Elliot Rudwick. *Along the Color Line.* Urbana: University of Illinois Press, 1976.

Moon, Elaine Latzman, ed. *Untold Tales, Unsung Heroes: An Oral History of Detroit's African-American Community, 1918–1967.* Detroit: Wayne State University Press, 1993.

Moss, Alfred, Jr. *The American Negro Academy, Voice of the Talented Tenth.* Baton Rouge: University Press, 1981.

National Association for the Advancement of Colored People. *Thirty Years of Lynching.* New York: Arno Press, 1968.

Neville, Ralph. *Days and Nights in Montmartre and the Latin Quarter.* London: H. Jenkins Limited 1927.

Newton, Michael and Judy Ann Newton. *The Ku Klux Klan: An Encyclopedia.* New York: Garland, 1991.

Orwell, George. *Down and Out in Paris and London*. London and New York: Harvest Book, 1933.

Osofsky, Gilbert. *Harlem: The Making of a Ghetto*. New York: Harper and Row, 1963.

Ottley, Roi. *The Lonely Warrior*. Chicago: H. Regnery Co., 1955.

Ovington, Mary White. *The Walls Came Tumbling Down*. New York: Schochen Books, 1970.

Oxford, William. *The Ferry Steamers: The Story of the Detroit-Windsor Ferry Boats*. Erin, Ontario, Canada: Boston Mills Press, 1992.

Quinn, Susan. *Marie Curie: A Life*. New York: Simon and Schuster, 1995.

Rand McNally Guide to Detroit and Environs. New York: Rand McNally, 1922.

Regaud, Claude, Dr. "Radium Institute of the University of Paris Departments of Radiophysiology and Medicine." *Methods and Problems of Medical Education*, 12th Series. New York: Rockefeller Foundation, 1929.

Reiser, Stanley Joel. *Medicine and the Reign of Technology*. Cambridge, Mass.: Cambridge University Press, 1978.

Rivers, Larry E. "Slavery in Microcosm: Leon County, Florida, 1824–1860." *Journal of Negro History* (February 1981).

Rosenberg, Charles E. and Morris J. Vogel. eds. *The Therapeutic Revolution: The Social History of American Medicine*. University of Pennsylvania Press, 1979.

Rosner, David. *A Once Charitable Enterprise: Hospitals and Health Care in Brooklyn and New York*. Cambridge, Mass.: Cambridge University Press, 1982.

Rudolph, Frederick. *The American College and University, A History*. New York: Vintage Books, 1962.

Rudwick, Elliot. *Race Riot in East St. Louis, 1917*. New York: World Publishing, 1966.

Rutkow, Ira M. "The Letters of William Halstead and Anton von Eiselsberg." *Archives of Surgery* 115 (August 1980), pp. 993–1000.

Sadoul, George. "Sambo Without Tears" in *Negro: An Anthology*. Nancy Cunard, ed. New York: Frederick Unger, 1979.

Scarborough, William Saunders. "Autobiography" [micro], Ohio Historical Society.

Seraile, Richard. *Voice of Dissent Theophilus Gould Steward (1843–1924) and Black America*. Brooklyn: Carlson, 1991.

Schneider, Mark. *We Return Fighting: The Civil Rights Movement in the Jazz Age*. Boston: Northeastern Press, 2001.

Scott, Emmett. "Letters of Negro Migrants of 1916–1918." *Journal of Negro History* 4 (July and October 1919).

Shorter, Edward. *Bedside Manners: The Troubled History of Doctors and Patients*. New York: Simon and Schuster, 1985.

Simmons, William J. *The Klan Unmasked*. Atlanta: W. E. Thompson Publishing 1923.

Sklar, Robert. *Movie Made America: A Cultural History of American Movies*. New York: Vintage, 1994.

Smith, Willie "the Lion" with George Hoeffer. *Music on My Mind: The Memoirs of an American Pianist*. New York: Doubleday, 1964.

Spann, Joe. "The South Florida Railroad." *Polk County Historical Quarterly* 12, no. 4 (March 1986).

Starr, Paul. *The Social Transformation of American Medicine*. New York: Basic Books, 1982.

Stern, Seymour. "Birth of a Nation." *Cinemages*, special Issue no. 1 (1955), Griffith Papers, MOMA, Film Library.

Stone, Irving. *Clarence Darrow for the Defense: A Biography*. New York: Doubleday, 1941.

Sugrue, Thomas J. *The Origins of the Urban Crisis: Race, Inequality in Postwar Detroit*. Princeton N.J.: Princeton University Press, 1996.

Tierney, Kevin. *Darrow: A Biography*. New York: Thomas Y. Crowell, 1979.

U.S. Congress. House Committee on Rules. *Hearings of the Ku Klux Klan*. New York: Arno Press, 1969.

Wade, Wyn Craig. *The Fiery Cross: The Ku Klux Klan in America*. New York: Simon and Schuster, 1987.

Warren, Francis H. *Michigan Manual of Freedmen's Progress*. Detroit, Michigan, 1915.

Washington, Booker T. *Black-Belt Diamonds: Gems from the Speeches, Addresses, and Talks to Students of Booker T. Washington*. New York: Negro Universities Press, 1969.

Washington, Booker T. *Up from Slavery*, in *Three Negro Classics*, John Hope Franklin, ed. New York: Avon Books, 1965.

Washington, Forrester B. "Part II: The Detroit Newcomers' Greeting," *Survey* (July 14, 1917), pp. 333–335.

———. "The Negro in Detroit: A Survey of the Conditions of a Negro Group in a Northern Industrial Center During the War Prosperity Period" (Detroit, 1920).

Waskow, Arthur I. *From Race Riot to Sit-Ins, 1919 and the 1960s*. New York: Doubleday, 1966.

Wechsberg, Joseph. *The Vienna I Knew*. New York: Doubleday, 1979.

Weinberg, Arthur. *Attorney for the Damned*. New York: Simon and Schuster, 1957.

Weinberg, Kenneth G. *A Man's Home, A Man's Castle*. New York: McCall Publishing, 1971.

Weiss, Nancy J. *The National Urban League, 1910–1940*. New York: Oxford University Press, 1974.

Wertz, Richard W. and Dorothy C. Wertz. *Lying-In: A History of Childbirth in America*. New York: Free Press, 1977.

White, Walter. *A Man Called White: The Autobiography of Walter White*. Athens: University of Georgia Press, 1995.

———. *Fire in the Flint*. New York: Alfred A. Knopf, 1924.

———. "Reviving the Ku Klux Klan." *Forum* (April 1921), pp. 426–434.

———. "Negro Segregation Comes North." *Nation* (October 21, 1925), pp. 458–460.

Who Was Who Among North American Authors, 1921–1939. Detroit: Gale Research Co., 1976.

Wilson, Sunny, with John Dohassey. *Toast of the Town*. Detroit: Wayne State University Press, 1998.

Woodward, C. Vann. *The Strange Career of Jim Crow*. New York: Oxford University Press, 1974.

Wright, Charles A. *The National Medical Association DEMANDS Equal Opportunity, Nothing More, Nothing Less*. Southfield, Mich.: Charro, 1995.

Young, Coleman. *Hard Stuff: The Autobiography of Coleman Young.* New York: Penguin, 1994.
Zangrando, Robert. *NAACP Crusade Against Lynching, 1909–1950.* Philadelphia: Temple University Press, 1980.
Zunz, Olivier. *The Changing Face of Inequality: Urbanization, Industrial Development, and Immigrants in Detroit.* Chicago: University of Chicago Press, 1982.

Author Interviews
Col. Hampton Green, July 10, 1999.
Ruth Manning, November 15, 1999.
Sam Silas, November 1, 1999.
Jacqueline Spotts, May 25, 1999; March 31, 2003; May 24, 2003.
Sherman Sweet, June 28–29, 1999, 2003.
Claude Woodruff, June 28, 1999.

Alex Baskin Interviews, Bentley Historical Library, University of Michigan, Ann Arbor, Michigan
Thomas F. Chawke, August 4, 1960.
John C. Dancy, July 27, 1960.
Charles Mahoney, August, 1960.
William Osby, Sr., July 27, 19[60].
Cecil L. Rowlette, August 1, 1960.
Dr. Otis Sweet, August 1, 1960.
Judge Robert M. Toms, November 28, 1959.

Legal Cases Cited
Buchanan v. Warley
245 U.S. 60 (1917)

Corrigan et al. v. Buckley
271 US 323 (1926)

Augustus Pond v. The People
8 Mich. 150 (1860)

People v. Lilly
38 Mich. 270 (1878)

ACKNOWLEDGMENTS

I STUMBLED OVER OSSIAN SWEET'S STORY WHILE I WAS researching my mother's family from Detroit. My grandparents were Russian immigrants who settled briefly in Canada before crossing separately into Michigan. My grandfather was a watchmaker. He owned one jewelry store on Woodward Avenue, another on Lafayette St. Both were in fashionable areas of an increasingly chic city. Then the depression wiped him out. That's about all I would learn about my mother's family before I was drawn to Ossian Sweet's story after reading Arthur Garfield Hays's *Let Freedom Ring*.

While writing is solitary, it is hardly an isolated endeavor. Along the way, I have incurred considerable debt to friends and family who tolerated demanding absences as well as a demanding presence. Thank you, first and always, to my husband, Gary Burke, for living this book with me, for sharing my burdens as his own, for reading and talking and listening not just once but for all time, and then again. And, to our children, Matt and Molly, who gave me the space to nurture this project lovingly if not always patiently.

Thank you to Anne Edelstein, my literary agent, for her gift of endless warmth, enthusiasm, and good judgment and for propelling me through alternating moods, successive drafts, and more than a few false starts.

I had the good fortunate to meet an extraordinary genealogist early in my research. Alvie Davidson, CGRS, thank you for opening doors to a labyrinth of records, answering queries on short demand, delivering me to archives I would have never imagined existed. Also, I am grateful for the help of Ruth McMahon and Ruth Lewis, genealogists in Chicago and Detroit, respectively; for Sharyn Thompson and Neira Marshall, in Tallahassee, Florida; for Eija Poluso and Kristen Gresh, in Paris, France. When I could not resolve a research question, Peter Edelman, Assistant Head Librarian, New York *Daily News,* speedily delivered me away from my confusion. I also thank: Matthew Burke and Jeremiah Quinlan for help with photoduplicating microfilm, and Linda Bulmer for secretarial assistance.

Alex Baskin, professor of history at Stony Brook, gave me access to his interviews on deposit at the Bentley Historical Library, University of Michigan. I thank him for his dedication to scholarship, and sharing handwritten, unpublished research notes on Detroit and the Sweet trial, which he painstakingly transcribed when a sharp pencil was a scholar's only tool.

Scores of librarians and archivists have answered requests, and I am grateful for the help of Judy Kucinski, Sarah Lawrence College; Sheila Darrow, North Central State, Wilberforce, Ohio; Jacqueline Brown and Jean Mulhern, Wilberforce University; Joe Spann, Polk Co. Historical and Genealogical Society, Bartow, Florida; Karen Jania, Bentley Historical Library, University of Michigan; Dr. Clifford Muse, Howard University Archives; Pat Zacharias, *Detroit News.* At the the Walter P. Reuther Library, Wayne State University, my sincere appreciation goes to Mary J. Wallace, audiovisual archivist, and William LeFevre, manuscript archivist. The entire staff at the Schomburg Center for Research in Black Culture, New York Public Library, provided steady, consistent help over the life of the project.

I cannot overstate my appreciation to my local library in Hastings-on-Hudson: Thanks to Sue Feir who granted me unconditional access, including during months of a dusty renovation when we all had to duck trailing electrical lines; to Janet Murphy for her indefatigable help at every stage, deftly managing the reference component of the interlibrary loan system, endlessly locating obscure titles; to Terri Fox, from the Westchester County Library System.

This would have been an entirely different book had the Sweet family not placed their trust in me. I owe my initial conversations with Jacqueline Spotts to the serendipity of friendship and thank Tom Tentler for the introduction. She has been exceedingly generous in sharing her memories, repeatedly answering questions about her family and Bartow to help me, as Clarence Darrow would say, "get it right." Sherman Sweet, Ossian Sweet's sole surviving brother, invited me into his community, shared his memories and provided access to other relatives including Colonel Hampton Green and Ruth Manning. My appreciation extends to Coach Claude Woodruff who escorted me through the town's east side pointing out markers weathered by time. For sharing their special knowledge of the Peace River Valley, I am most grateful to Canter Brown Jr., Joe Spann, Odell Robinson, Lloyd Harris, Clifton Lewis and Tom Sailor.

On numerous research excursions, friends welcomed me with hospitality and good cheer. I thank Ruth and Joe Bell in Washington, D.C.; Bill and Carol Joyce, in Princeton, New Jersey; and Tom and Leslie Tentler in Ann Arbor, Michigan.

The project benefited from people who shared their special knowledge or commented on chapters. I am especially grateful to Blanche Cook, Barbara Feinberg, Bill Goodman, Joann Kobin, Susan Meigs, Susan Olding, Elizabeth Pleck, Mark Schneider, Leslie Tentler, Marjory Waters, and Ellen Yaroshevsky. The family of Dr. Carl Rosenbloom generously gave me use of his personal correspondence during his years in Vienna. And I appreciate Eileen Berasi and Alison Kouzmanoff from Graphic Chart and Map for the exceptional job preparing the map.

Several people have left their impact on this project and on me. All that follows seems meager thanks considering their investment. I am grateful to: Marilyn Katz, my writing partner, for imbuing her careful critiques with grace, wit, and dedication and generously giving my needs equal billing to her own on-going projects; Sam Freedman for posing the early challenge to invest academic rigor with narrative style and to Jim Paul for forcing me back to the initial conception, first at Bread Loaf, later with comments on successive drafts; Jennifer Isenberg Nock for demanding clarity, precision, and compassion. I thank Paul Dodyk for reasons too extensive to enumerate, but include his encyclopedic knowledge about the law and history, his unique stylistic flair, his passion for social justice and his faith in this story. That plus his love for his hometown, Detroit, have influenced every page. All read the manuscript more than once, saved me from ungainly error, and invested my work with inestimable friendship which has enriched whatever merit accrued. Errors remain mine alone.

At Amistad/HarperCollins, the editorial team stands out: Dawn Davis, my editor, brought focus to the process with tenacious commitment and subtle, trenchant direction; Darah Smith graciously answered all too many questions with good cheer, assisted with countless details to tie up the project, which made my life, and toil, easier. I appreciate the help of Laura Blost and Betty Lew, who lent their brilliance to unifying the design; Eleanor Mikucki for the painstaking copy editing; and to Sue Llewellyn, who has led the wonderful team that worked behind the scenes. I thank you all.

INDEX